A TEXT BOOK OF

ELEMENTS OF CIVIL ENGINEERING

FOR

SEMESTER I

FIRST YEAR (F.E.) DEGREE COURSES IN ENGINEERING

STRICTLY AS PER THE NEW REVISED SYLLABUS OF
DR. BABASAHEB AMBEDKAR MARATHWADA UNIVERSITY, AURANGABAD
(EFFECTIVE FROM ACADEMIC YEAR – JULY 2013-2014)

U. S. PATIL
B.E. Civil, M. Tech. (Construction Management)
Associate Professor, Civil Engg. Deptt.
Bharati Vidyapeeth's Group of Institutes Technical Campus,
College of Engineering,
Lavale, PUNE

H. K. GITE
M.E. (Const. Mgt.), M.B.A. (H.R.D.)
Assistant Engineer Grade - 1
Water Resource Department, Govt. of Maharashtra
Formerly Assistant Professor, Civil Engg. Deptt.
JSPM's Rajarshi Shahu College of Engg.
Tathwade, PUNE

A. B. MORE
NEC, ISTE Delhi
Head, Civil Engg. Deptt.
JSPM's Imperial College of Engineering and Research
Wagholi, PUNE.

N2644

ELEMENTS OF CIVIL ENGINEERING (BAMU, F.E., SEM.-I)　　ISBN 978-93-83525-79-9

First Edition : September 2013

© : **Authors**

The text of this publication, or any part thereof, should not be reproduced or transmitted in any form or stored in any computer storage system or device for distribution including photocopy, recording, taping or information retrieval system or reproduced on any disc, tape, perforated media or other information storage device etc., without the written permission of Authors with whom the rights are reserved. Breach of this condition is liable for legal action.

Every effort has been made to avoid errors or omissions in this publication. In spite of this, errors may have crept in. Any mistake, error or discrepancy so noted and shall be brought to our notice shall be taken care of in the next edition. It is notified that neither the publisher nor the authors or seller shall be responsible for any damage or loss of action to any one, of any kind, in any manner, therefrom.

Published By :
NIRALI PRAKASHAN
Abhyudaya Pragati, 1312, Shivaji Nagar,
Off J.M. Road, PUNE – 411005
Tel - (020) 25512336/37/39, Fax - (020) 25511379
Email : niralipune@pragationline.com

Printed By :
REPRO INDIA LTD.
50/2 TTC MIDC Industrial Area,
MAHAPE
Navi Mumbai

DISTRIBUTION CENTRES

PUNE

Nirali Prakashan
119, Budhwar Peth, Jogeshwari Mandir Lane
Pune 411002, Maharashtra
Tel : (020) 2445 2044, 66022708, Fax : (020) 2445 1538
Email : bookorder@pragationline.com

Nirali Prakashan
S. No. 28/25, Dhyari,
Near Pari Company, Pune 411041
Tel : (020) 24690204 Fax : (020) 24690316
Email : dhyari@pragationline.com
bookorder@pragationline.com

MUMBAI
Nirali Prakashan
385, S.V.P. Road, Rasdhara Co-op. Hsg. Society Ltd.,
Girgaum, Mumbai 400004, Maharashtra
Tel : (022) 2385 6339 / 2386 9976, Fax : (022) 2386 9976
Email : niralimumbai@pragationline.com

DISTRIBUTION BRANCHES

NAGPUR
Pratibha Book Distributors
Above Maratha Mandir, Shop No. 3, First Floor,
Rani Jhanshi Square, Sitabuldi, Nagpur 440012,
Maharashtra, Tel : (0712) 254 7129

BENGALURU
Pragati Book House
House No. 1, Sanjeevappa Lane, Avenue Road Cross,
Opp. Rice Church, Bengaluru – 560002.
Tel : (080) 64513344, 64513355,
Mob : 9880582331, 9845021552
Email:bharatsavla@yahoo.com

JALGAON
Nirali Prakashan
34, V. V. Golani Market, Navi Peth, Jalgaon 425001,
Maharashtra, Tel : (0257) 222 0395
Mob : 94234 91860

KOLHAPUR
Nirali Prakashan
New Mahadvar Road,
Kedar Plaza, 1st Floor Opp. IDBI Bank
Kolhapur 416 012, Maharashtra. Mob : 9855046155

CHENNAI
Pragati Books
9/1, Montieth Road, Behind Taas Mahal, Egmore,
Chennai 600008 Tamil Nadu, Tel : (044) 6518 3535,
Mob : 94440 01782 / 98450 21552 / 98805 82331, Email : bharatsavla@yahoo.com

RETAIL OUTLETS

PUNE

Pragati Book Centre
157, Budhwar Peth, Opp. Ratan Talkies,
Pune 411002, Maharashtra
Tel : (020) 2445 8887 / 6602 2707, Fax : (020) 2445 8887

Pragati Book Centre
Amber Chamber, 28/A, Budhwar Peth,
Appa Balwant Chowk, Pune – 411002, Maharashtra,
Tel : (020) 20240335 / 66281669
Email : pbcpune@pragationline.com

Pragati Book Centre
676/B, Budhwar Peth, Opp. Jogeshwari Mandir,
Pune 411002, Maharashtra
Tel : (020) 6601 7784 / 6602 0855

PBC Book Sellers & Stationers
152, Budhwar Peth, Pune 411002, Maharashtra
Tel : (020) 2445 2254 / 6609 2463

MUMBAI
Pragati Book Corner
Indira Niwas, 111 - A, Bhavani Shankar Road, Dadar (W), Mumbai 400028, Maharashtra
Tel : (022) 2422 3526 / 6662 5254, Email : pbcmumbai@pragationline.com

www.pragationline.com　　info@pragationline.com

PREFACE

It gives us immense pleasure to present the book **"Elements of Civil Engineering"** to the students of first year degree course in engineering. The subject matter in the book is in accordance with the new revised syllabus prescribed by Dr. Babasaheb Ambedakar Marathwada University, Aurangabad, implemented from August 2012.

The subject matter is presented in a lucid, fluent and comprehensive manner. All efforts have been taken to present the text matter in Simple Language. Illustrative Figures, Exercise and Solved Problems have been added.

We take this opportunity to express our sincere thanks to Shri. Dineshbhai Furia, Shri. Jignesh Furia for publishing this book in time.

We specially appreciate special efforts taken by Shri. M. P. Munde and staff of Nirali Prakashan namely Mr. Santosh Bare (DTP), Mrs. Roshan Shaikh (Proof Reader), Miss. Chaitali Takale (Figure), Mrs. Prachi Sawant (Figure) and Staff of **Nirali Prakashan**, **Pune**.

We are also thankful to **Mr. Kumbheshwar Vibhute** (Marketing Executive, Beed Dist. office) and **Mr. Raju Shaikh** (Marketing Executive, Aurangabad and Ahmednagar Districts) for their valuable help and efforts for promotion of this book.

Any misprints or errors that have inadvertently crept in during the publication is solely our responsibility and we apologise for the same. We assure that constructive suggestions will be given attention for next reprint.

21th September 2013 **Authors**

Pune

SYLLABUS

UNIT I: BUILDING PLANNING AND CONSTRUCTION MATERIALS (5 Hrs.)

Site selection, plinth area, carpet area, floor space index, cost of building. Study of properties and uses of different engineering materials: (a) cement, (b) stone, (c) aggregates, (d) sand, (e) bricks, (f) concrete, (g) steel, (h) timber.

UNIT II: BUILDING AND ROAD CONSTRUCTION (10 Hrs.)

Loads coming on structure, types of construction: (a) load bearing structure, (b) framed structure. Functions of foundation, column footing, combined footing and machine foundation.

Superstructure and its components: Typical cross-section through load bearing wall. Masonry in superstructure and foundation in bricks and rubble, English and Flemish bond in one and a half brick thick wall, construction and precautions to be taken in brick masonry, coursed and uncoursed rubble masonry, construction and precautions to be taken in stone masonry.

Lintels: RCC lintels, cast in situ and precast concrete arch lintels.

Doors and Windows: Definitions and technical terms, location, sizes, study of doors and windows in public and residential buildings. Framed and paneled door, glazed doors. Casement windows and glazed windows.

Stairs: Definition and technical terms. Requirements of a good stair, bifurcated stairs and dog legged stairs. thumb rules of rise and tread.

Floors: Requirements, selection of flooring materials, flag stone and cement concrete flooring.

Roofs: Requirements of a roof, lean to roof, flat R.C.C. roof.

Road construction: Classification of roads, rigid and flexible pavements, typical road section, camber and function of camber.

UNIT III: EARTHQUAKE ENGINEERING (5 Hrs.)

Causes of earthquake, changes in earth crust during earthquake, technical terms related with earthquake such a focus, epicenter, magnitude, intensity and seismograph. Factors affecting damage, consideration of earthquake forces in design, general construction aspects, earthquake resistant low cost buildings, precautions to be taken before occurrence of an earthquake.

UNIT IV: SURVEYING AND LEVELLING (10 Hrs.)

Principles of survey, measurement of distance by chain and tape, chaining and ranging, direct and indirect ranging, base line and offset. Equipments: Ranging roads, pegs, line ranger and open cross-staff. Bearing, prismatic compass, measurement of bearings, calculation of included angles.

Levelling: Terms related to levelling, benchmarks, study and use of dumpy level, levelling staff, determination of reduced levels, height of instrument.

UNIT V: WATER RESOURCES ENGINEERING (5 Hrs.)

Definition of watershed, necessity of watershed management works. Different structures involved in watershed management. Roof top rain water harvesting and groundwater recharge. Classification of dams, typical section through a gravity dam and zoned earthen embankment. Necessity of irrigation and benefits of irrigation.

UNIT VI: ENVIRONMENTAL ENGINEERING (5 Hrs.)

Water demands, design period, per capita demand, methods of forecasting population: Arithmetic increase, geometric increase and incremental increase method. Treatment flow sheet for a typical water treatment plant, treatment units. Drainage of water from building. Construction of septic tanks and soak pits.

•••

CONTENTS

1. **Building Planning and Construction Materials**   1.1 – 1.38

2. **Building and Road Construction**   2.1 – 2.78

3. **Earthquake Engineering**   3.1 – 3.30

4. **Surveying and Levelling**   4.1 – 4.64

5. **Water Resources Engineering**   5.1 – 5.28

6. **Environmental Engineering**   6.1 – 6.22

•••

UNIT 1

BUILDING PLANNING AND CONSTRUCTION MATERIAL

1.1 BUILDING PLANNING: INTRODUCTION

Planning deals with the development of plan composition to facilitate in purely practical ways the purpose of the building. Sizes are decided according to accommodation and rooms are grouped in their functional sequence. For instance, factory buildings are planned according to their functional sequence and plans are made very simple. Location of structural members is determined so as not to disturb the function or its sequence and they are constructed to their correct size according to the structural design. This is the planning of a building or a structure.

The planner, before he actually begins planning, has to consider the requirements of accommodation. Site location and condition definitely indicate the layout and design of a building as well as the location of its entrance and exit etc.

1.2 SELECTION OF SITE

For optimum functional, economical planning and designing of a structure, proper selection of site is essential. It must however be clearly understood that, it is rarely possible to get a site which will satisfy all the criteria stated below. But given a choice, site should be so selected that it satisfies the following criteria to a greater extent.

1. Site should serve the intended purpose and scope of the building to be erected.
2. Size, shape, elevation and ground conditions.

(a) Site should be uniform in geometrical shape since with irregular shape land is wasted.

(b) Site should be spacious enough to cater for project and future functional requirements.

(c) The site should be relatively flat and should not be in depression. With site in depression problem of drainage and sanitation becomes difficult and plinth height is required to be raised.

(d) To reduce cost of foundation, hard and firm strata should be available at a shallow depth. Reclaimed, marshy, waterlogged, and black cotton soil, strata should be avoided.

3. **Facilities:** To the extent possible following facilities should be in proximity:
(a) Transport, electricity, water, school, shopping centres, recreation facilities, post and telecommunications, cooking gas, hospitals.
(b) Site should be safe and in well secured locality.
4. Ownership: Site should be free from legal litigations.
5. Site near river, nallah should be above the highest flood level of nearby river.
6. It should free from pollution due to smoke, dust, noise, insanitary conditions.

There are certain adverse elements listed below which may compel to reject the particular building site:
1. Immediate neighbourhood of rivers carrying heavy floods in monsoon;
2. Reclaimed soils, lands subject to subsidence or continuous settlement;
3. Smoke and obnoxious odours due to industrial vicinity; and
4. Noise.

Adverse effects of noise are not immediately noticeable. In fact, a quiet environment is an amenity. People get used to regular and continuous types of noises such as of local trains and noise due to heavy traffic thoroughfares. It is the occasional noises which are really disturbing such as factory sirens, whistles of loco-engines, aeroplanes flying at low altitudes. The relation of a site with its environment and the site itself would influence the moulding of the planner's scheme. He has to consider whether the proposed building would stand isolated amidst a vast field of agricultural lands or closely clustered around by a busy thoroughfare. The topographical features of the site with natural and artificial surroundings are to be taken into account while planning and designing a building. Also geophysical conditions, position of ground water table and vegetation should be considered.

1.3 DEFINITIONS

(i) **Plinth Area:** This is built-up covered area measured at the floor level of the basement or of any storey.

The following should be included in the plinth area:
1. Area of the walls at the floor level excluding plinth offsets, if any, when the building consists of columns, projections beyond cladding.
2. Internal shafts of sanitary installations, provided these do not exceed 2 m^2 in area, air-conditioning ducts, lifts, etc.
3. Proches and other cantilevers provided.
4. The area of *barsati* and the mumty at terrace level.

The following shall not be included in the plinth area:
1. Area of lofts.
2. Internal sanitary shafts provided these are more than 2 m^2 in area.

3. Unclosed balconies.
4. Towers, turrets, domes projecting above the terrace level unless they form a storey at the terrace level.
5. Architectural bands, cornices etc.
6. Vertical Sun breakers or box louvers projecting out.

(ii) Carpet Area: This is the floor area of the usable rooms at any floor level.

The carpet area of any floor shall be the floor area worked as per floor area and exclude the following portions of the building:

1. Sanitary accommodations
2. Verandahs
3. Corridors and passages
4. Kitchen and pantries
5. Stores in domestic buildings
6. Entrance hall and porches
7. Staircases and mumties
8. Shaft for lifts
9. Barsaties
10. Garages
11. Canteens
12. Air-conditioning ducts and air-conditioning plant rooms.

(iii) Floor Area Ratio (F.A.R.) or Floor Space Index (F.S.I.):

Necessity: In town planning schemes, one of the most important factors to be controlled is the density of population on a particular area of land. It is expressed as the number of persons living on a unit of land. Earlier, the method employed to control the density was indirect, i.e. by controlling widths of open spaces around buildings and their heights in relation to the widths of roads or by limiting the percentage of built up area to the plot area or by restricting the number of floors that could be built on the plot. Also by restricting tenement density the control was achieved.

F.A.R. or F.S.I. is a new concept to regulate population density and to control overcrowding in residential area.

Definition: It is defined as $\text{F.A.R. or F.S.I.} = \dfrac{\text{Total built up area on all floors}}{\text{Plot area}}$.

Thus, it is a ratio which indicates how much total area can be built with respect to plot size. For preventing overcrowding in a particular region only, the maximum permissible F.S.I. is specified by local governing authorities.

F.S.I. permitted varies depending on congested or non-congested regions. It also varies with the purpose of land use whether for residential or for commercial, educational and hospital use.

Let us assume that in a area, permissible F.A.R. is 1.5 and plot area is 1000 m². It means that total built up area should not be more than 1.5 × 1000 = 1500 m². The permissible F.A.R. in residential zones and for commercial buildings is given in the following table.

Limitations on built-up area:

Locality	Area of plot	Maximum permissible F.S.I. %
A residential area	< 200 m²	2 storied structure
	200 – 500 m²	50%
	500 – 1000 m²	40%
	> 1000 m²	33.5%
Industrial area		60%
Market area		75%

ILLUSTRATIVE EXAMPLES ON BUILDING PLANNING

Example 1.1: A plot owner proposed G + 1 storeyed construction with 175 m² built up area on each floor. The plot size is 16 m × 21 m. Find the ground coverage and FSI proposed, if all size margins are 2 m. If the FSI allowed in the area is 1.0, state with reasons whether the plan will be sanctioned or not.

Solution:

Data:

(i) Floor: G + 1 i.e. one ground and one first floor.

(ii) Built up area = 175 m².

(iii) Plot size = 16 m × 21 m.

(iv) All size margins = 2 m.

(v) FSI = 1.0.

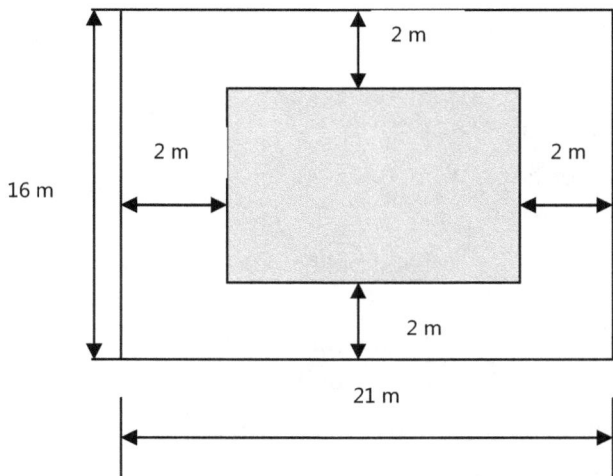

Fig. 1.1: Plan of a proposed building

Total built up area = 175 + 175 (For G + 1 i.e. for two floors)

$$= 350 \text{ m}^2$$

Plot area = 16 m × 21 m

$$= 336 \text{ m}^2$$

Now, $\quad$ FSI = $\dfrac{\text{Total built-up area}}{\text{Plot area}}$

Therefore, $\quad$ FSI = $\dfrac{350}{336}$

FSI = 1.04

This FSI i.e. 1.04 is greater than allowed FSI i.e. 1.0, therefore plan will not be sanctioned.

Example 1.2: Determine the carpet area per floor of a two storeyed building from the following data:

(a) Plot area = 800 m².
(b) FSI allowed = 1.0.
(c) Ratio of carpet area/built up area = 0.8.

Assume equal built up area per floor.

Solution:

Data:

(i) Two storeyed building i.e. one ground and one first floor.
(ii) Plot area = 800 m².
(iii) FSI allowed = 1.0.
(iv) Carpet area/Built up area = 0.8.
(v) Equal built up area per floor.

Built up area per floor:

$$\text{FSI} = \dfrac{\text{Total built-up area}}{\text{Plot area}}$$

$$1 = \dfrac{\text{Total built-up area}}{800}$$

Therefore, Total built up area = 800 × 1 = 800 m².

But equal area is consumed per floor.

Therefore, Built up area per floor = 800/2 = 400 m².

Carpet area per floor:

$$\frac{\text{Carpet area}}{\text{Built-up area}} = 0.8 \text{ (given)}$$

$$\text{Carpet area} = 0.8 \times \text{Built up area per floor}$$
$$= 0.8 \times 400$$
$$= 320 \text{ m}^2$$

Example 1.3: On a plot size 25 m × 30 m, the shorter side is facing the main road. The side margins are as follows: Front margin: 3 m, rear and side margins are all 2 m. Earlier FSI allowed was 0.75. However, only ground storeyed construction after leaving the margins was built by the owner. Now, as per the new norms, FSI allowed is increased to 1.5. If 2 more storeys are proposed by the owner, find the additional area to be built on each floor.

Solution:

Data:
(i) Plot size = 25 m × 30 m.
(ii) Shorter side of the plot is facing the main road.
(iii) Front margin = 3 m.
(iv) Rear and side margins = 2 m.
(v) FSI allowed (old) = 0.75.
(vi) FSI allowed (new) = 1.5.

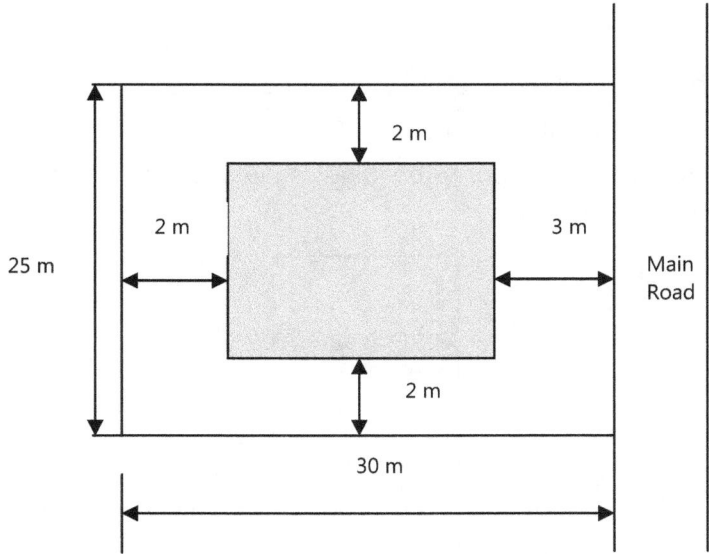

Fig. 1.2: Plan of a proposed building

$$\text{Plot area} = 25 \text{ m} \times 30 \text{ m}$$
$$= 750 \text{ m}^2$$

Ground floor coverage area:

Length of a building,   L = 30 – 2 – 3 = 25 m.

Width of a building,   W = 25 – 2 – 2 = 21 m.

Ground floor coverage area = L × W = 25 m × 21 m

                 = 525 m^2

Permissible construction:

(i)   As per old FSI

        Permissible construction = FSI × Plot area

                            = 0.75 × 750 = 562.5 m^2

(ii)   As per new FSI

        Permissible construction = FSI × Plot area

                            = 1.5 × 750 = 1125 m^2

The owner constructed only ground floor after leaving the margins i.e. 525 m^2.

Additional area can be constructed by the owner as per new allowed FSI and it is calculated as follows:

Additional construction:

Additional area available for construction = [Permissible constructional area as per new FSI –

                                                           Ground floor coverage area]

                                                           = 1125 – 525 = 600 m^2.

If this area is to be constructed equally on two more storeys,

Then built up area per each floor = 600/2 = 300 m^2

Fig. 1.3 shows elevation of a proposed building as per allowed new FSI.

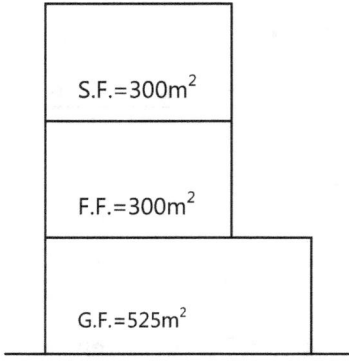

Fig. 1.3: Elevation of a proposed building

Example 1.4: A plot owner proposed G + 1 construction with 175 m² construction on each floor, on a plot size a 15 m × 20 m. If all margins are 2 m and FSI allowed = 1, find:
(a) Ground coverage
(b) FSI consumed
(c) Whether plan will be sanctioned or not.

If not, by how much amount the proposed area will be required to be reduced by the owner, so that the proposal will be sanctioned by the authorities.

Solution:

Data:
(i) Floor: G + 1 i.e. one ground and one first floor.
(ii) Built up area = 175 m².
(iii) Plot size = 15 m × 20 m.
(iv) All size margins = 2 m.
(v) FSI = 1.0.

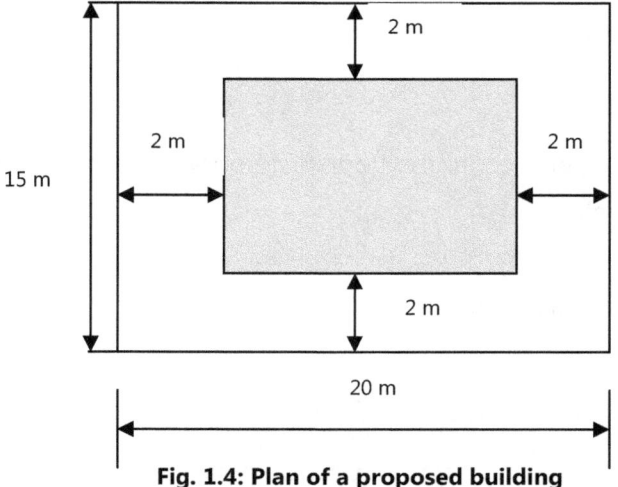

Fig. 1.4: Plan of a proposed building

$$\text{Total built up area} = 175 + 175 \text{ (For G + 1 i.e. for two floors)}$$
$$= 350 \text{ m}^2$$
$$\text{Plot area} = 15 \text{ m} \times 20 \text{ m} = 300 \text{ m}^2$$

Ground Coverage:
Length of a building, L = 20 − 2 − 2 = 16 m.
Width of a building, W = 15 − 2 − 2 = 11 m.
Ground floor coverage area = L × W
= 16 m × 11 m
= 176 m²

FSI Consumed:

$$FSI = \frac{\text{Total built-up area}}{\text{Plot area}}$$

Therefore,
$$FSI = \frac{(176 \times 2)}{(20 \times 15)}$$

$$FSI = 1.17$$

This FSI i.e. 1.17 is greater than allowed FSI i.e. 1.0; therefore plan will not be sanctioned. To consume the sanctioned plan, the consumed FSI must be 1.

Therefore,
$$1 = \frac{\text{Total built-up area}}{(20 \times 15)}$$

Total built up area = 360 m²

Therefore, reduced construction area = 352 − 300 = 52 m²

Example 1.5: Determine total carpet area of a three storeyed building from the following data:

(a) Plot area = 40 m × 30 m.
(b) FSI allowed = 0.9.
(c) Ratio of carpet area to built up area = 0.8.

Solution:

Data:

(i) Three storeyed building i.e. ground floor, first floor and second floor.
(ii) Plot area = 1200 m².
(iii) FSI allowed = 0.9
(iv) Carpet area/Built up area = 0.8.

Built up area per floor:

$$FSI = \frac{\text{Total built-up area}}{\text{Plot area}}$$

$$0.9 = \frac{\text{Total built-up area}}{800}$$

Therefore, Total built-up area = 800 × 0.9
= 720 m²

Total Carpet area:

$$\frac{\text{Total Carpet area}}{\text{Total Built-up area}} = 0.8 \text{ (given)}$$

Total Carpet area = 0.8 × Built up area
= 0.8 × 720
= 576 m²

1.4 STUDY OF PROPERTIES AND USED OF DIFFERENT ENGINEERING MATERIALS

The materials required for construction of structures are known as building materials. It is very essential for an engineer, builder, architect and contractor, to be thoroughly conversant with these building materials. The knowledge of different types of materials, their properties and uses for different purposes is very essential for the builder in achieving overall economy.

Building material accounts for about 70% of the total cost of construction. Thus, it is important that the building materials are easily and cheaply available. Civil engineering construction involves use of natural materials like stone, timber, sand, aggregates and manufactured materials like steel, plastic, cement etc. The correct use of materials leads to better structural strength, efficiency and economy in the long run. The commonly used materials required in civil engineering construction are discussed in this chapter in regards to their types, sizes, properties and uses etc.

1.5 CEMENT

The product obtained by burning and crushing to powder form, homogeneous and well proportioned mixture of lime stone and clay is known as cement. Commonly used greyish coloured cement is known as ordinary **Portland cement.**

1.5.1 Manufacture of Cement

"The raw materials required for manufacture of Portland cement are calcareous materials, such as limestone or chalk, and argillaceous material such as shale or clay. The process of manufacture of cement consists of grinding the raw materials, mixing them intimately in certain proportions depending upon their purity and composition and burning them in a kiln at a temperature of about 1300 to 1500°C, at which, the material sinters and partially fuses to form a nodular shaped clinker. The clinker is cooled and ground to a fine powder with the addition of about 2 to 3% gypsum. The product is known as cement. The oxide compounds in raw materials of cement are as follows.

Oxide	Content (%)
CaO	60 – 67
SiO_2	17 – 25
Al_2O_3	3 – 8
Fe_2O_3	0.5 – 6.0
MgO	0.1 – 4.0
Alkalies	0.4 – 1.3
SO_3	1.0 – 2.75

The oxide compounds mentioned in table are in the form of:

Tricalcium silicates (C_3S)   — $3\,CaO \cdot SiO_2$
Dicalcium silicates (C_2S)   — $2\,CaO \cdot SiO_2$
Tricalcium aluminates (C_3A)   — $3\,CaO \cdot Al_2O_3$
Tetracalcium alumino (C_4AF)   — $4\,CaO \cdot Al_2O_3\,Fe_2O_3$

1.5.2 Physical Properties of Cement

In order to judge suitability of cement, the following properties are important:

(i) Fineness: When cement is very fine, the number of cement particles present per gram of cement will be more and hence total surface area of all particles present in one gram of cement will be more. Therefore, more surface area will be available for chemical reaction. Hence, with finer cement more strength is developed.

Fineness of cement is measured either in terms of (i) surface area of cement in cm^2 per gm. or (ii) percentage of weight retained after sieving cement through 90 micron sieve.

As per I.S. surface area per gram of cement for ordinary Portland cement should not be less than 2250 cm^2/gm. I.S. specifies that the maximum residue after sieving through a 90 micron. I.S. sieve should be limited to 10% by weight for ordinary Portland cement.

(ii) Setting Time: The phenomenon by which the plastic cement paste changes into hard mass is called setting of cement. When cement and water are mixed to form paste, water combines chemically with the particles of cement to form hydrates. This process is known as hydration.

(a) Initial Setting Time: Cement paste is initially in plastic state, it sets slowly. Initial setting is that stage at which a crack that may appear will not reunite. This is not a sudden change, but it takes place gradually. Initial setting time of cement should not be less than 30 minutes.

(b) Final Setting Time: This is the term which relates to the completion of the setting process. The setting time is influenced by the percentage of water, its temperature, the temperature and the humidity of air. The setting time is controlled by adding a small quantity of gypsum in cement. Final setting time of cement is about 3 to 6 hours, but it should be greater than 10 hours.

(iii) Compressive Strength: Cement mortar cubes of surface area 50 cm^2 are prepared and kept wet for 3 days or 7 days. Then they are tested in a compression testing machine. For ordinary Portland cement, 3 days strength should be more than 16 N/mm^2 and 7 days strength should be more than 22 N/mm^2.

(iv) Soundness: Due to presence of lime and magnesium oxide, expansion of cement takes place as it comes in contact with water. Such expansion of cement is harmful and cement with less or no expansion is called sound cement. Expansion by Le Chatlier's apparatus should not be more than 10 mm.

1.5.3 Types of Cement

The various types of cements available in the market can be classified as follows:
1. Portland Cements
   (a) Ordinary Portland cement
   (b) Rapid hardening Portland cement
   (c) Low heat Portland cement
   (d) Sulphate resisting cement
   (e) Blast furnace slag cement
   (f) White and coloured cement
2. Super Sulphated cement
3. Natural cement
4. High Alumina cement
5. Special cements:
   (a) Portland Pozzolana cement
   (b) Masonry cement
   (c) Oil-well cement

1.5.3.1 Portland Cement

(a) Ordinary Portland cement: Nearly 60% of the cement used is ordinary Portland cement. It is admirably suited to all construction work. It is not affected by sulphates. It has medium rate of strength development and heat generation. It has adequate resistance to dry shrinkage and cracking, but has less resistance to chemical attack.

(b) Rapid hardening Portland cement: This cement is called rapid hardening Portland cement because the strength developed in a standard mortar cube after 3 days is the same as 7 days strength of ordinary Portland cement. This is because of higher percentage of C_3S present in this cement.

(c) Low heat cement: Percentages of C_3S and C_3A are lower in this cement while that of C_2S is higher. This results in a slower rate of reaction, lower evolution of heat of hydration and lower early strength, but the ultimate strength remains more or less unaffected.

(d) Sulphate resisting cement: In hardened cement, there exist two compounds which are sensitive to sulphate attack, viz. calcium aluminate hydrate which reacts with sodium sulphate and magnesium sulphate to form sodium-magnesium sulphoaluminate. This reaction results in an increase in volume of solid paste to the extent of 200 to 400% of the original calcium or magnesium aluminate hydrate. The surrounding concrete, therefore, slowly disintegrates.

(e) Portland blast furnace slag cement: Slag is a waste product in the manufacture of pig-iron. Slag is a mixture of lime, silica, and alumina. It is similar to ordinary Portland cement and can be used in all places where ordinary Portland cement is used. But in view of its low heat evolution it can also be used in mass concrete structures, such as dams, retaining walls, foundations, bridges and abutments. Blast furnace slag cement is more resistant to sulphate attack and is specified for marine works or pipe carrying water containing chemicals or sewage.

(f) White and coloured cement: White Portland cement is made from raw materials containing very little iron oxide and manganese oxide. China clay is used together with chalk or limestone free from impurities. Oil is used as a fuel instead of coal to avoid contamination. White cement is costly and is used only for interior decoration and architectural finish.

Coloured cement is obtained by mixing the pigments (oxide of lead etc.).

1.5.3.2 Super Sulphated Cement

Super sulphated cement is made by inter grinding a mixture of 80 to 85% of granulated slag with 10 to 15% of calcium sulphate and about 5% Portland cement clinker and ground to a fineness of 4000 to 5000 cm^2/g.

It is highly resistant to sea water and can withstand the highest concentration of sulphates normally found in soil or ground water and is also resistant to peaty acids and oils.

15.3.3 Natural Cement

It is obtained by calcining and grinding the so-called cement rock, which is a clayey limestone containing about 25% argillaceous material. The resulting cement is similar to Portland cement and it is really an intermediate product between Portland cement and hydraulic lime. Being heated at very low temperatures, it contains practically no C_3S and is, therefore, it slowly hardens. It is very rarely used, since manufacture of natural cement cannot be controlled.

1.5.3.4 High Alumina Cement

It is manufactured by the fusion of bauxite and limestone. Bauxite consists of hydrated alumina, oxide of iron and titanium with a small quantity of silica. It is not attacked by carbon dioxide dissolved in pure water and is, therefore, suitable for manufacture of RCC pipes.

1.5.3.5 Special Cement

(a) Portland Pozzolana Cement: This is a cement of inter-ground or blended mixture of Portland cement and pozzolana. Pozzolana is a natural or artificial material containing silica and alumina in a reactive form. Pozzolanic material is most found in volcanic ash, pumice, opal shale and cherts, burnt clay, fly ash etc.

The proportion of pozzolana used varies between 10 to 25% according to the weight of cement. Because free lime is removed, pozzolana concretes have high resistance to chemical attack. Portland pozzolana cement also has a lower rate of strength development. It is widely used for hydraulic structures such as dams, weirs etc.

(b) Masonry Cement: It is the product obtained by inter-grinding the Portland cement clinker with inert materials (non-pozzolana) such as limestone, dolomite and dolomite gypsum and an air-entraining plasticizer in suitable proportions so that the resulting product confirms to the requirements laid down by the Indian standards.

Masonry cement has been recently used in India because of its property of producing a smooth, plastic, cohesive, strong yet workable mortar when mixed with tint aggregate. Masonry cement is a good substitute for the normally used mortars.

(c) Oil-well Cement: A special type of cement is required for sealing oil-wells. Sealing is necessary to prevent the side of the freshly drilled well from collapsing and to keep ground water out of well shaft.

1.5.4 Field Testing of Cement

It is not always possible to check the quality of cement in a laboratory. In order to check the quality of cement on field, following methods are adopted:

1. When cement is thrown into a bucket of water it should float for sometime before sinking.
2. If one's hand is plunged into a bag of cement he should feel cool and not warm.
3. A thin paste of Portland cement with water should feel sticky between the fingers.
4. If the cement is found in the form of impalpable powder (felt between fingers by rubbing) the cement may be trusted. The quality of cement is suspected, if it is felt gritty.
5. Colour of cement should be greenish grey and should not show any visible lumps.

1.5.5 Uses

1. Ordinary Portland cement is used in the preparation of cement mortar and cement concrete in the construction of buildings.
2. It is used in the manufacturing of tiles.
3. It is used as a base in paints.
4. It is used for soil stabilization.
5. Rapid hardening cement is used in the construction of highway slabs.
6. Low heat cement is used in mass concreting of gravity dams, retaining walls.
7. White and coloured cement is used for ornamental works, face plastering to give a decorative finish.
8. Sulphate resisting cement is used in the construction of surfaces exposed to sulphate action.

1.6 STONE

1.6.1 Introduction

Stone has been used as a building material from very early times in the construction of buildings and other structures, both in India as well as in other parts of the world. Some of the ancient temples and forts are important examples of the extensive use of stone as a building material in our country over the ages. Today building stones are extensively used in various structures in different forms and can be used to fulfil a wide variety of requirements. Stone as a building material is the cheapest and most durable. It is quarried from rock.

1.6.2 Classification of Rocks

Stones are classified as per the classification of their parent rock:

1. **Geological Classification:** Igneous, sedimentary, metamorphic rocks.
2. **Physical Classification:** Stratified, unstratified, laminated rocks.
3. **Chemical Classification:** Siliceous, argillaceous, calcareous rocks.

(a) Igneous Rocks are formed by cooling the molten lava material which erupts from the interior of the earth. These are solid, massive and crystalline stones without stratification. For example: Basalt, granite and dolerite.

(b) Sedimentary Rocks are formed by denudation and deposition of existing rocks because of the weathering action of water, wind, frost, etc. Water is the most powerful medium of transportation of the disintegrated material from the primary rocks which ultimately gets deposited at the bottoms of lakes, streams and oceans. The consolidation of these deposited layers takes place under pressure by heat or by chemical agents acting as natural cements.

For example: Sand stone, lime stone and gravel.

(c) Metamorphic Rocks are originally either igneous or sedimentary rocks that have undergone considerable changes in their constitution, i.e. in their shape, structure, and sometimes, even in their mineral composition, under the influence of agents of metamorphism. There are three principal agents of metamorphism, viz. heat, pressure, and chemically acting fluids.

For example: Marble, gneiss, slate, Schist etc.

(d) Stratified Rocks: These rocks show a layered structure in their natural environment. They possess planes of stratification or cleavage and can be easily split up along these planes. Stratified rocks are derived from sedimentary rocks.

For example: Sand stone, lime stone, slate.

(e) Unstratified Rocks: Rocks which do not have strata and cannot be easily split into thin slabs fall into this category. Their structure may be crystalline or granular.

For example: Marble, granite, trap etc.

(f) Siliceous Rocks: These rocks have silica as their main component. They are hard, durable and not easily affected by weathering agents.

For example: Sand stone, granite, trap etc.

(g) Argillaceous Rocks: These rocks have clay or alumina as their main component. Although these rocks are dense, compact and hard; they are brittle and cannot withstand shock.

For example: Slate, laterite etc.

(h) Calcareous Rocks: These rocks have calcium carbonate as their main constituent. The durability of these rocks depends upon the atmospheric constituents as they are acted upon by hydrochloric acid.

For example: Marble, lime stone etc.

1.6.3 Uses of Stone

1. Slates are used for roofing and flooring material.
2. Stone blocks are mainly used in stone masonry in walls, foundations and ornamental facia work.
3. Granite is used for bridge abutments and pier, flooring, kitchen platform, steps, table top.
4. Marble is extremely suitable for ornamental and superior type of building work, monumental structures, floors, tiles.
5. Quartzite is used for rubble masonry, road metal, and aggregate for concrete.
6. Lime stone slabs are used for flooring, paving and roofing.

1.7 AGGREGATES

Aggregate is a general term applied to those inert or chemically inactive materials which, when bonded together by cement, form concrete. Most of the aggregates used are naturally occurring aggregates such as crushed rock, gravel and sand. Artificial and processed aggregates may be broken brick or crushed air-cooled blast furnace slag. Light weight aggregates, such as pumice, furnace clinker, coke, breeze, sawdust, foamed slag, expanded clays and shales, expanded slates, expanded vermiculite etc. are also used for the production of concrete of low density.

Classification:

Aggregate may be divided into two groups: (a) coarse aggregate, and (b) fine aggregate. Aggregates less than 4.75 mm are known as fine aggregates while those more than 4.75 mm in size are known as coarse aggregate. For large and important works it has become usual to separate the coarse aggregate also into two or more sizes, and these fractions are kept separate until the proper quantity of each has been weighed out for a batch of concrete. All-in aggregate, that is to say, aggregate as it comes from the pit or river bed, is sometimes used for unimportant works.

1.7.1 Quality of Aggregates

Natural aggregate used for concrete construction is required to comply with the norms laid down in IS: 383-1970 'specification for coarse and fine aggregates from natural sources for concrete'. Some of the important characteristics of aggregates are (1) strength (2) size (3) particle shape (4) surface texture (5) grading (6) impermeability (7) cleanliness (8) chemical inertness (9) physical and chemical stability at high temperatures (10) co-efficient of thermal expansion and (11) cost.

Aggregate should be chemically inert, strong, hard, durable, of limited porosity, free from adherent coatings, clay lumps, coal, and coal residues and should contain no organic or other admixture that may cause corrosion of the reinforcement or impair the strength or durability of the concrete.

The strength of concrete depends upon the strength of aggregate. Granite aggregate provides greater strength than pumice or burnt clay aggregates. The size of coarse aggregate used depends upon the nature of work. The coarse aggregate must be small enough to enable it to be worked between and around all reinforcements and into all corners of the work. For R.C.C. work, the maximum size of aggregate is limited to 20 mm to 25 mm. A coarse aggregate may have three shapes: rounded, irregular and angular. For a concrete of given workability, rounded aggregate require least water-cement ratio while angular aggregates require highest water-cement ratio. The particle shape is thus very important, since the water-cement ratio governs greatly the strength of concrete. Similarly, a concrete made with aggregates of rough surface is stronger than with smooth one. Grading of aggregates greatly affects strength and imperviousness of concrete. If the coarse and fine aggregates are well-graded, the percentage of void is considerably reduced. The voids of the fine aggregates are then occupied by the cement paste while the voids of coarse aggregate are filled with the mortar consisting sand, cement and water. The imperviousness of aggregates is an essential requirement, especially when the concrete is used for water retaining structures. This is also essential in other R.C. works of permanence, otherwise air and moisture would penetrate with the result that outer concrete would spall out. Aggregates must be clean and free from clay, silt, fine dust etc. so that proper mixing is possible. Dirt or other adherent coating would weaken the adhesion between the individual particles in a hardened concrete. Impurities, such as traces of sulphur or unburnt coal etc. may cause swelling due to chemical action, or may attack the reinforcement. The aggregate should have a thermal expansion similar to that of cement matrix. To summarise, the aggregate should be composed of inert mineral matter, should have high resistance to attrition, should be clean, free from any adhering coating, dense, durable and sufficiently strong to enable the full strength of the cement matrix to be developed.

1.7.2 Coarse Aggregate

The material retained on 4.75 mm sieve is termed as coarse aggregate. Crushed stone and natural gravel are the common materials used as coarse aggregates for concrete. Natural gravels can be quarried from pits where they have been deposited by alluvial or glacial action, and are normally composed of flint, quartz, schist and igneous rocks. Coarse aggregates are obtained by crushing, various types of granites (such as syenites, dolerites, diorites, quartzites etc.), schist, gneiss, crystalline hard lime stone and good quality sand stones. When very high strength concrete is required, a very fine-grained granite is perhaps the best aggregate. Coarse grained rocks make harsh concrete, and need high proportion of sand and high water/cement ratio to get reasonable degree of workability. Harder types of sand stones, having fine grained texture, are suitable as coarse aggregate, but softer varieties should be used with caution. Concrete made with sand stone aggregate gives trouble due to cracking, because of high degree of shrinkage. Similarly, hard and close-grained crystalline lime stones are very suitable for aggregate, is cheap, but should be used only in plain concrete. The bricks should be clean, hard, well-burnt and free from mortar and should not contain more than half percent of soluble sulphates. It should not be used for reinforced concrete work, since it is porous and may corrode the reinforcement. Blast furnace slag, coal ashes, coke-breeze etc. may also be used as aggregates to obtain light weight and insulating concrete of low strength.

1.7.3 Fine Aggregate

The material smaller than 4.75 mm size is called fine aggregate. Natural sands are generally used as fine aggregate. Sand may be obtained from pits, river, lake or sea-shore. When obtained from pits, it should be washed to free it from clay and silt. Sea shore sand may contain chlorides which may cause efflorescence, and may cause corrosion of reinforcement. Hence, it should be thoroughly washed before use. Similarly, if river sand contains impurities such as mud etc. it should be washed before use. Angular grained sand produces good and strong concrete, because it has good interlocking property, while round grained particles of sand do not afford such interlocking.

Grading of aggregates:

Gradation of the aggregates is almost as important as its quality is. The grading of the aggregates has a marked effect on the workability, uniformity, and finishing qualities of concrete. The grading of coarse aggregate may be varied through wider limits than that of sand without appreciably affecting the workability of concrete.

Fineness Modulus:

The fineness modulus of an aggregate is an index number which is roughly proportional to the average size of the particles in the aggregate. The coarser the aggregate, the higher the fineness modulus. The fineness modulus is obtained' by adding the percentage of the weight of materials retained on the following IS sieves and dividing it by 100.

80 mm, 40 mm, 20 mm, 10 mm, 4.75 mm, 2.36 mm, 1.18 mm, 600 micron, 300 micron, and 150 micron (total 10 sieves).

Table 1.1 illustrates the method of determining fineness modulus of both coarse and fine aggregates. It has been found that certain values of fineness moduli for the fine and coarse, aggregates give good workability, with a minimum quality of cement. The limits of fineness moduli are given in Table 1.2.

Table 1.1: Determination of fineness modulus

IS sieve	Coarse aggregate (10 kg)			Fine aggregate (1 kg)		
	Weight retained (kg)	Total weight retained (kg)	% weight retained	Weight retained (kg)	Total weight retained (kg)	% weight retained
80 mm	0.0	0.0	0.0	0.0	0.0	0.0
40 mm	0.0	0.0	0.0	0.0	0.0	0.0
20 mm	3.5	3.5	35.0	0.0	0.0	0.0
10 mm	3.0	6.5	65.0	0.0	0.0	0.0
3.75 mm	2.8	9.3	93.0	0.0	0.0	0.0
2.36 mm	0.7	10.0	100.0	0.1	0.10	10.0
1.18 mm	0.0	10.0	100.0	0.25	0.35	35.0
600 micron	0.0	10.0	100.0	0.35	0.70	70.0
300 micron	0.0	10.0	100.0	0.20	0.90	90.0
150 micron	0.	10.0	100.0	0.10	1.00	100.0
		Sum:	693.0		Sum:	305.0
Fineness modulus		$\dfrac{693.0}{100} = 6.93$			$\dfrac{305.0}{100} = 3.05$	

Table 1.2: Limits of fineness modulus

Maximum size of aggregate		Fineness modulus	
		Maximum	Minimum
(a) Fine aggregate	–	2.0	3.5
(b) Coarse aggregate	(i) 20 mm	6.0	6.9
	(ii) 40 mm	6.9	7.5
	(iii) 75 mm	7.5	8.0
	(iv) 150 mm	8.0	8.5
(c) Mixed aggregate	(i) 20 mm	4.7	5.1
	(ii) 25 mm	5.0	5.5
	(iii) 32 mm	5.2	5.7
	(iv) 40 mm	5.4	5.9
	(v) 75 mm	5.8	6.3
	(vi) 160 mm	6.5	7.0

1.8 SAND
1.8.1 Introduction

Sand is a granular form of silica (SiO_3). The grains vary in size and shape and they may be round or angular. Good sand is one whose mineralogical composition approaches pure quartz. Natural sand is the weathered and worn out particles of stones and rocks.

There are two types of sand: natural and artificial. Natural sand is obtained from pits, river beds and sea shores. Artificial sand is obtained by crushing gravel and/or stones. Sand may be divided into two categories depending upon its fineness. Sand passing through 4.75 mm sieve is **fine sand** and sand retained on 4.75 mm sieve is **coarse sand**.

1.8.2 Importance of Sand

Sand increases the volume of mortar thereby making the mortar economical and also prevents excessive shrinkage of cement paste, thereby, avoiding cracks during setting. Fine sand occupies the voids in coarse aggregates. This helps in making concrete solid and waterproof.

1.8.3 Advantages of Artificial Sand

Due to advancement in technology, it is now possible to manufacture artificial sand which has the following advantages:

1. Well graded
2. Superior surface texture.
3. Lesser quantity of coating material (cement) is required.
4. Required quantity and quality of sand can be produced in a short time.
5. Wastage of sand is less.
6. If economy at large is considered, artificial sand proves to be economical.

1.8.4 Bulking of Sand

When moisture content in sand is raised up to 5%, the volume of sand (dry) increases to about 25%; this phenomenon is called 'bulking of sand'. This occurs because the sand grains become surrounded by a thin film of water, which prevents them to come in contact with each other and consequently the sand, swells up. But, bulking decreases with the addition of water beyond 5%, and ultimately the volume of sand saturated with water becomes equal to that of dry sand.

1.8.5 Requisites for Good Sand

1. The grains should be sharp, angular and coarse.
2. The sand should be free from clayey materials and organic matters.
3. The grains should be made of durable minerals.
4. It should be free from salts.
5. The gradation of grain sizes should be such that it will give minimum voids.

1.8.6 Uses of Sand

1. Sand is used in cement mortar, lime mortar for stone masonry, brick masonry.
2. Sand is used in plain cement concrete, reinforced cement concrete, precast concrete, pre-stress concrete.
3. Coarse sand is used for face plaster on external walls.
4. Fine sand is used in plastering to give a smooth surface to the wall.
5. Sand serves as a drainage material and is therefore used in filtration plants, filling behind retaining wall, around foundation, filling well foundation, as a filter to drain seepage water from earthen dams.
6. Sand is used below flooring material (tiles) to provide a hard and levelled surface.

1.9 BRICKS

1.9.1 Introduction

Brick is a rectangular block of regular shape obtained by moulding a mixture of clay and sand, and generally burnt at high temperature. Bricks are easily moulded from plastic clays, also known as brick clay or brick earth.

Brick earth is derived by the disintegration of igneous rocks. Potash feldspars, orthoclase or microcline ($K_2O: Al_2O_3\ 6SiO_2$) is mainly responsible for yielding clay mineral in the earth. This mineral decomposes to yield kaolinite, a silicate of alumina which on hydration gives a clay deposit $Al_2O_3 2H_2O$ known as kaolin.

A good brick earth should be a mixture of pure clay and sand that when prepared with water can be easily moulded and dried without cracking or warping. It should contain a small quantity of lime which causes the grains of sand to melt and helps bind the particles of brick clay together.

1.9.2 Chemical Composition of Brick Earth

According to IS: 2117-1975, the clay selected should preferably confirm to the following mechanical composition:

      Clay   : 20 - 30% by weight
      Silt   : 20 - 35% by weight
      Sand : 35 - 50% by weight

The total content of clay and silt may preferably be not less than 50% by weight.

1.9.3 Functions of the Constituents of Brick Earth

1. Silica or sand prevents shrinkage in brick earth, and cracking and warping of bricks.
2. Clay or alumina makes brick earth plastic and makes bricks hard.
3. Lime and oxides of iron both act as fluxes helping the grains of sand to melt and bind the particles of clay together.

4. Oxides of iron also impart a red colour to the brick but if in excess, it makes the bricks dark blue.
5. Magnesia present in clay, combined, with oxide of iron makes the brick yellow.

1.9.4 Manufacture of Clay Bricks

Bricks are made by treating suitable brick earth or clay, moulding it to shape and size, drying it, and then baking it at high temperatures in order to fuse the constituents to a hard, homogeneous mass. The process of manufacture is as follows:
1. Selection of site
2. Preparation of clay
3. Moulding of bricks
4. Drying of bricks
5. Burning of bricks

1.9.5 Properties of Bricks

As per IS: 1077-1976, the following are the standard properties of burnt clay bricks:

1. Size and Shape of Brick: Hand moulded or machine moulded bricks should be free from cracks, flaws and from nodules of free lime. Bricks of 9 cm height may be moulded with a frog 1 to 2 cm deep on one of its flat sides. Bricks should have smooth rectangular faces and sharp corners. The standard size of common building bricks is 19 cm (length) × 9 cm (width) × 9 cm (height).

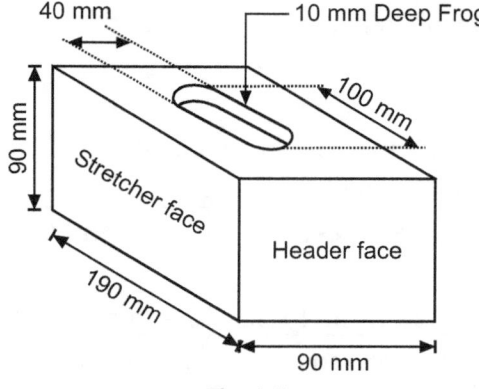

Fig. 1.5

2. Water Absorption of Bricks: After immersion in cold water for 24 hours, the average water absorption of common building bricks should not be more than 20% by weight and 15% by weight for higher classes.

3. Efflorescence: Salts such as sulphates of sodium and potassium, if present in bricks, are dissolved by the absorbed water. As and when drying conditions prevail, evaporation takes place at the outer face of the wall and the water previously absorbed is drawn to the face and along with it the salts also. As evaporation proceeds, the concentration of the salt in solution increases until a point is reached when the salt crystallizes out. According to

IS: 3495-1976, the rating of efflorescence should not be more than moderate and slight for higher classes. The liability of efflorescence is reported as follows:

    Nil   :   When there is no perceptible deposit of efflorescence.

    Slight   :   When not more than 10% of the area of the brick is covered with a thin deposit of salts.

    Moderate :   When there is a deposit that is heavier than that mentioned under slight, and covering up to 50% of the exposed area of the brick surface, but unaccompanied by powdering or flaking of the surface.

    4. Strength of Bricks: Bricks often have to withstand great compressive stresses. The durability of the masonry depends upon the strength of the bricks. The common building bricks should have a minimum strength of 35 kg/cm^2.

1.9.6 Types of Bricks

Bricks can be classified into two types:

(i) Modular brick: The bricks confirming to LS 1077-1976 are known as modular brick. The size of brick is 19 cm × 9 cm × 9 cm. With mortar joint the size becomes 20 cm × 10 cm × 10 cm.

(ii) Traditional brick: These bricks are manufactured traditionally or right from ancient times. There is a slight variation in the size of the brick from place to place. The common size is 23 cm × 11.4 cm × 7 cm.

Classification of Bricks:

    The bricks are also classified as per their quality. The comparison of properties of different classes of bricks is given in table.

Sr. No.	Description	First Class	Second Class	Third Class
1.	Moulding	Machine and Table	Hand and Table	Hand
2.	Colour and burning	Uniform red	Uniform red, may be slightly over burnt.	May be slightly over burnt or under burnt.
3.	Shape	Sharp straight edges, plain rectangular faces.	May have slightly blunt edges.	May have distorted round edges.
4.	Absorption of water by weight	Less than 20%	Less than 22%	Less than 25%
5.	Efflorescence	Nil	Slight	Moderate
6.	Compressive strength	Greater than 10.5 N/mm	Greater than 7 N/mm	Greater than 3.5 N/mm

1.9.7 Uses of Bricks
1. Bricks are used in brick masonry as a load bearing or a partition wall.
2. Bricks are used as flooring material.
3. Special refractory bricks are used as refractory lining.
4. Broken bricks are used as aggregates in lime concrete.
5. First class bricks are used in architectural compositions and face work of building.
6. Bricks are also used in the construction of roads.

1.10 TYPES OF CONCRETE

Cement concrete is the most important artificial building material being commonly used in present day construction. Concrete is a mixture of cement, sand and coarse aggregates with water. Just after mixing, concrete is in plastic stage and it takes the shape as given by mould.

1.10.1 Grades of Concrete

Concrete was specified by volumetric proportions such as 1 : 2 : 4 or 1 : 3 : 6 or 1 : 4 : 8 showing proportions of cement, sand, and coarse aggregates. Indian Standard specifies seven grades of concrete designated as M 10, M 15, M 20, M 25, M 30, M 35, and M 40, where M stands for concrete mix and the number specifies 28 day's compressive strength of a 15 cm cube in N/mm^2.

Sr. No.	Grade	Proportion of mix	Specific Uses	Compressive Strength N/mm^2
1.	M10	1: 3: 6	For mass concrete work in culverts, retaining walls, concrete flooring, compound and foundation walls, parapet, ordinary machine base etc.	10
2.	M15	1: 2: 4	For general R.C.C. work such as stairs, columns, beams, slabs, lintels, damp proof course at plinth level, machine foundations, R.C.C Piles.	15
3.	M20	$1: 1\frac{1}{2}: 3$	For water tanks, bridge construction and sewers, under water construction.	20
4.	M25	1: 1: 2	For heavily loaded R.C.C. members, R.C.C. arches of long span.	25
5.	M30	–	For heavily loaded structures with special purpose.	30
6.	M35	–	For heavily loaded structures with special purpose.	35
7.	M40	–	For radiation shielding	40

1.10.2 Types of Concrete

Concrete can be broadly classified into the following:

I. Plain cement concrete (P.C.C.):

It is obtained by mixing cement, sand and coarse aggregates with an adequate quantity of water. P.C.C is very strong in compression and very weak in tension. It has good weathering resistance and is impervious. It has good resistance to abrasion and is hard and durable.

Uses:
1. It is used in foundation masonry, base for foundation, flooring base.
2. Mass concrete work in construction of gravity dams and retaining wall.

II. Reinforced cement concrete (R.C.C.):

It is obtained by reinforcing steel in the mixture of cement, sand and coarse aggregate with an adequate quantity of water. R.C.C is equally strong in compression and tension. It is hard, durable and can bear all type of stresses. R.C.C is used for columns, beams, slabs, foundations, retaining wall, water and oil tanks, road pavements, concrete pipes.

Uses of R.C.C:
1. It is used in construction of multi-storied building.
2. It is used for construction of water and oil tanks, bridges, concrete pipes.
3. It is used for construction of road pavement.
4. It is used for marine structures, hydraulic structures with some anticorrosive admixtures.

Advantages of R.C.C.:
1. The fluidity of concrete and flexibility of reinforcement make it possible to mould the member into a desired number of shapes.
2. Its monolithic character provides more rigidity to the structure.
3. It is highly durable and fire-resisting. It is not affected by vermin, termites, fungus, or such other insects.
4. Care and cost of maintenance of R.C.C. is almost negligible.

III. Precast Concrete:

When a large number of components of similar dimensions are required, the best option is to use precast concrete units produced in a factory. Individual concrete units or members of various types which are cast in separate form before they are placed in a structure is known as precast concrete members.

Hollow concrete blocks, tiles, pipes, roof slabs, electric poles, fencing posts, staircase railing balusters are the common examples.

Uses of Precast Concrete:
1. In the production of building components like beams, columns, slabs, stairs, water tanks, partition walls, septic tank, step units, cladding panels, manholes, water supply and drainage pipes, fencing posts etc.
2. In the production of industrial elements such as girders, funicular trusses, portal frames, shells, domes, pressure vessels etc.
3. In the production of electric poles, piles, caissons, shaft lining, wharfs, road dividers, traffic barriers, tetra pods etc.

Advantages of Precast Concrete:
1. The use of precast concrete proves to be advantageous when there are many individual members to be cast, because the same form can be used many times.
2. Concrete of superior quality can be produced because it is possible to have better quality control on the production in factory.
3. Smoother exposed surfaces can be achieved and hence plastering may not be required.
4. Precast members of desired shape can be made with greater accuracy.

IV. Pre-stress Concrete:

It is a modification of reinforced concrete, which not only eliminates the weakness of concrete in tension but also makes it possible to take full advantage of compressive strength of concrete. The concrete is subjected to compressive stresses, before the external loads are applied by inducing tensile stresses in the reinforcement to counteract tensile stresses in the concrete caused by external loads.

Methods of Pre-stressing: There are two methods as follows:

(A) Pre-tensioning: In this method, for pre-tensioning the member, the tendons are pre-stressed in place in the form, before the concrete is poured. The tendons consist of small diameter high tensile steel wires. These tendons are first stretched to the desired tension in the form by hydraulic jack and then anchored at their ends. Concrete is now poured in the form or mould and then allowed to harden for 28 days. The tendons are then released from their anchorages. These tendons being high tension wires, try to return to their original position. However, because of the bond between concrete and tendon, these tendons can not return back to their original position and therefore induce a compressive force in the concrete member.

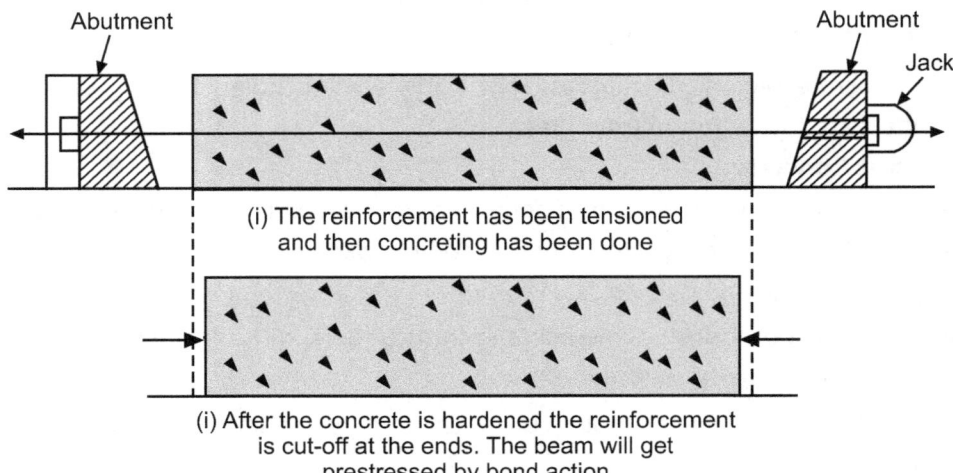

Fig. 1.6

(i) The reinforcement has been tensioned and then concreting has been done

(i) After the concrete is hardened the reinforcement is cut-off at the ends. The beam will get prestressed by bond action

(B) Post-Tensioning: In this method, the tendons are given the required tension after the concrete has attained the desired strength. In this system, the tendons are enclosed in ducts or metal sheets which prevent them from bonding with concrete. After the concrete has attained the required minimum strength the tendons are stretched through ducts by special jacks acting against the end of the side of the precast member. After stretching, the tendons are anchored at the ends of the concrete member, inducing compressive stress in it.

Uses:

1. Pre-stress concrete girders are used in bridge construction.
2. The large span beams are possible with pre-stress concrete.
3. Railway sleepers and electric poles are examples of pre-stress concrete.
4. Used in construction of nuclear power stations, steel plants, piles, transmission poles and silos.

Advantages:

1. The size of structural members is reduced.
2. These members can sustain effects of impact, shocks, and vibrations.
3. It permits the use of large spans (greater than 30 m) with shallow members, even when heavy loads are encountered.
4. High quality materials are used.

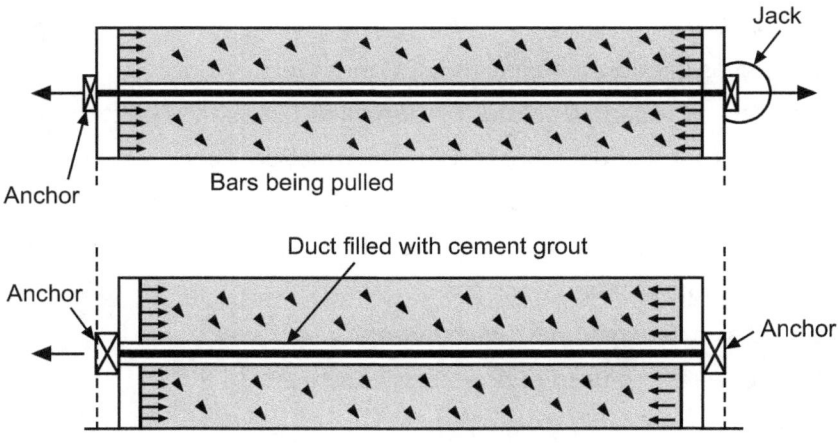

Fig. 1.7

1.11 STEEL

Reinforcing steel consists of bars, usually circular in cross section. These are available in three different grades viz. Fe 250, Fe 415 and Fe 500. Fe refers to ferrous metal and the number refers to the specified guaranteed yield stress in N/mm^2.

Steel is an intermediate form between cast iron and wrought iron. It is an alloy of iron and carbon containing carbon from 0.25 to 1.25%. Steels are highly elastic, ductile, malleable, forgeable, weldable.

1.11.1 Classification of Steel

Based on the physical and mechanical properties, the following three types of reinforcements are mainly used in reinforced concrete construction:

(a) Mild steel: Mild steel is used as structural and non-structural steel in the form of various sections like I-section, channel, angle, flat and also in the form of round bars as reinforcement in concrete. It is designated as Fe 250 due to the yield strength of 250 N/mm^2.

(b) Tor steel: These bars are usually of steel which do not possess a well defined yield point. These bars have low ductility and low bend ability. Tor steel is extensively used as reinforcement in R.C.C work. It is available in two grades: Fe 415 and Fe 500 and a variety of diameters ranging from 8 mm to 40 mm.

(c) High tensile steel: Wires of high tensile strength (tendons) are used in pre-stress concrete. The diameter of wires is 1.5 mm to 8 mm with their ultimate stress ranging from 1500 N/mm^2 to 2350 N/mm^2. Tendons are grouped in the form of cables containing 7 to 8 wires.

1.11.2 Uses of Steel

1. Mild steel is used as distribution steel in R.C.C members.
2. Mild steel is used as rolled structural sections like I-section, T-section, channel section, angle iron, plates; round and square rods in construction work.
3. Plain and corrugated sheets of mild steel are used as roof coverings.
4. Mild steel is also used in the manufacture of various tools and equipments, machine parts, towers and industrial buildings etc.
5. Tor steel is used as main steel in R.C.C members.
6. High tensile steel wires are used in pre-stress concrete.
7. In the fabrication of steel tank, steel pipes.
8. In the fabrication of structural steel in trusses, stanchions, beams in the form of various sections.
9. In the fabrication of non-structural steel component for grills, door frame, windows and stairs.

1.12 TIMBER

1.12.1 Introduction

Timber is an age old building material. In fact as per old English word timber means "to construct or build." Timber is used in building construction in various locations such as beams, trusses, rafters, as joists in floors, doors, window frames, shutters, stair cases, poles, piles, columns. There is hardly any part of building, where timber can not be used. Therefore, word timber appropriately means "to construct or to build."

However, day by day, use of timber is decreasing due to scarcity, high cost of labour and timber, availability of cheaper and stronger material.

1.12.2 Classification of Timber

Timber is classified in variety of ways. Some of these are as under:

1. Growth of tree i.e. whether growth of tree is outwards (i.e. EXOGENOUS) as in sal teak etc. or inwards (i.e. ENDOGENOUS) as in Cane, Bamboo, etc.

2. Durability: i.e. average life of timber.

3. Strength of Timber.

4. Refractiveness i.e. resistance to defects during seasoning.

5. Classifications according to **IS 399.**

1.12.3 I. S. Classification of Timber: [IS 399 -1963]

I. S. classification of timber takes into account, details of zonal distribution, various uses, availability, durability, treatability and refractiveness.

(a) Zones: For this classification, India is devided into five zones: North, South, East, West and Central zone.

(b) Uses: Uses are classified under the following categories: (i) Construction purpose, (ii) Furniture and cabinet making, (iii) Light packing cases, (iv) Heavy packing cases for machinery and similar stores. (v) Agricultural implements and tools handles. (vi) Turnery articles and toys. (vii) Veneers and ply-woods.

(c) Availability: Availability of timber is categorised as under: (i) X: Most common; (1000 tones or more per year. (ii) Y: Common - 250 to 1000 tons per year. (iii) Z: Less common - Less than 250 tons per year.

(d) Durability and refractoriness to air seasoning.

(e) Comparative strength co-efficients: The figures for comparative strength co-efficients for various uses for all the timbers have been arrived at, by suitably grouping the various important mechanical properties that come into play for any particular use, and giving due weightage to the relative importance of these properties.

Certain timbers are prone to developing of defects during air seasoning, whereas certain timbers offer resistance to development of such defects. Timbers are classified according to the resistance offered. Resistance to air seasoning is called as "Refractiveness." Accordingly timbers are classified as under:

(a) Class "A" or Highly Refractory Timber: Timbers which can be air seasoned, without developing any defects are classified under this category.

(b) Class "B" or Moderately Refractory Timber: Timbers under this class can be seasoned with suitable precautions against rapid drying Teak, Sheesam come under this class.

(c) Class "C" or Low Refreactory Timber: These timbers require special precautions during seasoning.

1.12.4 Defects and Decay in Timber

Usefulness and strength of timber for Engineering usage gets reduced due to: (i) defects in tree during its growth, (ii) defects in tree after felling, (iii) defects in tree during seasoning (iv) decay and diseases in tree.

There are more than 24 types of defects and it is difficult to get a tree free from all the defects. Depending upon whether timber is to be used for structural usage or non-structural usage, I. S. classifies defects into two categories viz. (a) Prohibited defects and (b) Permissible defects.

Some of the important defects and diseases are explained below:

(a) Centre Heart/Heart Shakes: This defect develops in matured trees due to shrinkage of heart wood or if tree is *cut* and *kept unbarked for a long time*. The cracks are wide at centre and go on reducing along medullary rays. *This defect is permissible if it* is not farther than 25 to 50 mm from the nearest edge. [Ref. Fig. 1.8 (a)]

(b) Bow: This is a prohibited defect in non-coniferous timber and may develope after felling tree or during conversion and seasoning. Converted timber shrinks, bends in the direction of length. [Refer Fig. 1.8 (b)].

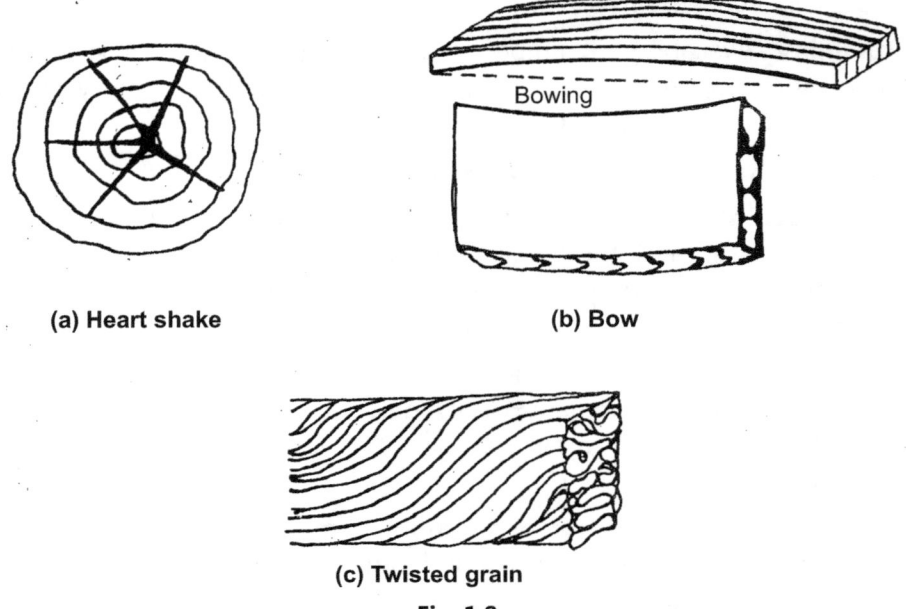

(a) Heart shake   (b) Bow

(c) Twisted grain

Fig. 1.8

(c) Twisted Grain: Timber with twisted grain is unsuitable for sawing and *hence it is a prohibited defect*. However, such timber *can be used in unsawn condition* for using as post or pole. This defect is found in trees, which are subjected to constant strong wind in one direction. [Fig. 1.8 (c)].

(d) Knots: A knot is a part of branch incorporated in the body of a tree.

When knot is intact with surrounding wood, free from any defect, it is called as "Live knot." When it is not held firmly it is called as "dead-knot" or "Loose knot". Knots make the working of wood difficult. In respect of intergrown knots, the annual growth rings are completely intergrown with the surrounding wood. If large, these knots may check, but these do not loosen or drop out, since they are integral part of wood. Encased knot is one, whose annual rings of growth are not intergrown with those of surrounding wood. [Fig. 1.9].

Permissible maximum size of live knot corresponding to different widths of face (ranging from 75 mm to 600 mm) depends upon whether knot is located in the central width of section and whether it is nearer to top or bottom edge. In general, knot of small size is permitted if it is nearer to edge than if it is in central width.

Timbers containing large dead knots, decayed knots, or cluster of knots are rejected as they are poorer in strength.

 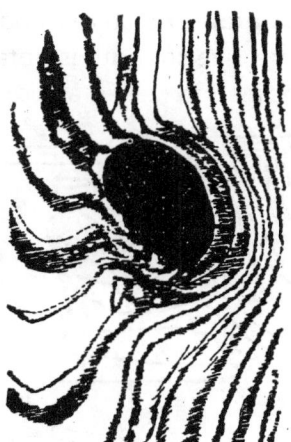

Fig. 1.9

Knots do not decrease strength, because of any inferiority in their quality, but because
(i) The grain of the piece is destorted in passing around them.
(ii) Growth of knot is at a large angle to the grain of the piece.
(iii) During drying checking may occur in and around the knot.

The weakening effect of knot is more in tensile strength than on compressive strength. In simply supported beams, bottom fibres will be subjected to tensile stresses, hence it is advisable to place knot on upper side than on lower side. *Knots do not have any effect on shear strength.*

In short columns, reduction in strength is proportional to the size of knot.

(e) Wane: Lack of wood or bark from any cause at edge or corner of piece is called wane. [Fig. 1.10].

This is a not a serious defect. The following are the permissible limits for grade I, II, III timbers for structural use.

Grade of Timber	Permissible fraction of width of face occupied by width of wane
Grade I timber	1/8 th of width
Grade II timber	1/6 th of width
Grade III timber	1/4 th of width

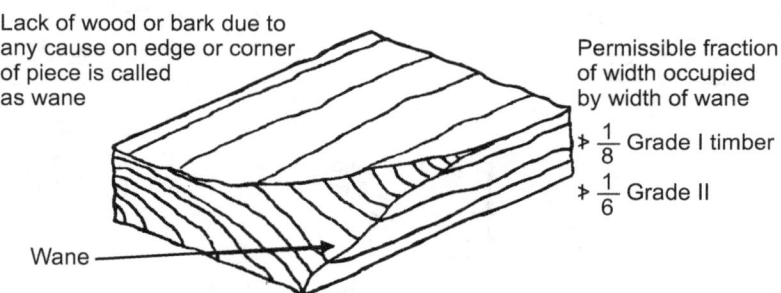

Fig. 1.10: Wane

(f) Slope of grain: As stated above, grain refers to the direction of fibres. Maximum tensile and compressive strength is obtained along the grain. Strength of timber is reduced if load acts at an inclination (called as slope of grain) to the longitudinal axis.

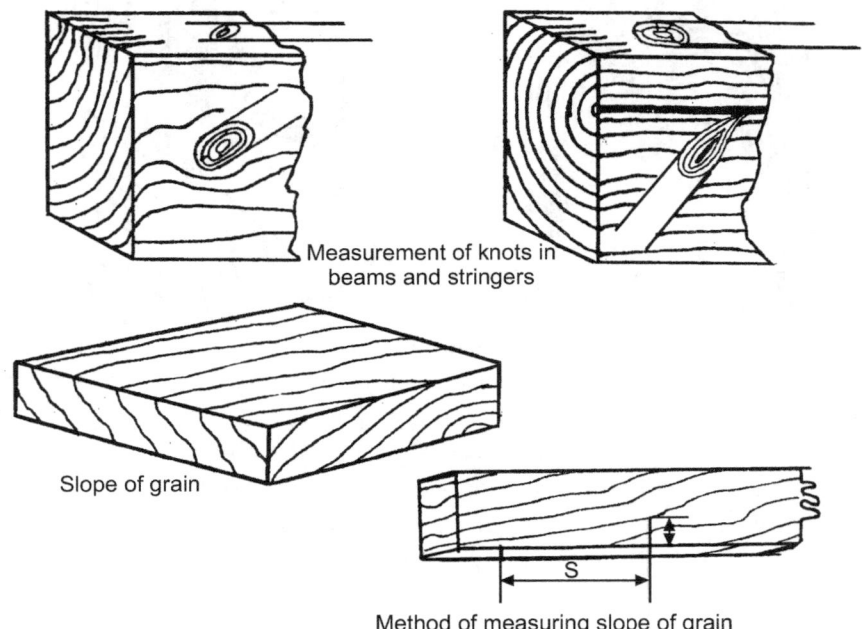

Fig. 1.11: Slope of Grain and measurement of slope of grain

Maximum permissible slope of grain in timbers of structural use for grade I, II and III timbers is 1 in 20; 1 in 15 and 1 in 10 respectively.

(h) Foxiness: Generally, this defect developes due to lack of ventilation during storage and is caused by action of fungi. In this defect, yellowish reddish stains are caused by water soluble material, in over matured trees.

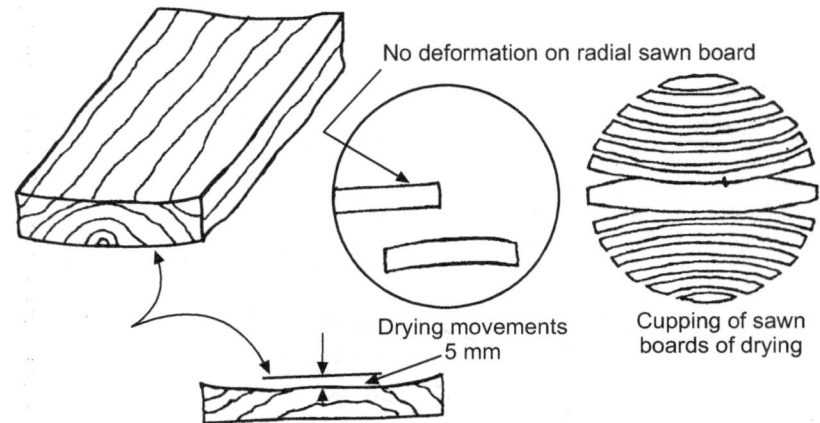

Maximum sag or 5 mm is permitted for grade I timber of any width

Fig. 1.12

(i) Cupping: It is distortion of a board in which the face is convex or concave transversely.

It is considered as prohibited defect in special grade, and grade I non-coniferous sawn timber. In respect of grade 2 timber maximum 5 mm sag is permitted in any width.

1.12.5 Seasoning

Removal of moisture from timber so as to be in equilibrium with moisture in surrounding atmospheric conditions, where timber is likely to be used, is called as seasoning. Seasoning is done to achieve the following objectives:

Objectives of Seasoning Timber:
- (a) Seasoning improves following properties: (i) strength, durability, (ii) working qualities including polishing, painting and gluing. (iii) Resistance to attack of insects, fungus.
- (b) Proper seasoning reduces tendency to split, shrink, and warp.
- (c) Seasoning reduces weight of timber and is easy to handle.
- (d) Timber becomes fit to receive preservative treatment.

Preparing timber for seasoning:

Before actual seasoning timber is treated as under:

(a) Girdling: In respect of trees which are resistant to attack of fungus about 5 to 8 cm deep and 15 cm wide around cut is made at the bottom of the tree, about 2 to 3 years prior to felling of tree. During the interval, tree dies and moisture is removed.

(b) Thick sections of some timbers are likely to be subjected to end splitting. Ends of logs of such timbers are coated with thick layers of moisture proof substances such as coal tar, bituminous paint, paraffin wax.

(c) Water seasoning: When it is not possible to cut logs into planks scantlings, first bark is removed; and then logs are completely submerged in running water, for about a fortnight. If water is stagnant, then, it is changed once in a fortnight. Partial immersion in water is harmful. By this method, sap in timber is washed away; and possibility of cracking and warping of timber is reduced; however, strength of wood is reduced. Afterwards timber is air dried to bring down moisture content to 40% and then it is seasoned in kiln.

Seasoning of Timber:

Seasoning may be either air (natural) seasoning or artificial seasoning.

(a) Air seasoning: Area selected for seasoning should be elevated, drainable, dry and should have free access to air. Timber is stacked about 30 to 45 cm clear of ground. The sawn pieces are stacked alternate in longitudinal and transverse direction in such a way that free circulation of air is ensured. Timber is protected from the direct sun. Hard wood which dry out slowly is stacked in winter, whereas soft woods which dry out quickly is stacked in Summer. Air seasoning is a economical method, and renders good quality timber. However, following are the disadvantages:
- (i) Seasoning takes long lime. As a result more area and capital is blocked.
- (ii) Reduction in moisture content is not less than 18% and where less moisture is required, air seasoned timber cannot be used.

(iii) During the prolonged period of seasoning, the timber is likely to be attacked by fungi and insects.

(iv) There is no effective control over moisture content in timber.

(b) Kiln seasoning:

(i) The kiln used for seasoning consists of brick masonry chamber (usually hollow bricks) and is lined with refractory lining to reduce loss of heat.

(ii) Heating system is arranged in such a way that, temperature of kiln can be raised to maximum or can be lowered smoothly.

(iii) Arrangement is made to provide sufficient humidity and it can be controlled smoothly.

(iv) Propeller fans are arranged in such a way that, air circulation is uniform and has sufficient velocity. Air can be changed and controlled as desired.

Method: Timber to be seasoned, is stacked on rail mounted trolley and is taken inside kiln. Doors are closed, steam is injected and heating system is adjusted for low temperature; and full humidity is maintained to avoid evaporation of moisture from timber surface. Gradually temperature of kiln is raised and humidity is reduced. Proper air circulation is maintained by fans. By proper control of humidity and temperature, sterilisation of timber can be achieved.

Advantages of Kiln Seasoning are:

(i) Timber can be seasoned thoroughly, as desired in a short period.

(ii) Less space is required and turn out is more. As a result, capital is not blocked.

(iii) Timber can be sterilised and is less liable for shrinkage.

Disadvantages:

(i) Skilled labour is required.

(ii) If there is no proper control over humidity, temperature etc. timber is liable for seasoning defects like end split, warping etc.

(c) Other methods of seasoning:

Chemical seasoning: Some varieties of timber which are difficult to season in a kiln due to development of surface split and checks are painted with hygroscopic chemicals such as sodium chloride, urea etc. The chemicals keep the moisture content of the surface layer of wood, above fiber saturation point and hence prevent shrinking even at low humidity and high temperature. After applying the chemical treatment, the timber is subjected to kiln seasoning.

Note: As stated before depending upon the behaviour of timber during seasoning, timber is classified as Highly Refractory, Moderately Refractory and Non-Refractory.

Table 1.3: Properties and uses of important timbers in Maharashtra

	Babul	Khair	Rakta Rohida	Phanas	Aini	Shisam	Kusumb	Jambhul	Mango	Teak	Chir	Deodar	Suru
1. Availability	y	y	y	z	y	y	z	y	y	x	x	z	y
2. Density kg/m^3	785	1010	690	595	595	770	1105	850	690	640	575	519	850
3. Durability	Low	H	H	H	Low	H	Low	M	Low	H	Low	Low	Low
4. Treatability	b	-	-	-	-	-	a	e	a	e	b	c	c
5. Refractiveness to air seasoning	M	H	M	M	M	M	H	H	L	M	L	M	H
6. Compare strength on basis of teak as 100:													
(a) As a beam	105	120	90	75	90	90	140	95	90	100	70	60	90
(b) As a column	105	-	-	75	95	115	140	95	75	80	75	85	-
(c) Shock absorption	170	-	-	75	90	145	155	105	100	85	80	60	-
Suitability for													
1. Constructional purpose	✓	✓	✓	✓	✓	✓	✓	✓	✗	✓	✓	✓	✓
2. Furniture making	-	-	✓	✓	✓	✓	-	-	✓	✓	✓	✓	-
3. Packing Cases:													
(a) Light	-	-	-	-	✓	-	-	✓	✓	✓	-	✓	-
(b) Heavy	-	✓	-	-	-	-	-	-	✓	✓	-	✓	-
4. Agricultural Implements	✓	-	✓	-	-	✓	-	-	-	-	-	-	-
5. Turnery Articles	✓	-	-	✓	✓	✓	-	✓	✓	✓	-	-	-
6. Veneers and Plywoods	-	-	-	✓	✓	✓	-	✓	✓	✓	-	-	-

EXERCISE

1. Explain the various criteria for the selection of site for the building (residential).
2. Define the following terms:
    (a) Plinth area.
    (b) Carpet area.
    (c) Floor space index.
    (d) Cost of building.
3. Write short note on floor space index.
4. What are the various factors to be considered for the selection of site ?
5. What is F.S.I. ? Give typical values of space requirements around a building in your area.
6. State any two uses of basic construction materials.
7. Write short note on classification of stones and bricks.
8. State importance of sand in construction.
9. Explain the following terms:
    (i) P.C.C., (ii) P.C., (iii) R.C.C., (iv) P.S.C.
10. Enlist any four basic materials used in construction and give two uses of each of them.
11. Mention any two uses of any three types of concrete.
12. Differentiate between pre-tensioning and post tension.
13. Give two practical applications of the following:
    (i) Pre-stress concrete.
    (ii) Plain cement concrete.
14. Sketch a conventional brick showing a frog. Also state the importance of frog.
15. State four uses of bricks.
16. State any two uses of each:
    (i) Stones, (ii) Cement, (iii) I class brick.
17. Write a short note on classification of bricks. Also state any three requirements to ascertain the quality of good bricks for a building.
18. Write a note on classification of stones and state any two uses of first class bricks.
19. Give two practical examples of
    (i) Plain cement concrete.
    (ii) Precast concrete.
20. Write short notes on the following:
    (i) Aggregates, (ii) Timber, (iii) Types of steel, (iv) Sand as a construction material.

21. Differentiate between the following:
    (i) Aggregate and sand.
    (ii) P.C.C. and R.C.C.
    (iii) Brick and stone.
    (iv) Timber and steel.
22. What is cement ? State any two types of special cements. Also state their suitability.
23. How will you check quality of cement in the field without sending sample of cement to the laboratory ?
24. What is the importance of sand in construction ? State any four advantages of artificial sand.

❑❑❑

UNIT 2

BUILDING AND ROAD CONSTRUCTION

2.1 LOADS COMING ON STRUCTURE

The basic requirement of any structural member of a building is that it should be strong enough to carry or support all the possible types of loads which are liable to be subjected on it. Different types of load act on the building and try to deform it. Hence, a proper assessment of the loads coming on the structure has to be made carefully. Design load is the load generally taken as the worst possible combination of forces and loads which a structure has been calculated to sustain. The different types of load are as follows:

1. Dead Load:

It is defined as the force whose magnitude, position and direction remain constant. Thus the weight of all the permanent parts of a building such as walls, columns, beams, floors, roofs, stairs, doors, windows etc. is considered as dead load. Dead load of different parts of a building can be determined by multiplying its volume by the unit weight of the materials. The unit weight of common materials used in building construction is given in IS - 1911: 1967.

	Building material	Unit Weight (kN/m^3)
(i)	Stones	20 to 28
(ii)	Bricks	20 to 24
(iii)	Steel	78
(iv)	Plain Cement Concrete	22
(v)	Reinforced Cement Concrete	24
(vi)	Structural Timber	7
(vii)	Tiles	18
(viii)	Sand and Loose gravel	16 to 20

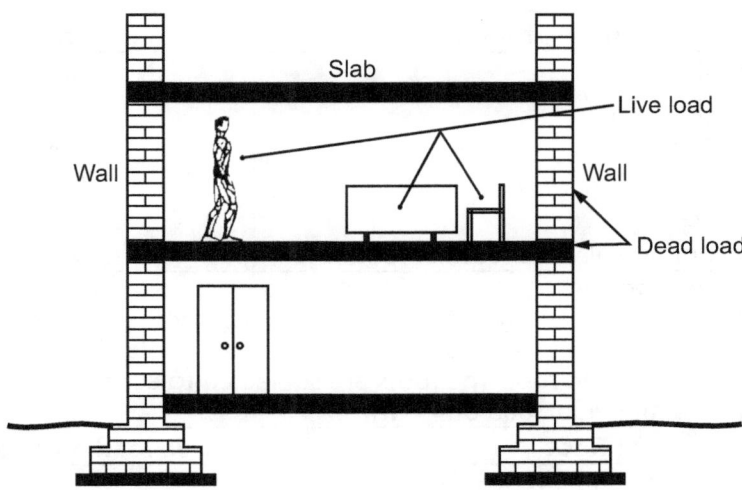

Fig. 2.1: Dead load and live load

2. **Live Load:**

(a) **Live load on Floors:** These loads are also known as superimposed loads. They consist of moving or variable loads due to occupants, weight of furniture, home appliances, equipments and stores. For design of a building their maximum magnitude, worst position and direction should be taken into account. IS 875-1964 gives minimum live load per square metre of floor area as equivalent static uniformly distributed loads. Some of these are given below:

	Type of floor	Minimum live load (kN/m^3)
(i)	Residential building, hospital wards	2.00
(ii)	Office rooms, Small work places	2.50
(iii)	Bank and Reading room	3.00
(iv)	Shops, Classrooms, Assembly Halls	4.00
(v)	Warehouses, Workshops, Factories, Dance halls for light weight	5.00
(vi)	Warehouses, Workshops, Factories for medium weight	7.50
(vii)	Warehouses, Workshops, Factories for Heavy weight	10.00

For multi-storeyed buildings, while designing columns, walls and foundation, reduction in live load is considered, as all floors are not likely to be simultaneously loaded. The live load for upper floor is reduced by applying reduction factor as shown in the table.

Number of floors		Reduction in Live Load
(i)	One floor	No reduction
(ii)	Two floor	10%
(iii)	Three floor	20%
(iv)	Four floor	30%
(v)	Five floor	40%
(vi)	Six floor and all other subsequent floor	50%

(b) Live Load on Roof: Roofs may be flat, sloping or curved and are used for frequent or incidental assembly purposes. Live load on the sloping roof is calculated by taking into account slope, accessibility. On the roofs, snow load is taken as 25 N/m² of roof area per cm depth of accumulated snow on roof. The roofs are subjected to accumulation of snow or rain and are designed for a minimum load of 4 kN/m².

Type of Roof	Live load on a roof plan
1. Flat or Sloping roof (slope up to 10°) (i) Access provided (ii) Access not provided	 1.5 kN/m² 0.75 kN/m²
2. Sloping roof with slope 10° (i) For roofs with sheets, purlins (ii) For trusses, beams, etc.	 $(9.5 - 0.2\theta)$ $2/3 (9.5 - 0.2\theta)$ Subject to min. of 4 kN/m²

3. **Wind Load:**

When wind is obstructed by the structure, it exerts a pressure on the structure known as wind pressure. Wind pressure acts horizontally on the exposed vertical faces of the structure and is expressed in terms of basic wind pressure P which is an equivalent static pressure in the direction of wind. Basic wind pressure may be obtained by

$$P = KV^2$$
P = wind pressure in kg/m²
V = wind velocity in kmph
K = coefficient which depends on wind velocity, air temperature, size of the building.

When the height of building is less than three times its effective width and further, wind load may be neglected.

For a height 12 m of the structure, wind pressure is taken as 0.5 kN/m² and 0.7 kN/m² for 24 m height. Snow load may be considered if necessary.

4. **Earthquake Load:**

The effect of an earthquake is taken equivalent to imparting acceleration to the foundation of the building in the direction in which the wave is travelling. Earthquake waves may reach in any direction and for design purposes it has to be resolved in vertical and horizontal components.

The magnitude of earthquake force is given by:

$$\text{Earthquake force} = W \cdot \alpha/g$$

α = acceleration due to an earthquake adopted from historical available data is 1/20 g to 1/10 g where g is the gravitational acceleration.

W = weight of the structure.

2.2 TYPES OF CONSTRUCTION

2.2.1 Load Bearing Structures

In load bearing structures, the entire load of the superstructure is transmitted through the walls to the firm soil below the ground. These walls are supported on continuous foundations that rest on hard strata. Thickness of such walls is large. This type of construction is restricted to four storeys but practically only two storeys are constructed. If the number of storeys is increased, the thickness of the walls increases considerably. This not only reduces the carpet area but even increases the cost. This type of construction, therefore, cannot be used for multi-storeyed buildings.

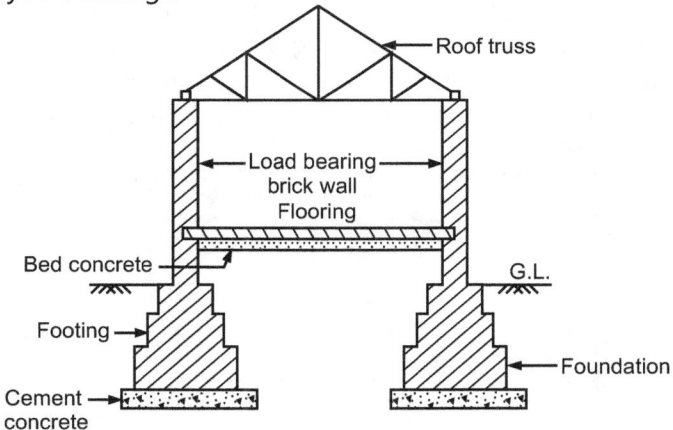

(a) Load bearing structure

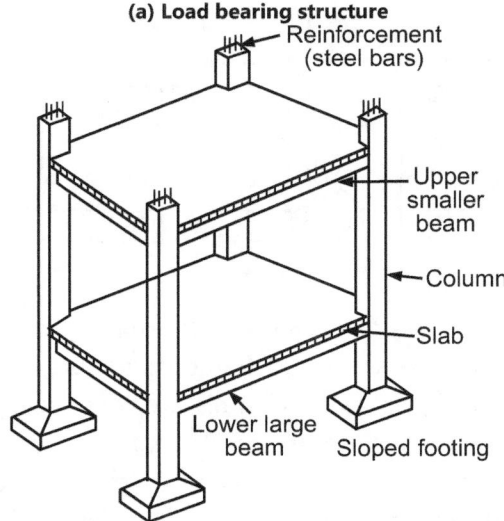

(b) Framed structures

Fig. 2.2

2.2.2 Framed Structures

Framed structure comprises a frame made up of beams and columns. While beams are the horizontal members of the frame, columns are its vertical members. All the loads on a floor as well as those of walls are supported by beams. The beams transmit the load to the columns. Columns transmit the load to the foundation, which rests on a hard soil below the ground.

In comparison with the load bearing structures, here more carpet area is available. A higher degree of flexibility can be exercised as the partition walls can be easily shifted in case of framed structures. The walls are used for enclosing and dividing the space, hence these walls are called partition walls.

Framed structures are suitable for medium and multi-storeyed buildings. The frames can be constructed using R.C.C. or Steel. Steel framed structures are widely used for industrial and factory sheds and R.C.C. for residential and commercial complex. The speed of construction is fast as compared to load bearing structures. Construction time can also be reduced by use of precast concrete members and ready mix concrete. It can be constructed on any type of soil by using pile and raft foundations. They have good earthquake resistance.

2.2.3 Composite Structures

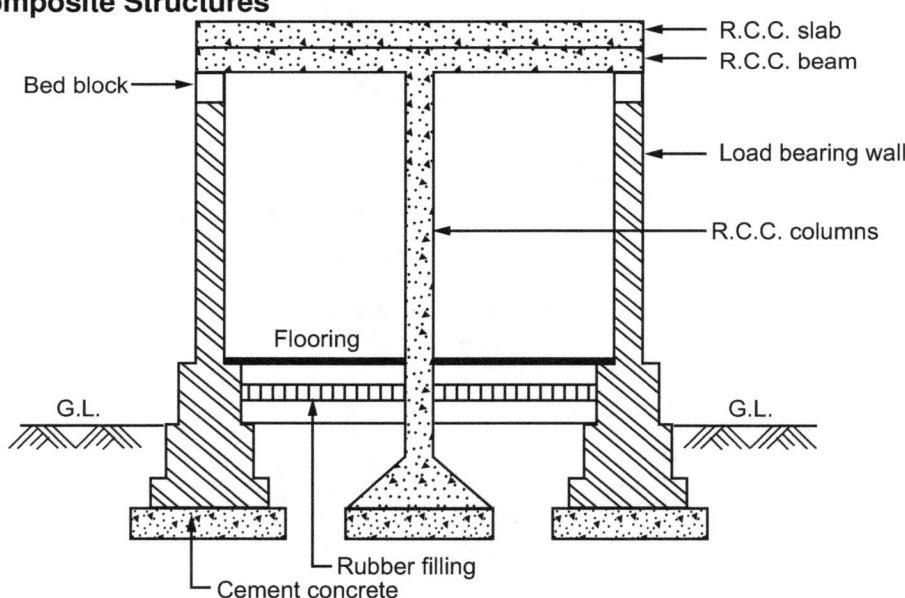

Fig. 2.3: Composite Structures

It is a combination of load bearing and framed structure so that advantages of both types can be enjoyed. In this type, external walls are load bearing type and the internal supports are in the form of columns. Roofs and floors are supported by load bearing walls and internal columns. The design and construction of this type of structure may become difficult and complicated. Composite structures are preferred for buildings having large spans such as warehouses, workshops, etc.

Comparison of between Load Bearing and Framed Structures

	Items for comparison	Load Bearing Structures	Framed Structures
1.	Sub-soil condition	It can be constructed on hard strata available at shallow depth	It can be constructed on any type of soil. E.g. black cotton soil, reclaimed soil, soft soil.
2.	Floor space	Less floor area is available for use because of thick wall	More floor area is available for use because of thin wall
3.	Number of stories	Height is limited and it is suitable for 2 to 3 storeys	No restriction on height. Suitable for multi-storeyed building
4.	Dead load	More, due to thick wall	Less, due to thin wall
5.	Time of construction	For the same number of storeys, time required is more	For the same number of storeys, time required is less because different construction activities can be carried out at the same time
6.	Flexibility in planning	Less	More
7.	Earthquake resistance	Susceptible to earthquake	Can be designed to resist more earthquake vibrations
8.	Economy	In general cheaper up to 2 storeys.	Economical for multi-storeyed building

2.3 FUNCTIONS OF FOUNDATION

1. To distribute the load of structure over a larger area.
2. To distribute the load on underlying soil evenly thus to prevent unequal or differential settlement of foundation.
3. To provide a levelled and hard surface for supporting the superstructure.
4. To increase the stability of the structure as a whole against sliding, overturning and other disturbing forces like wind, rain etc.

2.4 TYPES OF FOUNDATIONS

Foundations are broadly classified as follows:

2.4.1 Shallow Foundation

When depth of foundation is less than or equal to the width of foundation, then the foundation is known as shallow foundation. (SB)

Following are the types of shallow foundation:

1. Spread Footing:

It is the most common shallow foundation used to transfer the load of a wall or an isolated column. The base of the wall or column is spread to distribute the load over a larger area (i.e. to reduce the intensity of the load). Spread footing does not directly rest on the soil. Usually about 15 to 30 cm thick plain concrete of mix 1: 3: 6 or 1: 4: 8 called foundation concrete is laid as a base course. Base course provides a levelled and hard surface for spread footing. Different types of spread are discussed below:

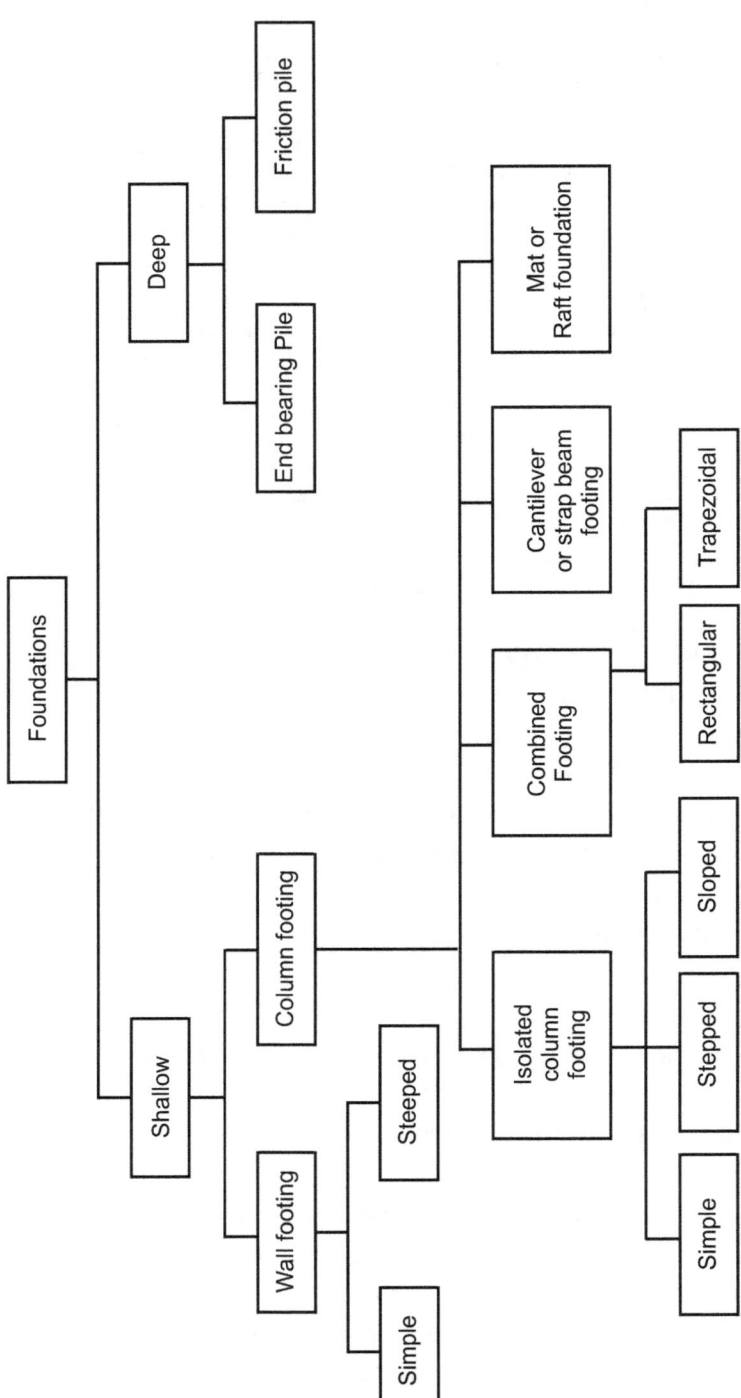

Fig. 2.6 : A Block diagram of classification of foundation

2. Wall Footing:

Wall footing can be either simple or stepped. The base course of these footings is generally made of concrete. Simple footings are used for light structures. Simple footings have only one projection beyond the width of the wall on both sides. The base width of the concrete base course should be at least twice the wall thickness. The projection provided is usually about 15 to 20 cm and the concrete mix is 1: 3: 6 or 1: 4: 8.

Stepped footings are similar to simple footing except that they have more than one projection or step. Stepped footings are used to transfer heavy loads. The depth of the footing is taken about 1.0 m, but in case of expansive soil it is taken up to that depth where there is no shrinkage and cracks.

If the load coming on the wall is heavy and there is a probability of differential settlement instead of providing P.C.C. bed, foundation concrete is reinforced by providing steel reinforcement. If projection of footing beyond the wall is excessive, the footing may crack due to soil pressure in the cantilever portion and hence stepped footing becomes essential.

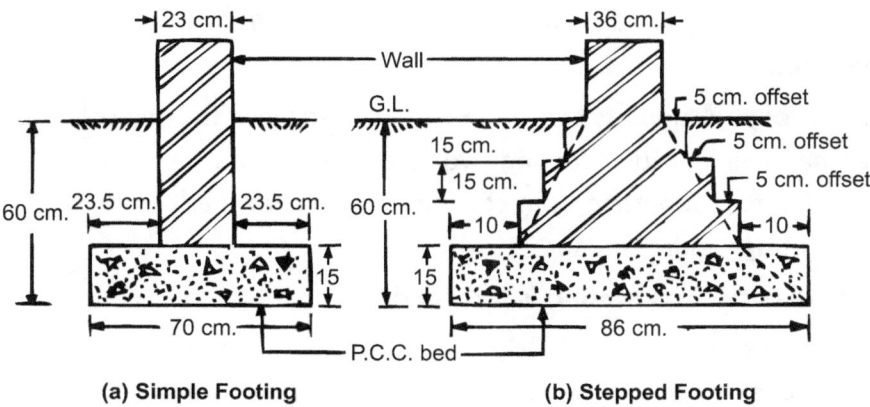

(a) Simple Footing   (b) Stepped Footing

Fig. 2.5: Wall footing

3. Isolated Footing Column:

Isolated or column footings are used to support individual columns. They can be either of stepped type or have projections in the concrete base. In case of heavy loaded columns, steel reinforcement is provided in both the directions in the concrete bed. In case of brick masonry columns, an offset of 5 cm is provided on all the four sides in regular layers. The footing of concrete columns may be simple, stepped or sloped.

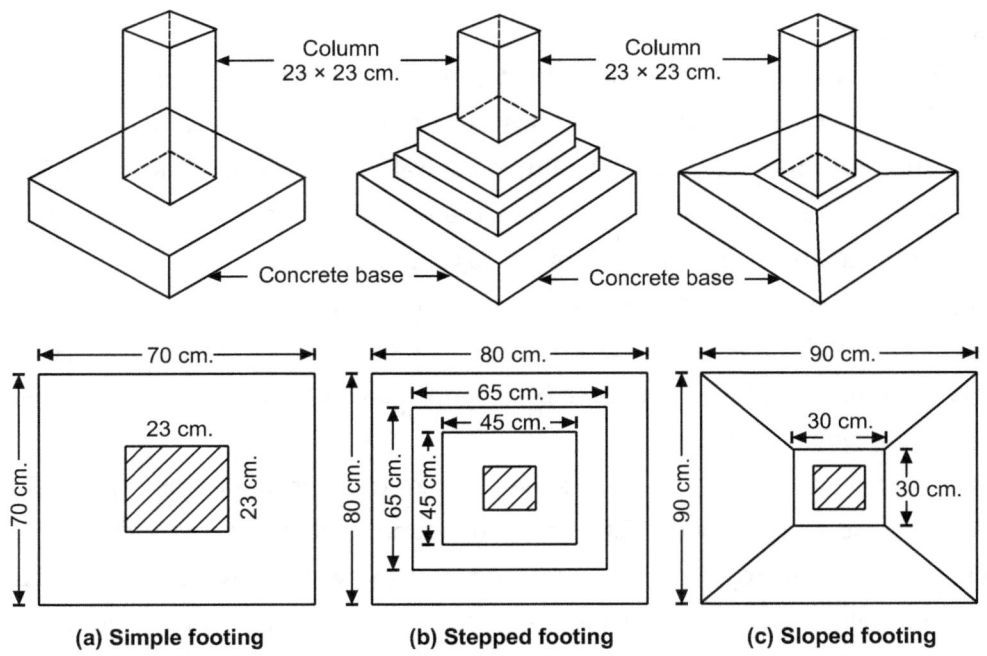

Fig. 2.6: Types of column footing

4. Combined Footing:

A combined footing supports two columns. It is used when the two columns are so close to each other that their individual footings would overlap, so to avoid overlapping a common footing is provided for supporting both columns. This is known as combined footing. It may be rectangular or trapezoidal in shape.

Situations where combined footing is provided:

1. When the property line is so close to one column that an isolated spread footing would be eccentrically loaded when kept entirely within the property line. By combining it with that of interior column the load is evenly distributed.

2. Rectangular combined footing is used if sufficient space is available beyond each column and if load on both the columns is same and the distance between the columns is less.

3. Trapezoidal combined footing is used when load on the columns is different, so more footing area is required for supporting the column carrying heavy load and also if the distance between the columns is large.

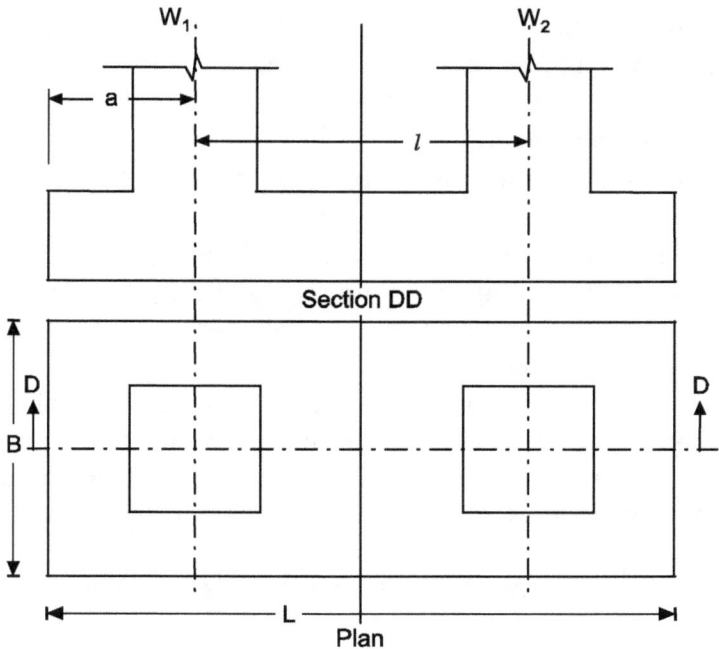

Fig. 2.7: Combined rectangular footing

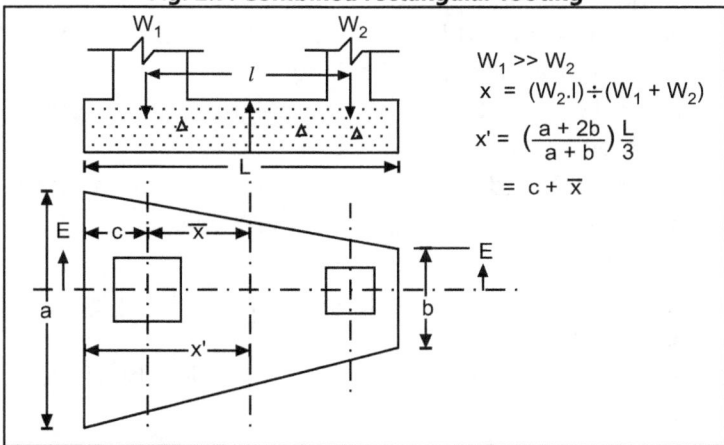

Fig. 2.8: Trapezoidal footing

2.5 MACHINE FOUNDATION

The machine is mounted on a foundation block which is supported on foundation layer of soil or rock. Under the influence of dynamic forces caused due to the operation of machine, the foundation block vibrates. Hence the design of machine foundation is more complex than that of foundation which supports only static loads. Type of machine determines the nature of force acting on the machine foundation. It may be reciprocating type machine or centrifugal type machine or impact type machine. The foundation must be designed for acceleration, reversal of forces, differential settlement, vertical and lateral forces, moments, torques, temperature variations, dead weight etc. They are generally raft type or mat type. Manufacturing companies generally make recommendations for foundation layout and design which should be properly followed.

(I) Requirements of Machine Foundation:
1. The foundation should sustain the imposed loads without causing shear or crushing failure.
2. Settlement of foundation should be uniform and within permissible limits.
3. In case of dynamic loads the natural frequency of foundation soil system should be either too small or too large compared to the operating frequency of the machines. No resonance should occur.
4. The amplitudes of motion at operating frequency should be within permissible limits.
5. The combined centre of gravity of machine and foundation should lie in the same vertical line as the centre of gravity of the base plane. All the rotating and reciprocating components of machine should be balanced so as to reduce the unbalanced forces or moments, and vibrations.

From practical point of view, the machine foundation should fulfil the following requirements:
1. The level of machine foundation should be taken below the level of foundations of adjacent buildings.
2. The ground water table should be very low and should be deep by 1/4 the width of foundation, to control the vibration circulation.
3. They should normally be isolated from the neighbouring structures with a gap and separated by cushions.
4. Weight of foundation should be 2 to 3 times the weight of machine.
5. Foundation should be strong, rigid and should not yield.

General Guidelines:
1. The machine should be fixed to the foundation block using base-plate and anchor bolts, or rag bolts.
2. Bolts must be correctly positioned in the foundation block corresponding to the holes in the base plate.
3. Holes should be left in the formwork to form pockets in concrete for anchor bolts. Concreting is done upto the level of base-plate and is allowed to harden.
4. Holes should be grouted with dense rich cement mortar after the anchor bolts are aligned properly.
5. The filling should be allowed to hardon after which the machine can be fixed to the anchor bolts firmly by means of nuts, washers and then operated.
6. Shock absorbents such as rubber, cork, felts, should be used to absorb the vibration.
7. To much sound, causing noise nuisance should be reduced.
8. The foundation block should be poured in one operation without any construction joints.

9. Machine foundation should be built in with M 15 to M 20 grade concrete.
10. Minimum 50 kg of steel per cubic metre of concrete should be provided. Foundation should be reinforced in all direction to resist tensile stresses.

(II) Types of Machine Foundations:

1. Block foundation is adopted for reciprocating machines and light rotary machines. See Fig. 2.9 (a).

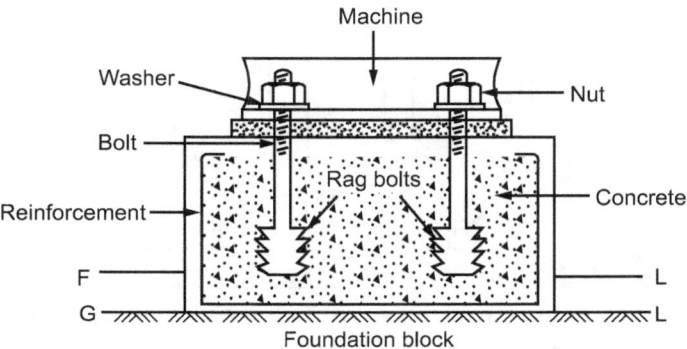

Fig. 2.9 (a): Block type

2. Blocks of greater depths and box or trough foundation are adopted for impact machines such as drop forge hammers. See Fig. 2.9 (b).

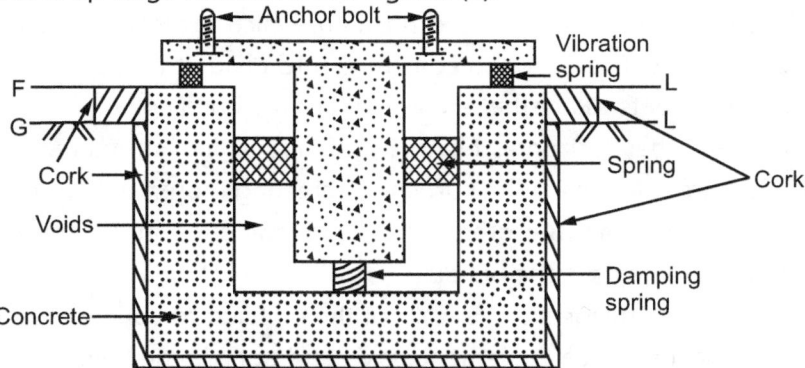

Fig. 2.9 (b): Box type

3. Wall type foundation is used for light high speed machines. See Fig. 2.9 (c).

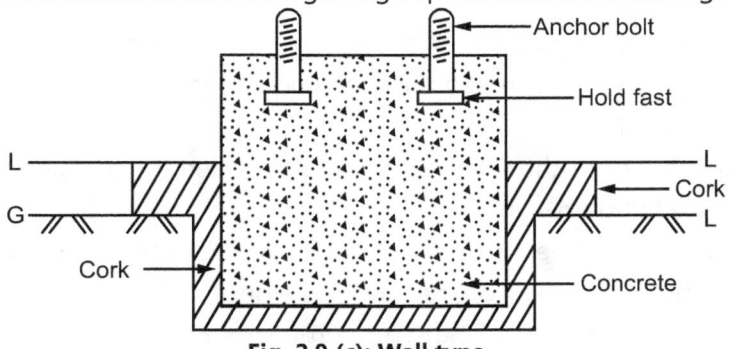

Fig. 2.9 (c): Wall type

4. Frame foundation is adopted for heavy rotary centrifugal type machines to take up shocks and vibration. See Fig. 2.9 (d).

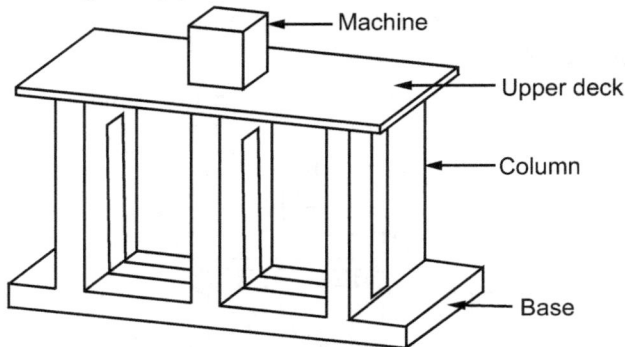

Fig. 2.9 (d): Frame type

2.6 SUPERSTRUCTURE

It is that part of the structure which is constructed above the plinth level or ground floor level. The various components of superstructure are walls, floors, doors and windows, roofs, stairs, sill, lintel, weather sheds, finishes for wall, utility fixtures, etc. The functions of various components of superstructure are as follows:

1. **Walls:** The vertical components of the building, which are constructed to enclose the space, are called walls. They are also constructed to divide the space into various rooms and small compartments as per the requirement of the building.
2. **Floors:** Floors are the horizontal elements of a building structure which divide the building into different levels for the purpose of creating more accommodation within the restricted space one above the other and to provide support for the occupants, their furniture and requirements in the building.
3. **Doors:** The openings provided in the walls of the building to connect the internal rooms, to be used as a means of free movement inside and outside the building.
4. **Windows:** The openings provided in the outer walls of the building for the purpose of light and air.
5. **Roofs:** The uppermost horizontal or inclined part of a building provided to cover the space enclosed by the walls is called the roof. Roofs protect living spaces from direct sun, rain or snow and wind.
6. **Stairs:** The component of the building which is provided for climbing from one floor to another floor is called stairs.
7. **Lintel:** Lintel is the component of the building provided over the openings i.e. doors and windows. It supports the load of the brick or stone masonry above the opening and transfers the same on either side of the supporting walls.

8. **Sill:** Sill is the component of the building provided between the bottom of a window frame and the wall below it. It protects the top of the wall from wear and tear. Window sill are usually weathered and throated to throw the rain water off the face of the wall.
9. **Weather sheds:** The horizontal slabs projecting from the external wall just above the doors, windows, verandas, etc. are called weather sheds or sun shades or chhajjas. They are monolithically constructed with the lintels. They protect the doors, windows, etc. from the direct effects of the sun and rain.

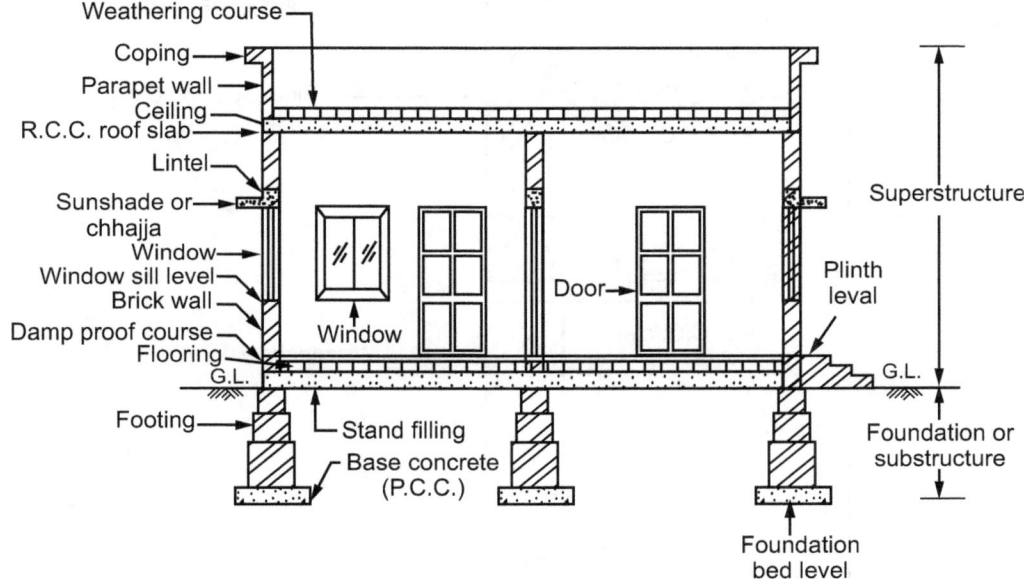

Fig. 2.10: Components of a building

10. **Finishes of Wall:** Finishes are of several types such as pointing, plastering, distempering, decorative colour washing, etc. that are applied on the walls. The main functions of these finishes are as follows:
    (i) They provide an even and smooth finished surface and also improve the aesthetic appearance of the structure as a whole.
    (ii) They rectify, rather cover to some extent, the poor or defective workmanship.
    (iii) They protect the structure from the effects of weather, such as rain, sun.
11. **Utility Fixtures:** These are built in items of immovable nature, which add to the utility of a building and hence, are termed as utility fixtures. The most common of such built-in fixtures are cupboards, shelves, smokeless chulas, etc.

2.6.1 Components of Substructure

The following are the components of substructure:

1. Foundation: It is the lowest artificially prepared part of a structure below the ground level which provides base for superstructure and transmits all loads from the component parts of the building to the soil on which the building rests.

2. Plinth: It is the portion of a structure between the surface of the enclosing ground and the surface of the floor first above the ground.

3. Damp Proof Course (DPC): It is the layer between superstructure and the substructure. It does not allow the moisture to move from the foundation level to the superstructure.

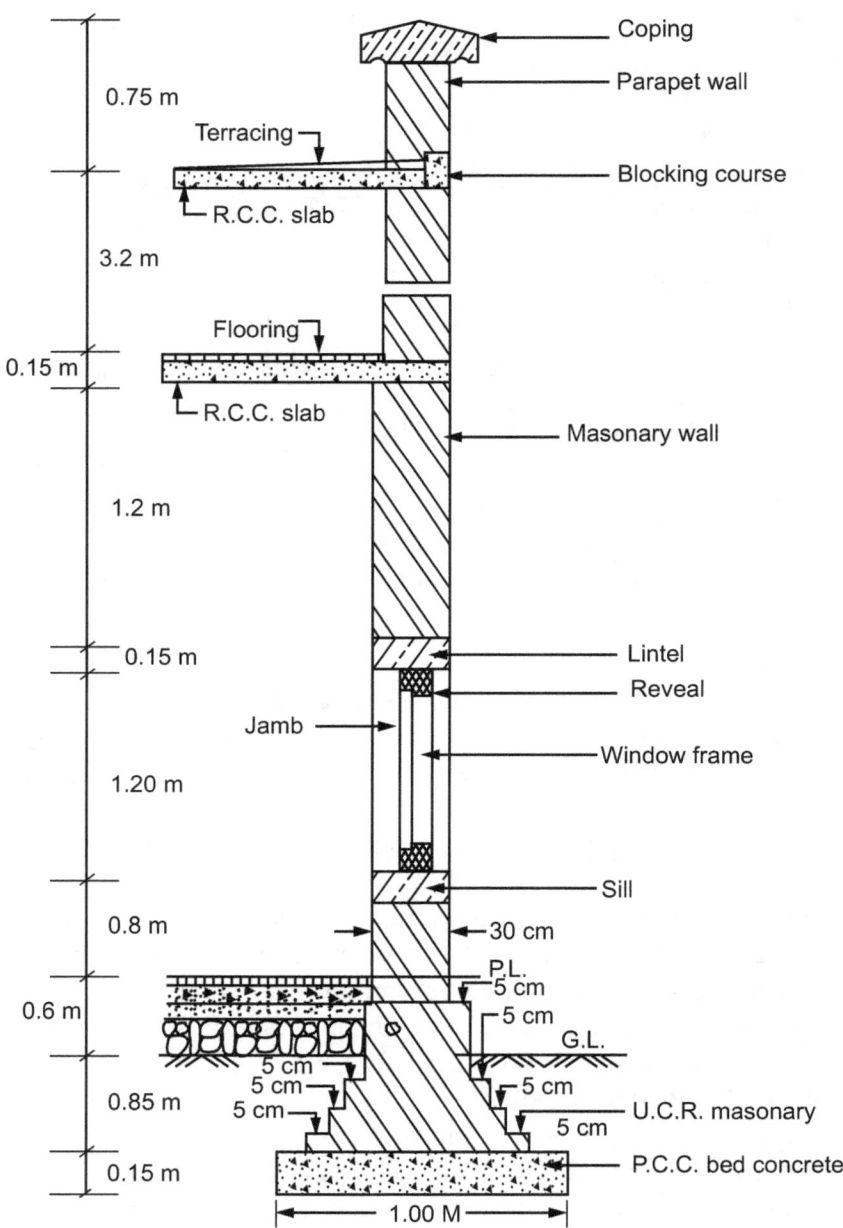

Fig. 2.11: Cross-section through a load bearing wall

2.7 MASONRY

Masonry may be defined as the systematic arrangement of bonding together of building units, usually in horizontal courses with some form of mortar. The building units may be stone, bricks or precast concrete blocks. These building units are bonded together to form a homogeneous mass in such a manner that they can withstand the loads and transmit them without failure.

Masonry is normally used for the construction of foundations, walls, columns etc. Masonry performs a variety of functions in load bearing structures such as supporting load sub-dividing space, providing thermal and acoustics insulation and fire resistance etc.

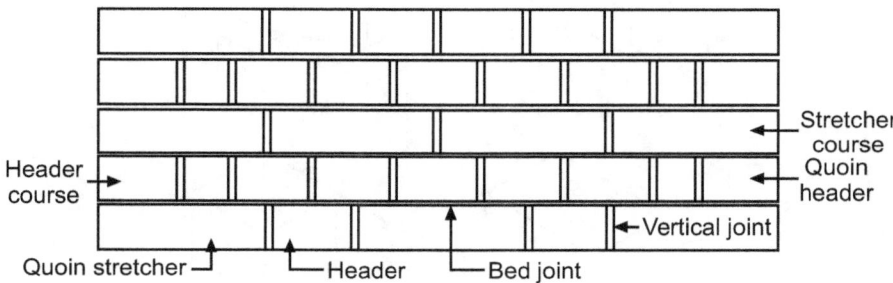

Fig. 2.12: Illustration of various terms used in masonry

2.7.1 Important Terms Used In Masonry

1. **Course:** It is a horizontal layer of masonry units, the thickness of which is equal to the thickness of the stone or brick or concrete block plus the thickness of the bed joint.
2. **Stretcher:** It is the full stone or brick or concrete block unit, laid in such a way that its length is **parallel** to the face of wall.
3. **Header:** It is the full stone or brick or concrete block unit, laid in such a way that its length is **perpendicular** to the face of wall.
4. **Bed:** Bed is a lower surface of a brick or stone in each course.
5. **Bond:** Bond is defined as an arrangement of bricks or stones in alternate courses by overlapping so that the individual units are tied together and no continuous vertical joints are formed.
6. **Quoin:** The corner or exterior angle of a wall is known as quoin. If the length of the quoin is parallel to the face of wall, it is known as stretcher quoin and when the length of quoin is perpendicular to face of wall, it is known as header quoin.
7. **Closer:** A closer is the portion of a brick cut in such a manner that its one long face remains uncut. It can also be defined as a header of small width.

8. **Queen closer:** Queen closer is that portion of a brick obtained by cutting a brick along its length into two equal parts.
9. **King closer:** King closer is obtained by cutting off the triangular portion between the centre of one end and centre of the adjacent side.
10. **Bat:** Bat is obtained by cutting a brick along its width. A bat is smaller in length than the full brick and accordingly known as three quarter bat and half bat.

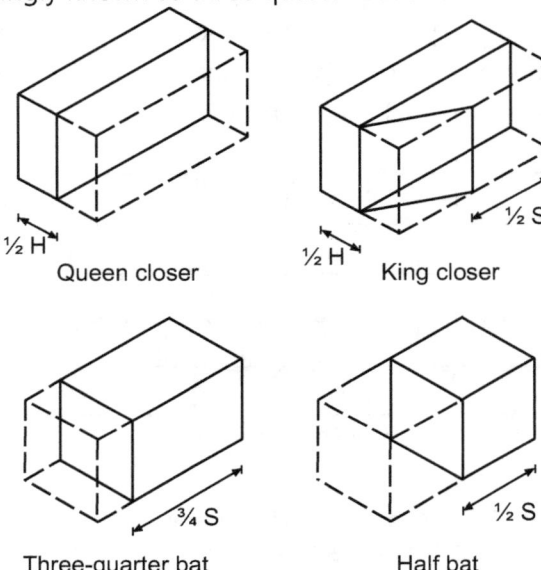

Fig. 2.13

2.7.2 Classification of Masonry

2.7.2.1 Stone Masonry

When stones are used as building units and are bonded together with mortar, it is known as stone masonry. Stone masonry is stronger, durable and weather resistant than other types of masonry. Stone masonry is used in the construction of walls, footings, columns, dams etc. and is economical at places where stones are available in abundance.

Depending on the arrangement of stones in the construction and the degree of refinement used in shaping and finishing the stone, stone masonry may be classified as follows:

1. Rubble masonry
2. Ashlar masonry

1. Rubble Masonry: Stones used in this type of masonry are either undressed or roughly dressed having wider joints. This is further sub divided as uncoursed, coursed, flint and dry rubble masonry.

(i) Uncoursed Rubble Masonry: This is the cheapest, roughest and poorest form of stone masonry. The stones used in this type of masonry are of different shapes and sizes and are directly obtained from the quarry. Stones are arranged carefully to distribute the load over a larger area and long continuous vertical joints are avoided. The interior of the wall is properly filled with chips and mortar, though stones are provided at regular intervals. It may be either uncoursed random rubble or uncoursed square rubble. This type of masonry is commonly used in construction of foundations for load bearing structures.

(A) Uncoursed Random Rubble: In this type of masonry, weak corners and edges of the stones obtained from the quarry are removed by the mason's hammer. Larger stones are used as quoins and jambs to increase the strength of masonry, though stone is provided in every one square metre of the face work. Continuous vertical joints are avoided.

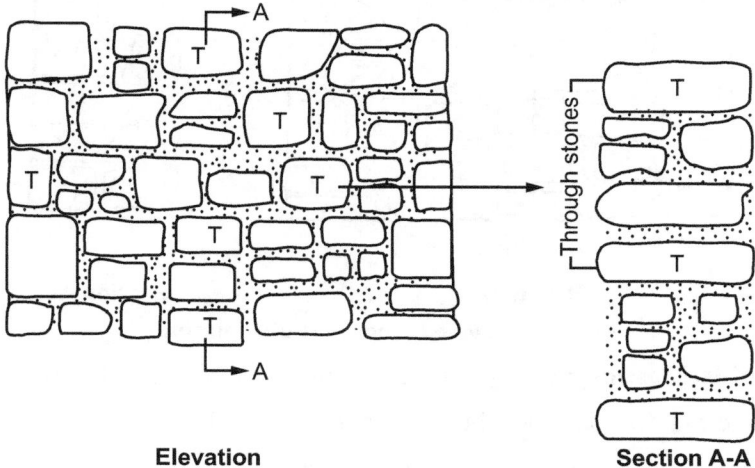

Elevation   **Section A-A**

Fig. 2.14: Uncoursed random rubble masonry

(B) Uncoursed Square Rubble: In this type of stone masonry, stone blocks are made roughly square using a hammer. Stone blocks are of varying sizes and are placed in different irregular patterns. Facing stones are given hammer dressed finish.

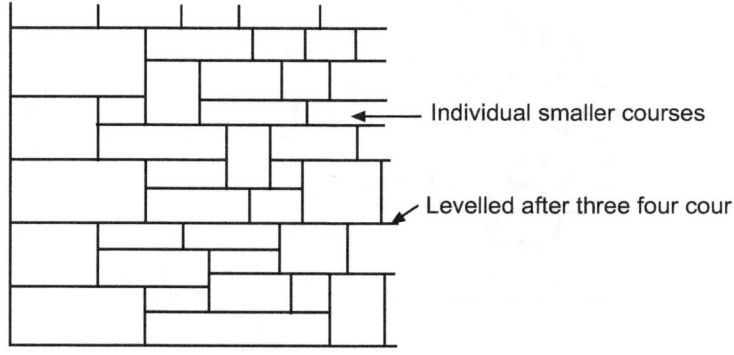

Fig. 2.15: Uncoursed squared rubble masonry

(ii) Coursed Random Rubble Masonry: This masonry is commonly used in the construction of low height walls of public buildings, residential buildings etc. the stones used are of 5 cm to 20 cm size. In each course, stones of equal height are used, though all the courses may not be of the same height. In construction of this type of masonry, quoins are built first and a string is stretched between the tops of the quoins. The remaining wall is then brought up to this level by using different sizes of stones, though stones are introduced at appropriate places.

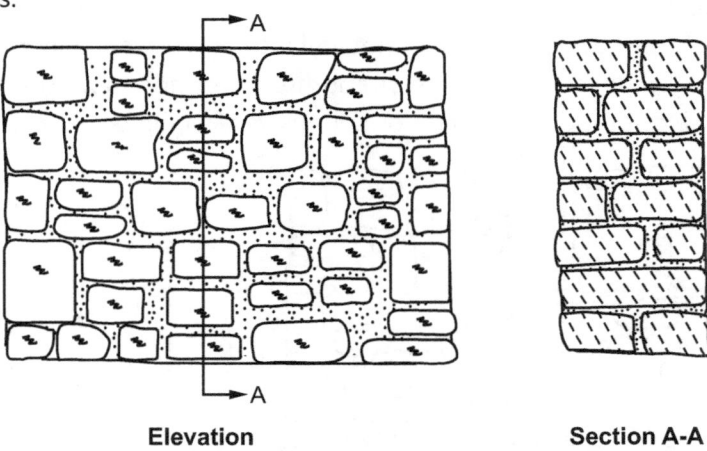

Elevation   Section A-A

Fig. 2.16: Coursed random rubble masonry

(iii) Dry Rubble Masonry: In dry rubble masonry, stones are placed in courses without using mortar in joints for binding the stones together. This type of construction is the cheapest and is used for non load bearing walls such as compound walls or protection walls of agriculture farms. Stones used in this type of construction should have maximum bedding area.

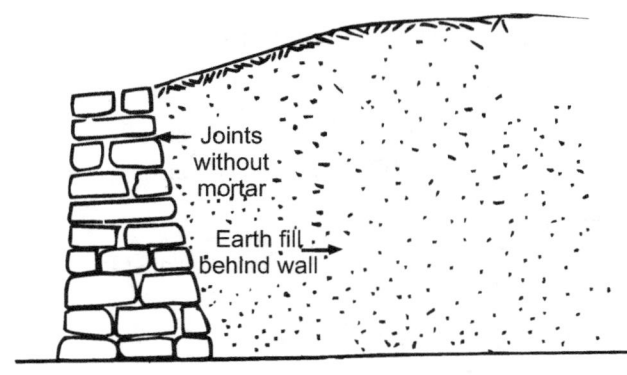

Fig. 2.17: Dry rubble masonry

2. Ashlar Masonry:

Ashlar masonry is built from accurately dressed stones with uniform and very fine bed and end joints. The height of stones varies from 25 to 30 cm. The height of stones in each course is kept equal. It is a costlier, higher grade and superior quality of masonry. Ashlar masonry may be of the following types:

(i) Ashlar fine tooled
(ii) Ashlar rough tooled
(iii) Ashlar chamfered

(i) Ashlar Fine Tooled: This is the finest type of stone masonry. Perfectly dressed stones are used to get the desired pattern. Bed joints and faces of stones are chisel dressed to obtain a fairly smooth surface. Headers and stretchers are laid alternately in each course; in such a way that the header comes under the middle of the stretcher, of the subsequent course. The thickness of the mortar joints should be less than 5 mm.

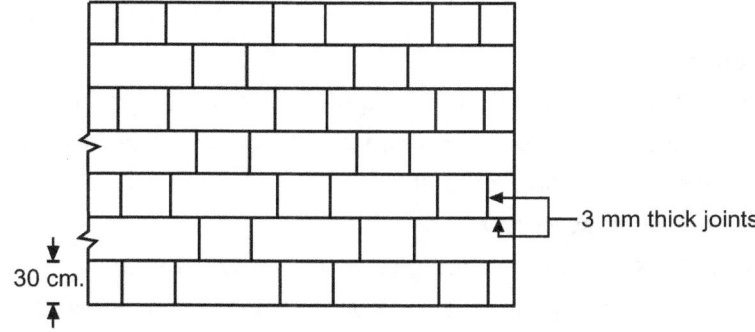

Fig. 2.18: Ashlar fine

(ii) Ashlar Rough Tooled: The same stones used in ashlar fine masonry are also used here, but the exposed face is dressed by rough tooling. A strip of about 25 mm width made with a chisel is provided around the perimeter of the rough dressed lice of each stone.

(iii) Ashlar Chamfered: In this type of masonry, a strip provided around the perimeter of the exposed face is chamfered at an angle of 45 to a depth of 25 mm. Thus a groove is formed between the adjacent blocks of stone. Around this chamfered strip another strip of 10 cm is dressed with the chisel.

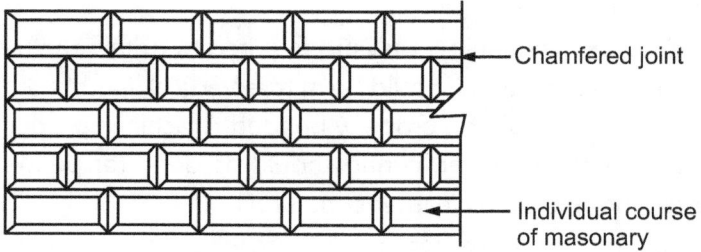

Fig. 2.19: Ashlar chamfered

General Principles for Stone Masonry:
　Following precautions should be taken in stone masonry construction:
1. Stones should be free from defects like cracks, cavities, flaws etc. and should be strong, tough, hard and uniform in texture.
2. Stones should be well watered before use so that it does not absorb water from the mortar.
3. All stones should be laid upon their natural beds.
4. Proper bond should be maintained throughout the masonry.
5. Masonry work should be raised uniformly to avoid non-uniform distribution of load on foundation.
6. Vertical surfaces of wall should be perfectly in plumb.
7. Mortar to be used should be of proper quality and proportion.
8. After the construction of masonry, curing should be done at least for two weeks.

2.7.2.2 Brick Masonry

　In brick masonry, brick units are bonded together with mortar. Strength of brick masonry depends upon the type of mortar used. Brick masonry is widely used for the construction of walls, footings, columns, floors and arches etc.

General Principles for Brick Masonry:
　Following precautions should be taken in brick masonry construction:
1. Bricks should fulfil all the requirements of a good brick i.e., they should be well burnt and possess uniform size, shape and colour.
2. Bricks should be properly soaked in water for at least 2 hours before laying them in cement mortar or lime mortar.
3. Brick work, throughout the length of wall, should be raised uniformly with proper bonding to avoid any unequal settlement. No portion of the wall should be raised higher than 1 m than the rest of the wall.
4. In one day, brick masonry should not be constructed more than 1.5 m height.
5. Bricks should be laid on their bed with their frogs pointing upwards to have good bond strength between the different courses.
6. Brick bats should not be used unless they are required to obtain the required bond.
7. Vertical joints in alternate courses should be in true vertical line.
8. The junctions of the wall should be properly bonded to achieve proper strength.
9. For brick work with cement mortar, curing should be done for period of at least one or two weeks, depending upon the weather conditions.
10. All the joints should be raked to a depth of 10 mm when the mortar is green, for pointing or plastering.

Necessity of a Proper Bond:

A proper bond in brick masonry is provided for the following purposes:
1. To break the continuity of vertical joints in the adjacent courses.
2. To ensure both longitudinal and lateral strength of the brick structure.
3. To produce a pleasing appearance of the unplastered surfaces of the walls.
4. To enable the structure to act as a solid compact mass.
5. To distribute the load uniformly to the foundation, if the structure is a load bearing one.

Types of Bonds in Brick Work:

On account of their uniform size and shape, bricks can be arranged in variety of patterns giving rise to different types of bonds. Bonding is essential to eliminate the continuous vertical joints, both in the body as well as on the face of the wall thereby, imparting strength of masonry.

A wall having defective arrangement of bricks reduces the strength and the stability of the structure. A wall having continuous vertical joints does not act as a homogeneous mass to distribute the superimposed load.

The different types of bonds commonly adopted are given below:
1. Stretcher bond
2. Header bond
3. English bond
4. Flemish bond
5. Dutch bond
6. Raking bond

2.8 TYPES OF BOND

Following are some of the types of bonds used in brick masonry:
1. English bond
2. Single and double Flemish bond
3. Header bond
4. Stretcher bond
5. Herring bone bond
6. Diagonal bond
7. Garden wall bond.

2.8.1 English Bond

This bond is considered as the strongest in brick work and is used extensively. Following are the features of English bond. (Refer Fig. 2.20 and 2.21).

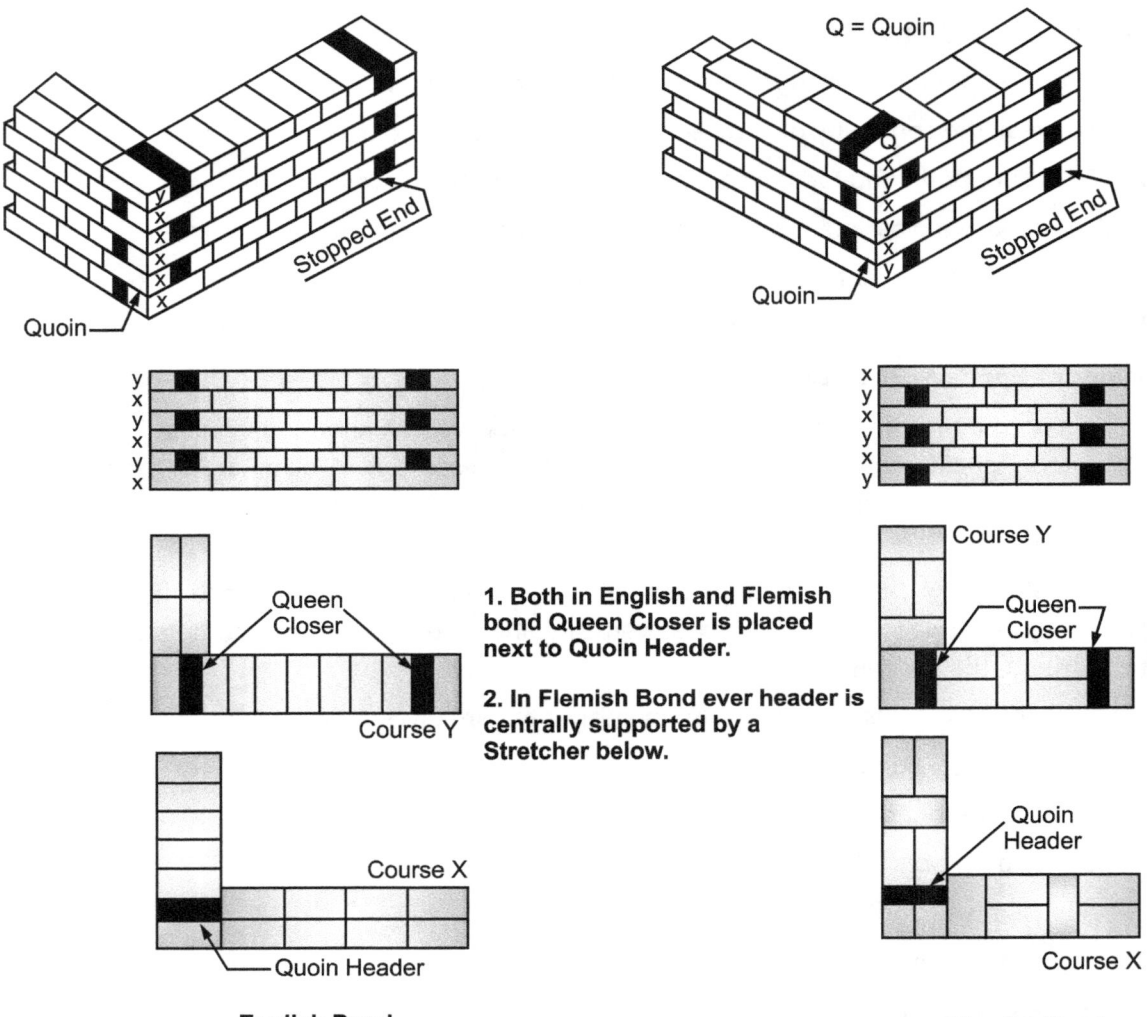

Fig. 2.20: Brick wall with corner and stopped end

1. Queen closer is placed next to Quoin header and Queen closer is not required in stretcher course.
2. In alternate courses headers and stretchers are provided.
3. No continuous vertical joint is formed.
4. Lap between header and stretcher course in successive courses is not less than $1/4^{th}$ of length of brick.
5. For 1, 2 and 3 brick thick wall in both front and rear elevation, the same course shows headers or stretchers.

   However, for $1\frac{1}{2}$, and $2\frac{1}{2}$ thick brick wall, if header is in front elevation, stretcher will be seen in rear elevation for the same course.

6. Since, the number of joints in header courses are double than that in stretcher course, these joints should be thin, so that desired lap is maintained.

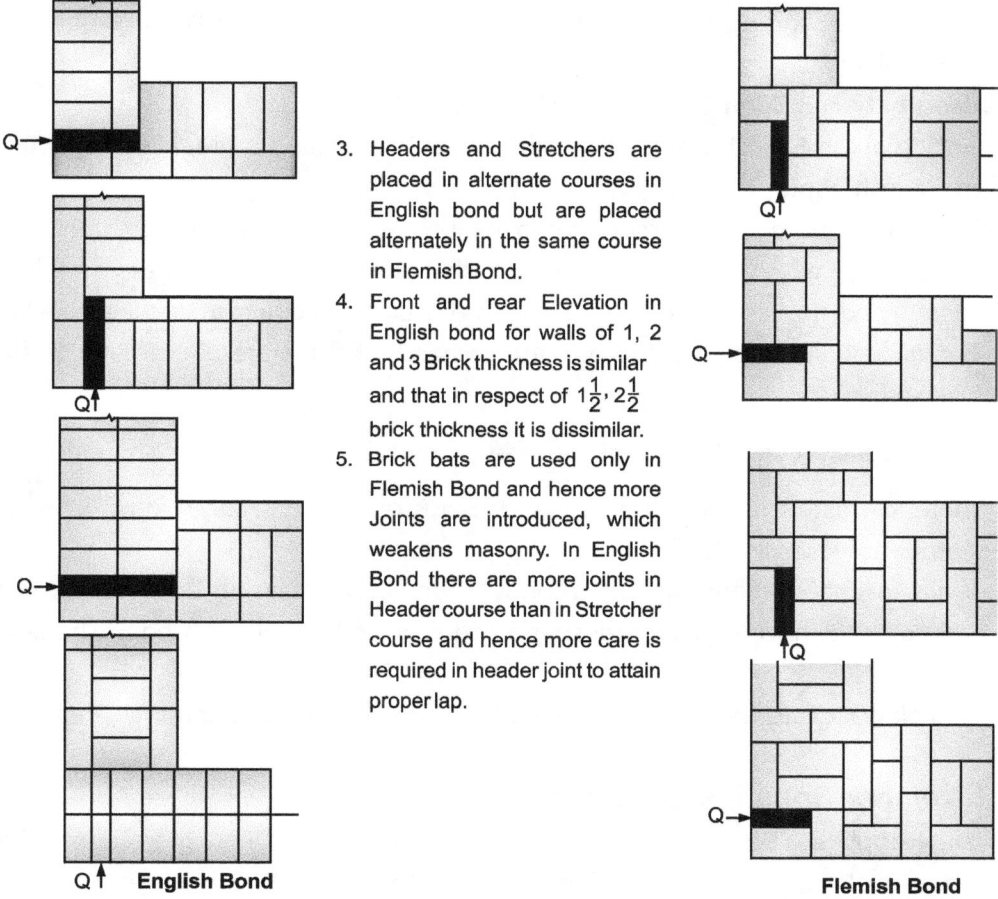

3. Headers and Stretchers are placed in alternate courses in English bond but are placed alternately in the same course in Flemish Bond.
4. Front and rear Elevation in English bond for walls of 1, 2 and 3 Brick thickness is similar and that in respect of $1\frac{1}{2}$, $2\frac{1}{2}$ brick thickness it is dissimilar.
5. Brick bats are used only in Flemish Bond and hence more Joints are introduced, which weakens masonry. In English Bond there are more joints in Header course than in Stretcher course and hence more care is required in header joint to attain proper lap.

Fig. 2.21 (a): Plans of alternate courses in English and Flemish bond for $1\frac{1}{2}$ and 2 brick thick walls

2.8.2 Flemish Bond

The following are the main features of this bond:

1. In this bond, in the same course, headers and stretchers are placed alternately.
2. As in English bond, Queen closer is placed next to Queen header.
3. Every header is centrally supported by a stretcher below; and hence gives pleasing appearance in elevation.
4. In English bond, in case of walls of thickness of 1, 2 or 3 bricks, only front and back elevation is similar; and is dissimilar in case of $1\frac{1}{2}$, $2\frac{1}{2}$ thick walls. However, in Flemish bond, walls of all thickness have similar elevation both in front elevation and rear

elevation. Only difference is that, for walls of thickness of $1\frac{1}{2}$, $2\frac{1}{2}$ bricks, quarter bat is used in the hearting portion, whereas no such bats are required in respect of 2 or 3 brick thick wall.

Comparison between English and Flemish Bond:
1. Brick work in English bond having thickness 2 bricks and more, is stronger than that in Flemish bond.
2. In general more care is required to be taken while using Flemish bond. Pleasing appearance which can be had in Flemish bond is lost, if thickness of joint is not maintained. In case of English bond, more care is required to taken while laying header course, since number of joints in header course are double that in stretcher course.
3. While constructing $1\frac{1}{2}$, $2\frac{1}{2}$ walls, use of bats is made in Flemish bond. As such, material cost is less in Flemish bond. But strength is reduced due to increase in number of joints in Flemish.
4. Walls in English bond are monotonous bond have pleasing appearance. However, unless bricks have regular size, shape and sharp edges, Flemish bond should not be used.
5. If brick work is to be plastered, it is advisable to use English bond than Flemish bond.

2.8.3 Stretcher Bond For 1/2 Brick Walls

As name implies, all courses are laid as stretchers only; and that there are no headers. From plan and elevation, it is clear that, with this bond only 1/2 brick thick walls, (as in partition walls) can be constructed.

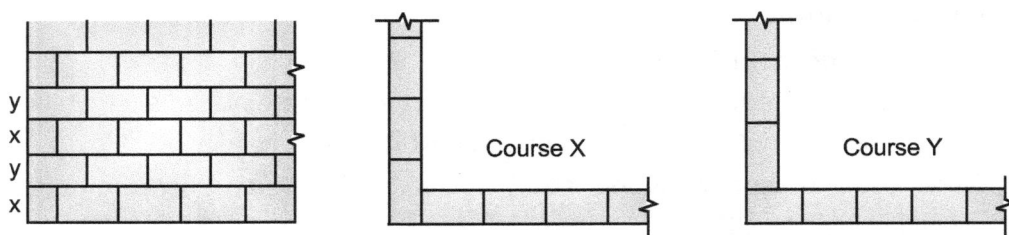

Fig. 2.21 (b): Stretcher bond

2.8.4 Header Bond For 1 Brick Wall

In this bond, as the name implies, the bricks are laid with their ends towards the face of wall (like headers). There are no stretchers; and hence, wall of 1 brick thickness only can be constructed. The bond does not possess sufficient strength to transmit load, in the direction of the length of wall. However, with this bond, walls having curvature can be constructed as headers can be cut to suit curvature; whereas cutting of stretchers is quite inconvenient.

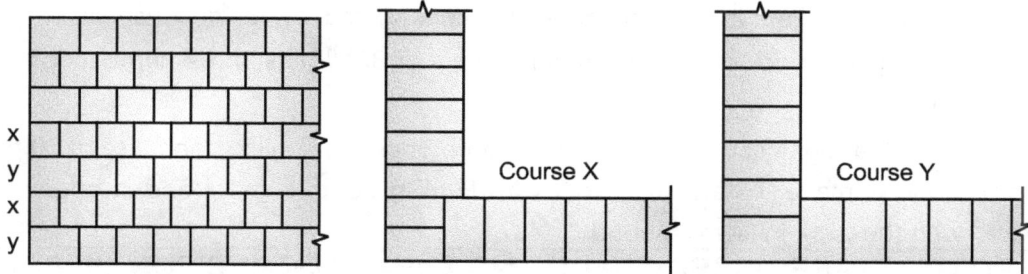

Fig. 2.21 (c): Header bond

2.9 COLUMNS IN ENGLISH AND FLEMISH BONDS

Following are the features of square columns in English and Flemish bond:

(a) One Brick Thick Column

(i) In English bond, it can be constructed by laying two bricks side by side. Each of the next course is laid at right angles to the previous course.

(ii) It may be noted that one brick pier in flemish bond is not possible.

(b) $1\frac{1}{2}$ Brick Thick Column:

(i) In English bond, it can be constructed either by laying 2 numbers of $3/4^{th}$ bat side by side and 3 numbers of full bricks. It can also be constructed by using 6 numbers of $3/4^{th}$ bats.

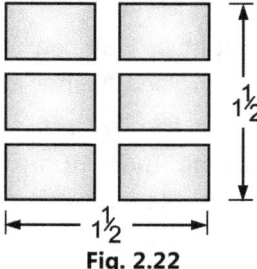

Fig. 2.22

However, columns constructed by using this second alternative, are not strong, hence are avoided.

(ii) In Flemish bond, $1\frac{1}{2}^{th}$ brick columns can be constructed by using 4 numbers of $3/4^{th}$ bat and centrally placed half bat. This column in Flemish bond is comparatively weaker than that in English bond, since, more number of joints are introduced.

(c) 2 Brick Thick Column in English Bond:

(i) Here use of 6 bricks of full length and 4 Queen closers is made 2 brick thick column. Each of the next course is laid at right angles to the previous course.

(ii) Two brick columns in Flemish bond are constructed by making use of 10 pieces consisting of 4 brick of full length, 4 numbers of $3/4^{th}$ bats and 2 numbers of queen closers.

It is clear that, as against 6 numbers of full length bricks, in English bond, use of 10 pieces in flemish bond is made. As a result, work with English bond is faster and stronger, when compared with the work in Flemish bond.

2.10 POINTS TO BE OBSERVED DURING THE CONSTRUCTION OF BRICK MASONRY

1. The bricks to be used in the work should be of appropriate quality as regards size, shape, burning, strength, efflorescence etc.

2. In order that brick do not absorb water from mortar, bricks should be soaked in water at least for 2 hours before use. This also helps in spreading of mortar uniformly, washing of kiln dust and proper adhering of mortar to bricks.

3. Next to quoin header, queen closer is placed.

4. Mortar is spread over the first course to a thickness of 1 cm. End stretcher is placed in position and hammered down till thickness of joint is one cm.

5. Corners of wall are built upto certain height first, and then by making use of reference monuments, "line dori" and "plumb bob", wall are constructed in line, level and in plumb.

6. When wall is built upto the height of wall near corner, brick work near the corner is raised further and construction is raised further and work proceeds further.

7. All the walls should be raised uniformly and difference between levels of any two portions of walls, should not be more than 1 metre. This will ensure uniform distribution of load and will avoid uneven settlement.

8. As work proceeds, joints in the brick work should be raked out to depth of about 1 cm. This will help in having proper key to plastering or pointing.

9. As far as possible double scaffolding should be provided, so as to avoid making holes in masonry to support cantilever scaffolding.

10. In order to have proper grip with previous brick work, either steps are provided or toothing is provided.

11. Previous days work is roughened and cleaned, while starting next day's work.

12. Brick work should be cured for 2 to 3 weeks.

2.11 GENERAL POINTS TO BE OBSERVED DURING THE SUPERVISION OF STONE MASONRY WORK

Various points as regards thickness of joints, quoins, through stones, dressing, height of course, hearting have been summarized and given in the chart for Random Rubble and Square Rubble Masonry and in the specifications for DCR and CR masonry. In addition to this, the following points should be observed:

1. The stones should be properly wetted so that stones do not absorb moisture in mortar.
2. The stones should be dressed as per requirement, before placing in position.
3. Positioning, spacing of centre line of walls must conform as per drawings; during the entire construction of the wall. The same must be checked with the help of reference points located outside.
4. Verticality of the wall should be checked from time to time, with the help of plumb bob. This is to ensure that, the loads acting on the wall is concentric.
5. The various courses should be brought to level with the help of thin string stretched between the ends of walls.
6. Construction of stone masonry should commence at prominent corners of walls. Masonry between corners should be raised gradually, uniformly and in plumb.
7. Good and bad examples of (i) Stretcher stone, (ii) Quoins, (iii) Through stones and (iv) Faulty construction are shown in the following sketches. Faulty materials and methods should be avoided.
8. All surfaces should be kept wet while the work is in progress. After completion of work, the masonry should be cured in 2 to 3 weeks.

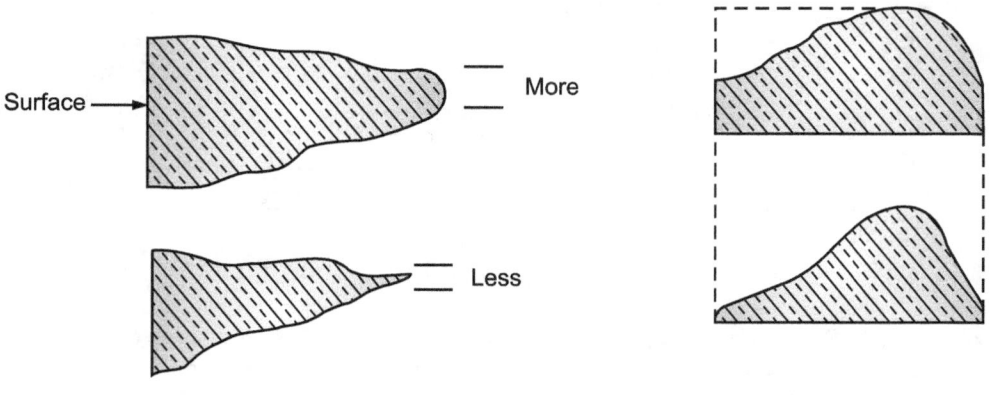

(a) Good and bad header   (b) Good and bad stretcher

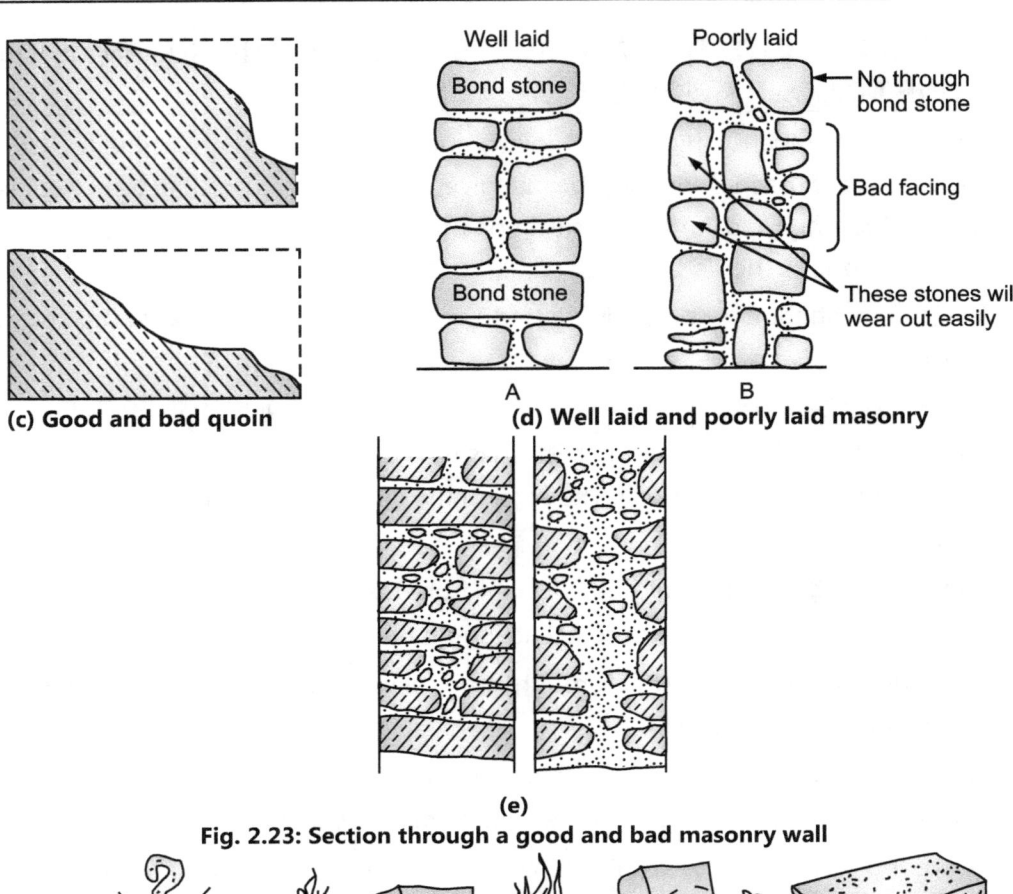

(c) Good and bad quoin

(d) Well laid and poorly laid masonry

Fig. 2.23: Section through a good and bad masonry wall

Fig. 2.24: Avoid (i) Stones absorbing more water (ii) Rounded (iii) Soft and stone composed of sand and soil (iv) Irregular flat pointed (v) Likely to affected by weather (vi) With dark spots and bonds of different colours

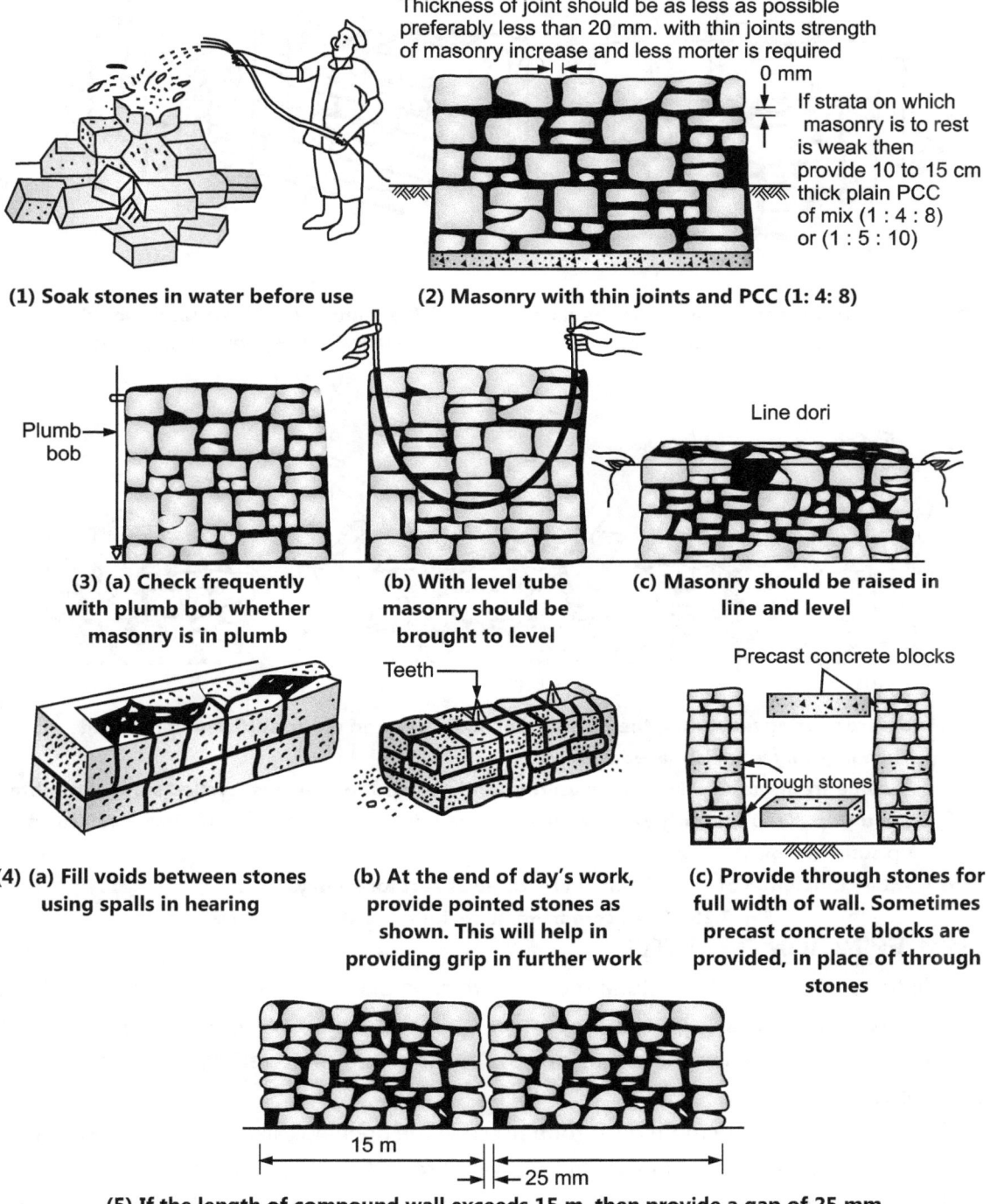

Fig. 2.25: Seven commandments for good stone masonry (continued)

(6) (a) In one day masonry should not be raised to height more than 0.6 m

(b) The joints should break and should not be vertically one above other, as in (c)

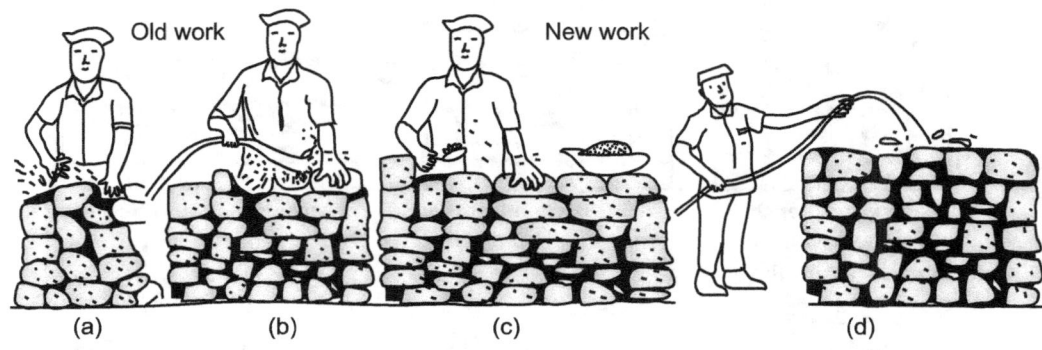

(7) (a) Before starting new work, the old mortar should breaked out to sufficient depth and
   (b) Then masonry work is soaked with water
   (c) Provide fresh mortar "into the masonry" and not on the previous levelled surface to obtain good grip. Keep mortar just near the work (and not at far away and too low level) to speed up construction.
   (d) After completion of work, it should be cured atleast for 15 days.

Fig. 2.26: Seven commandments for good stone masonry

2.12 DEFINITION OF LINTEL

A lintel is a horizontal structural member which is placed across an opening viz. doors, windows, recesses etc. to support the portion of the structure above it. Though the lintels perform exactly the same function as arches, but they are preferred to arches due to the following reasons:

(i) The arches require more head room to span the openings, like doors, windows, etc.

(ii) The arches require strong abutments (walls) to withstand the arch thrust.

(iii) Lintels are more stable as they support the load by beam action and transfer the loads vertically to the walls.

(iv) The lintels are simpler in construction.

The ends of lintels are built into the masonry and thus, the load carried by lintels is transferred to the masonry in jambs. In general, it should be seen that the bearing of lintel i.e. the distance upto which it is inserted in the supporting wall, should be the minimum of the following three considerations.

(i) 10 cm; or

(ii) height of lintel; or

(iii) one - tenth to one - twelth of the span of lintel.

Reinforced Cement Concrete Lintels: Reinforced concrete lintels are extensively used and practically R.C.C. has replaced all other materials used for lintels. The R.C.C. lintels are fire-proof, durable, strong, economical and easy to construct. No relieving arches are necessary when the R.C.C. lintels are adopted. R.C.C. lintels may be either precast or cast in-situ. Precast R.C.C. lintels are preferred for small span upto 2 metres or so, and they are economical as the same mould can be used to prepare a number of lintels. The precast R.C.C. lintels increase the speed of construction and allow sufficient time for the curing before fixing. One precaution to be taken in case of precast R.C.C. lintels is that the top of lintel should be properly marked with tar or paint.

For large spans, the lintels should be cast in-situ. Details of lintels are as follows:

(i) **Depth of Lintel:** For ordinary loads, adopt 15 cm depth for span upto 1.2 m and add another 2.5 cm for every additional 40 cm span.

(ii) **Reinforcement in Lintels:** As a rule, for thickness of wall 10 cm (half-brick), adopt 2 bars and for every additional 10 cm thickness, one main bar should be added. The diameter of bar varies with the span and is adopted as follows, as a general rule (Alternative central bars are bent up).

$\qquad$ 6 mm ϕ for spans upto 1 metre

$\qquad$ 8 mm ϕ for spans upto 1 to 1.5 metres

$\qquad$ 10 mm ϕ for spans upto 1.5 to 2.0 metres

$\qquad$ 12 mm ϕ for spans upto 20 to 30 metres

(iii) **Concrete:** The usual concrete mix for R.C.C. lintel is 1: 2: 4.

For cast in-situ, R.C.C. lintels, the centering is prepared, reinforcement is placed and concreting is done as usual.

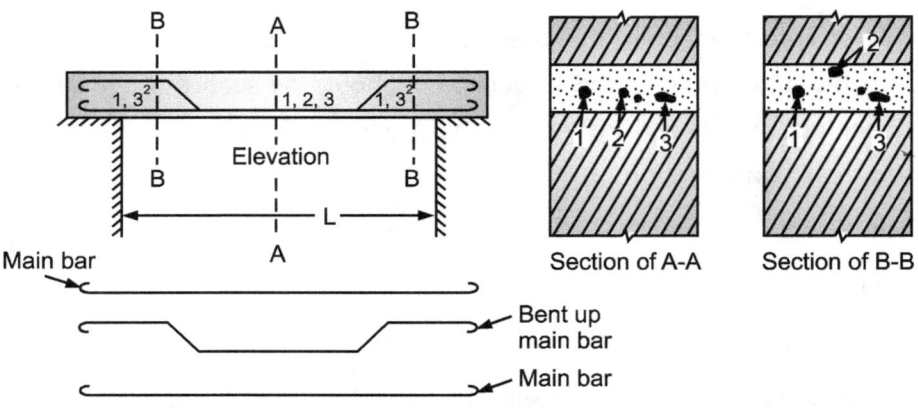

Fig. 2.27: R.C.C. lintel - details for small spans (L < 2 metres)

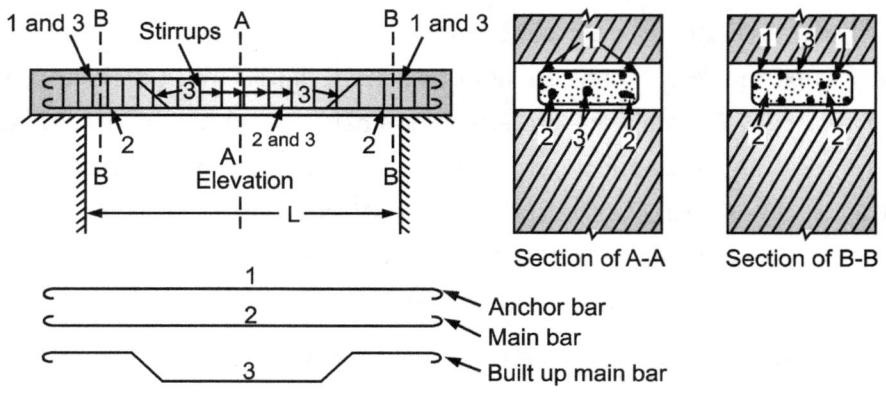

Fig. 2.28: R.C.C. lintel - details for large spans (i.e. span > 2 metres)

The projection, in the form of weather shed Chajja can be easily taken out from R.C.C. Lintels, as shown in Fig. 2.29. The weather shed throws the rain water away from the wall.

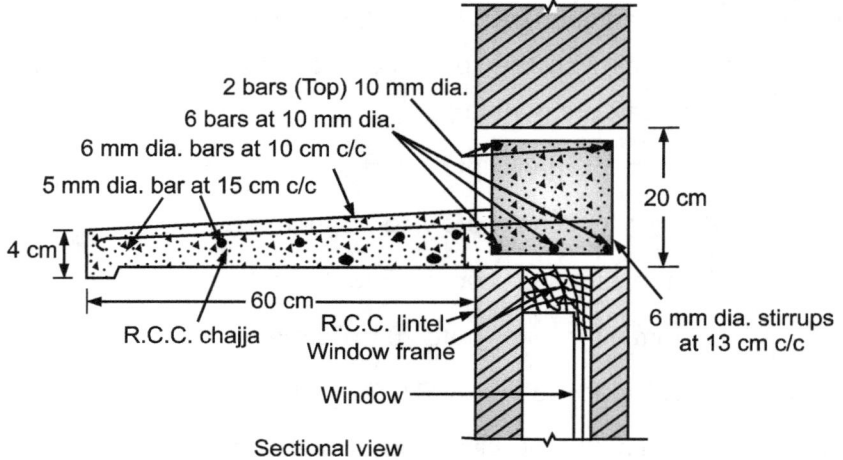

Fig. 2.29: R.C.C. lintel with weather shed or chajja

2.13 CAST IN SITU AND PRECAST CONCRETE ARCH LINTELS

R.C.C. lintels may be either pre-cast or cast in-situ. Pre-cast R.C.C. lintels are preferred for small spans upto 2 metres or so and they are cast in wooden moulds and cured well in advance. Pre-cast lintels prove to be economical as the same mould can be used to prepare a number of lintels. Moreover, the use of pre-cast R.C.C. lintels assures speedy construction as no more time is needed for their curing. However, while laying a pre-cast lintel, special care should be exercised to see that the marked face of the lintel is on the top or upper side. (All pre-cast lintels are marked with tar or paint at the top after pouring concrete in the mould so as to distinguish it from the bottom. This is essential because if the faces are reversed in position (i.e., reinforcement is reversed) then structural failure may occur).

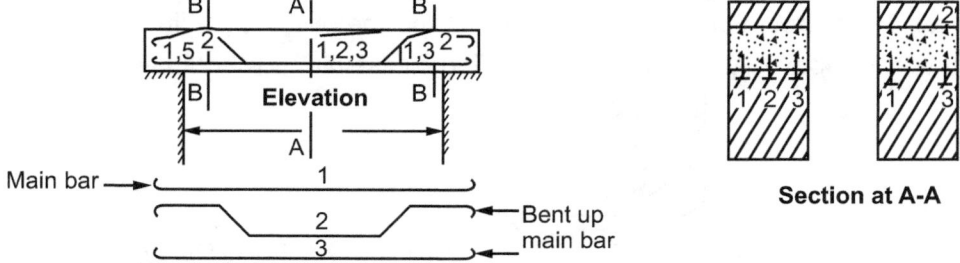

Fig. 2.30: R.C.C. lintels – details for small spans (L < 2 metres)

For larger spans, the lintels should be cast in-situ. Under special lifting tackle or cranes are available in cast in-situ. R.C.C. lintels, erection of centering, placing of reinforcement and concreting is done as usual. The ends of the bars are hooked as shown in Fig. 2.31 to increase the bond or grip between them and the concrete. For lintels, the depth and reinforcement requirements may be computed as below:

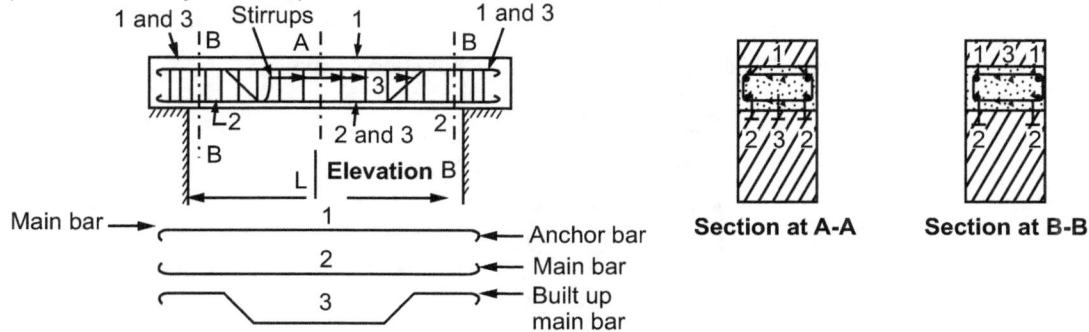

Fig. 2.31: R.C.C. lintel – details for large spans (i.e., span > 2 metres)

(i) Depth of lintel: For ordinary loads, adopt 15 cm depth for span up to 1.2 metre and add another 2.5 cm for every additional 40 cm spans.

(ii) Reinforcement in lintels: The number of main bars depends upon the load to be carried from the wall above the span of opening. As a rule, for thickness of wall 10 cm (half-brick), adopt 2 bars and for every additional 10 cm thickness, one main bar should be added. The diameter of the bar varies with the span and is adopted as follows, as a general rule (Alternate central bars and bent-up).

6 mm ɸ for spans upto 1 metre.

8 mm ɸ for spans 1 to 1.5 metres.

10 mm ɸ for spans 1.5 to 2 metres.

12 mm ɸ for spans 2.0 to 3.0 metres.

The details of chajja projection or weather shed along with lintel are shown in Fig. 2.32.

In case of cavity walls, an R.C.C. boot lintel over the openings may be provided, the details of which are shown in Fig. 2.33. This type of lintel is better in appearance as well as economical. But it should always be ensured that the toe of the boot lintel is strong enough to bear the loads above. A flexible damp-proofing course (D.P.C.) should also be provided.

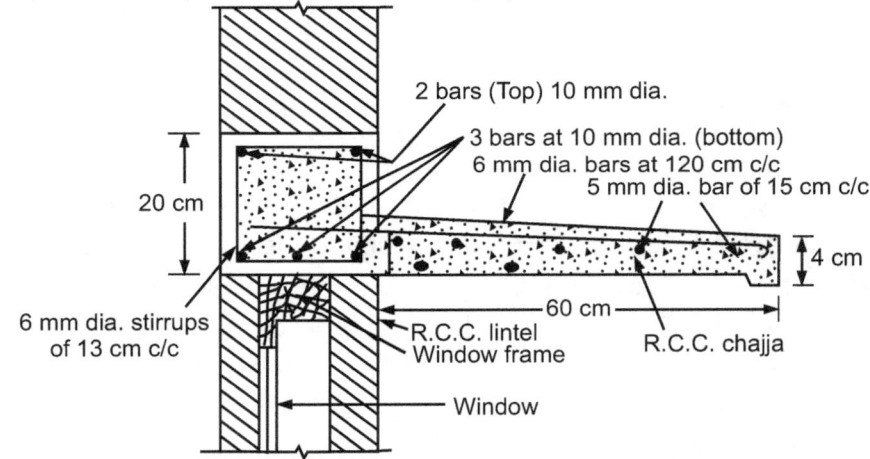

Fig. 2.32: R.C.C. lintels with weather shed or chajja

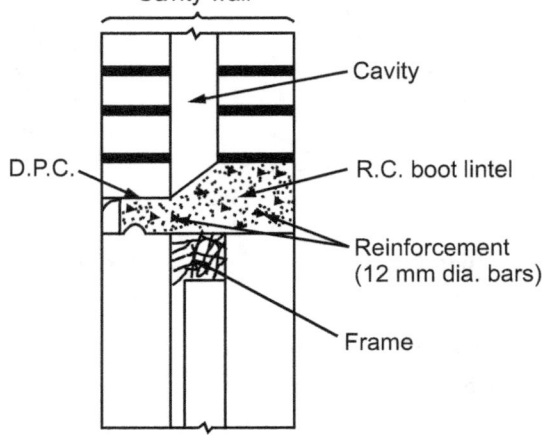

Fig. 2.33: R.C.C. boot lintel details.

2.14 DOORS AND WINDOWS

To enter into a volumetric space of a room what we need is an openable barrier known as a **Door**. To provide light and ventilation and better vision what we need is a **Window** and when these are closed for partial or full privacy what we need is a **Ventilator**.

Location, positioning and total number of doors and windows have a great impact on planning of a building.

General Guidelines for Location and Number of Doors:
- The number of doors should be kept minimum so as to increase the circulation area thereby increasing utility of space.
- Normally (preferably) the door be located near the corner of the room, at around 20 cm from it.
- If it is customary to have two doors for a room, place them in opposite walls, facing each other for good ventilation and free circulation within the room.
- Other governing factors for location, number and size are desired day light, desired vision of surrounding privacy, natural ventilation, heat loss and other local climatic factors etc.
- Also in today's context interior decoration is to be considered while positioning the doors.

For locating the windows and for deciding their number one must concentrate upon the following factors; climatic condition, floor area, distribution of light within the room, ventilation control, privacy, interior decoration, outside vision etc.

General guidelines:
- The windows should preferably located in opposite walls, facing each other.
- Fresh air and continuous diffused daylight entry is achieved if northern side placement is worked out for windows.
- Windows should be located in prevalent wind direction.

Thumb Rules:
- For residential buildings the sill height ranges from 0.7 to 1.0 m from floor level.
- $B_W = \frac{1}{8}$ (Width of room + Height of room).
- Total area $-\frac{1}{10^{th}}$ (min.) to $\frac{1}{5^{th}}$ of floor area (max. in case of public buildings).
- Area of opening = Residential 1 sq. m for 30 to 40 cu. m of inside volume.
- For admittance of light → glazed panel area = 8 to 10% of floor area.

(A) Doors:
1. A door may be defined as an openable barrier secured in a wall opening OR

2. It can also be defined as a movable barrier, secured in an opening, known as doorway through a building wall or partition, for the purpose of providing an access to the building or rooms of a building.

Purposes Served:

(a) Access,

(b) Connecting link for various sections specially in case of commercial buildings,

(c) Security and privacy as and when needed.

(B) Windows:

A window is a barrier secured in a wall opening.

Purposes Served:

(a) Admittance of natural light and air.

(b) For viewing outside scenario.

Materials Used: Wood, Glass, Steel, Plastic and combinations of these etc.

Designation of Door, Window and Ventilators: Frames are designated by symbols denoting width, type and height in succession.

Width: It is indicated by the number of modules of 10 cm; (initial number in the designation - Refer examples a, b, c).

Type: It is indicated by an abbreviated letter/alphabet (middle term).

Height: It is indicated by number of modules of 10 cm (final number).

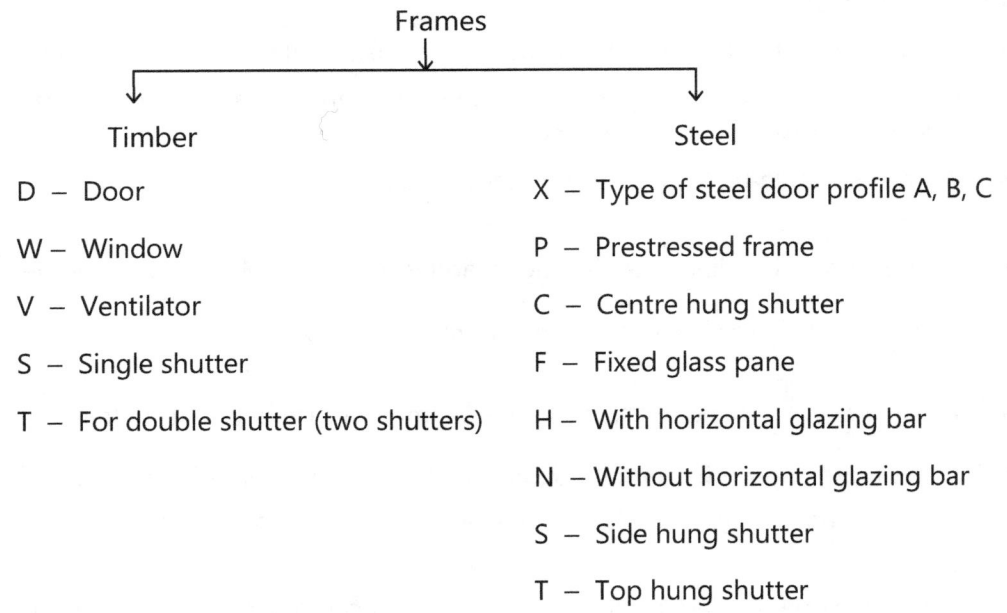

Examples:

(a) 8 DS 20 indicates single shutter door with;

$$\text{Width} = (8 \times 10) - 1 = 79 \text{ cm}$$
$$\text{Height} = (20 \times 10) - 1 = 199 \text{ cm}$$

(b) 10 P X 20 indicates prestressed steel frame with, profile X (i.e. X – A, X – B or X – C).

$$\text{Width} = (10 \times 10) - 1 = 99 \text{ cm}$$
$$\text{Height} = (20 \times 10) - 1 = 199 \text{ cm etc.}$$

(c) 6 WS 12 indicates single shutter window with 60 cm as width and 120 cm height for opening.

∴
$$\text{Clear width} = (6 \times 10) - 1 = 59 \text{ cm}$$
$$\text{Clear height} = (12 \times 10) - 1 = 119 \text{ cm}$$

Table 2.1

Designation	Size of Opening	Frame Size	Shutter Size (Total)	Remark
8 DS 20	80 × 200	79 × 199	70 × 190.5	
9 DS 20	90 × 200	89 × 199	80 × 190.5	
10 DS 20	100 × 200	99 × 199	90 × 190.5	→ Each shutter 56 cm wide with 2 cm overlap.
12 DT 20	120 × 200	119 × 199	110 × 190.5	
8 DS 21	80 × 210	79 × 209	70 × 200.5	
9 DS 21	90 × 210	89 × 209	80 × 200.5	
10 DS 21	100 × 210	99 × 209	90 × 200.5	→ Each shutter 56 cm wide with 2 cm overlap.
12 DT 21	120 × 210	119 × 209	110 × 200.5	
6 WS 12	60 × 120	59 × 119	50 × 110	
10 WT 12	100 × 120	99 × 119	90 × 110	Shutter width 46 and 56 cm respectively with 2 cm overlap.
12 WT 12	120 × 120	119 × 119	110 × 110	
6 WS 13	60 × 130	59 × 129	50 × 120	
10 WT 13	100 × 130	99 × 129	90 × 110	Shutter width 46 (1st case) and 56 cm (2nd case) respectively with 2 cm overlap.
12 WT 13	120 × 130	119 × 129	110 × 120	
6 V 6	60 × 60	59 × 59	50 × 50	
10 V 6	100 × 60	99 × 59	90 × 50	
12 V 6	120 × 60	119 × 59	110 × 50	

Nominal sizes adopted – (Residential buildings):

External door	– 1.0 × 2.0 m
Internal door	– 0.9 × 2.0 m
Bath/W.C. doors	– 0.7 × 2.0 m/0.9 × 2.0
Public buildings	– 1.2 × 2.25 m
Garages etc.	– 2.5 × 2.25 m

Note: Minimum height should not be less than 1.8 m.

2.14.1 Technical Terms

(A) Frame:

An assemblage of vertical members (post/upright/jambs/gramps) and horizontal members (Top - head, Bottom - sill) forming an enclosure, to which shutters are attached.

Materials Used: (a) Timber, (b) Steel sections, (c) Aluminium sections, (d) Concrete, (d) Stone.

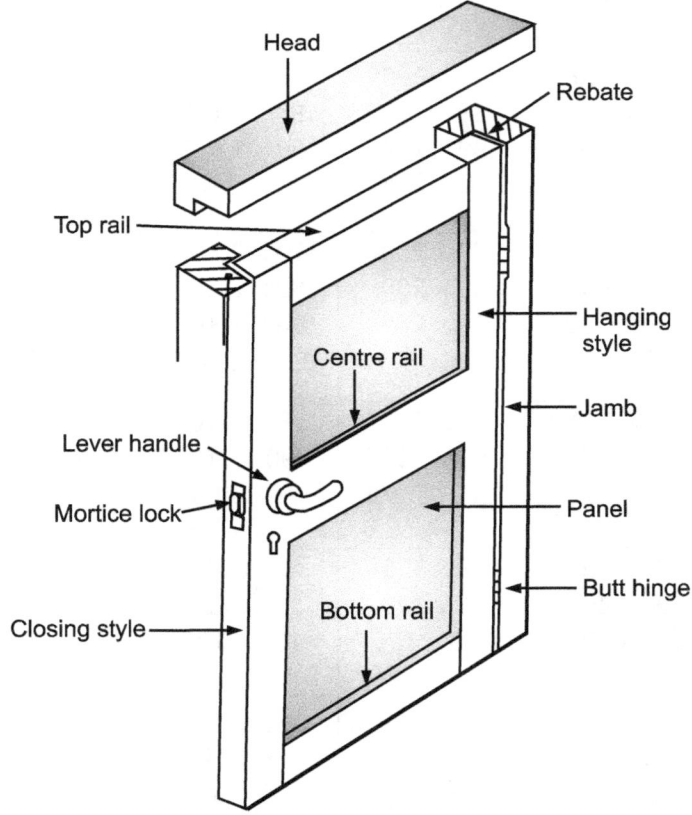

Fig. 2.34: Parts of standard door

Details:
1. **Head:** The top horizontal member to be connected with vertical posts with horns on either side (15 cm in length beyond vertical members) for securing the frame with masonry.
2. **Sill:** The bottom horizontal member to be connected with vertical posts (in case of window).
3. **Jambs or Posts:** The vertical parts of the frame attached to head (and sill of window) with tenon and mortise joint. The shutter rests on jambs (inner side).
4. **Reveal:** The external jamb or right angles to the face of the wall. Hence, it represents a narrow cross surface of the wall on both sides of the opening on the outside of the frame.
5. **Rebate:** A cut or a recess made inside a frame all around on one side to which the shutter is attached through rivets/hinges.
6. **Holdfasts:** To provide additional fixity to the frame, M.S. flats 30 mm × 6 mm and 20 cm in length are provided, which remain embedded in the masonry.
7. **Threshold:** Wooden fixture, fixed to the floor under door frame, thereby enabling the door to be cut short enough to clear floor coverings on the inside.

(B) Shutters:

A movable barrier of the door or window attached to the frame with assembly of styles, rails, panels or planks or otherwise.

Materials Used: Timber, Plywood, Plastic, Decorative or plane glass, Pressed boards, Hard boards and combinations of above.

Details:
1. **Styles (style/stile):** These are outer vertical members of shutter:
   (a) **Hanging style:** Attached with the frames with hinges, the door hangs on it.
   (b) **Closing style:** Which holds the latch.
   (c) **Meeting style:** Provided for two shutter doors, where they meet.
2. **Rails:** These are the horizontal members attached with styles at different levels and are classified depending upon the positions or functions. They are going to serve:
   Types: (a) Top rail, (b) Intermediate rail, (c) Frieze rail, (d) Lock rail, (e) Bottom rail.
3. **Sash Bar or Glazing Bar:** Light weight member of shutter receiving or holding the glass.
4. **Mullion:** It is the vertical member used to subdivide door or window shutter vertically.
5. **Transom:** It is the horizontal member used to subdivide the window or door shutter horizontally.
6. **Panel:** It is the area enclosed between the rails and styles. Glass or timber is usually used.

7. **Louver:** An inclined piece of wood or glass positioned in such a way to maintain privacy but ventilation is possible through number of louvers.
8. **Architrave:** This is a strip of wood, usually moulded or splayed, which is fixed round a door frame to improve its appearance at the joint with masonry, without leaving any reveal.
9. **Putty:** This is a mixture of linseed oil and whiting chalk. It is used for fixing glass panels.

2.14.2 Classification of Doors and Windows

Doors are generally classified on the basis of:

(A) Functional:
1. **Entrance Doors:** The door provided at the Principal entrances of a building are called **entrance doors**.
2. **Ordinary Doors:** The main function of which is to permit passage of persons are called **ordinary doors or exterior and interior doors**.
3. **Screen Doors:** The light doors which are provided in conjunction with main doors and mounted on the outside of the frames of exterior doors are called **screen doors**.
4. **Fire Doors:** The doors specially designed to resist the passage of fire are called **fire doors**.
5. **Wicket Doors:** A small size door provided within a large door to permit the passage without opening the large door.

(B) Operational:
1. **Swinging Doors:** Shutters are hung to the door frame with hinges on one side and they swing about a vertical axis. Type - single swing or double swing.
2. **Sliding Door:** Horizontal or vertical sliding action.
3. **Folding or Accordian Door:** Shutter leaves fold on one or either side.
4. **Revolving Door:** Door revolves around central pivot.
5. **Rolling Door:** Vertical rolling of shutter.
6. **Collapsible Door:** Door collapses on one side or on either side.

(C) Materials Used:
1. Timber/Wooden doors.
2. Plywood - Veneer - particle boards as types of timber.
3. Glazed doors.
4. Steel doors.
5. Aluminium framed doors etc.

Classification of Windows:

(A) Functional:
1. For admitting light only - fixed - glazed window.
2. For admitting light and air - ordinary windows.
3. For admitting air and maintaining privacy - louvered windows.
4. Projecting windows - outward/inward projections.
5. Ventilator - special category.

(B) Operational:
1. Side hung - hinges on sides.
2. Top hung - hinges on top.
3. Bottom hung - hinges at bottom.
4. Sliding - horizontal and vertical.
5. Folding - normally on either side.
6. Pivoted - horizontal and vertical pivots.

(C) Materials Used:
Wooden, Aluminium, Steel, Glazed etc.

2.14.3 Types of Doors

Following are the usual types observed in rural and urban areas in India.

1. Battened and ledged doors.
2. Battened, ledged and braced doors.
3. Battened, ledged and framed doors.
4. Battened, ledged, braced and framed doors.

(**Note:** Above types are becoming obsolete for many reasons such as - unpleasant elevation, scarcity of timber, it can be used only for narrow openings etc.)

5. Framed and panelled doors.
6. Glazed or sash doors.
7. Sliding doors.
8. Flush doors.
9. Collapsible doors.

10. Revolving doors.
11. Swing doors.
12. Rolling steel shutter doors.
13. Louvered doors.
14. Folding doors.
15. Plastic doors.

(A) Framed and Panelled Doors:

Characteristics: These are commonly used as their appearance is pleasing and tendency of shrinkage is reduced. Also if the panel area is partially occupied by glazing it admits additional natural light inside the room. The ratio of glazed to panelled portion is 2: 1. The styles run vertically for the whole height and are most important as all other parts are connected to it. If the width is more, then additional vertical member, mullion is also provided to give additional strength.

Minimum number of rails is three i.e. top rail, lock rail and bottom rail. The available space between styles and rail is termed as panel. The minimum width of style is kept as 100 mm and for bottom and lock rail it is 150 mm. The thickness of shutter depends on various factors such as size of the door, type of work, position of door, number of panels, moulding size etc. Usually, it ranges from 30 mm to 50 mm. Internal edges are grooved to receive the panels and mortised-tenoned joint is preferred for framework. Total number and pattern of panel depends upon designer's aspect or owner's choice.

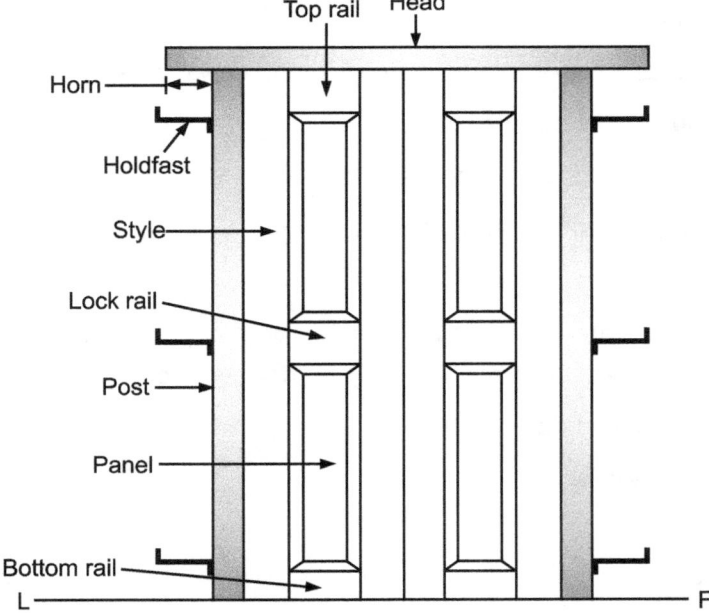

Fig. 2.35: Doors frame and panelled shutters

(B) Glazed and Sash Doors:

If employed, this door gives very good effect, hence specially provided for private bungalows or in case of public buildings such as hospitals, colleges, libraries, showrooms etc. For fully glazed door, a single glass panel (plate glass) is received into the rebates along the inner edge of styles and secured by nails and putty or by wooden beads. Sometimes the glazed area is subdivided into number of small areas by providing sash bars. The glass panes are secured in the rebates of framework of sash bars.

To increase the area of glazing, width of style above lock rail is sometimes reduced. These reduce dimensioned styles are known to be diminished or gunstock styles.

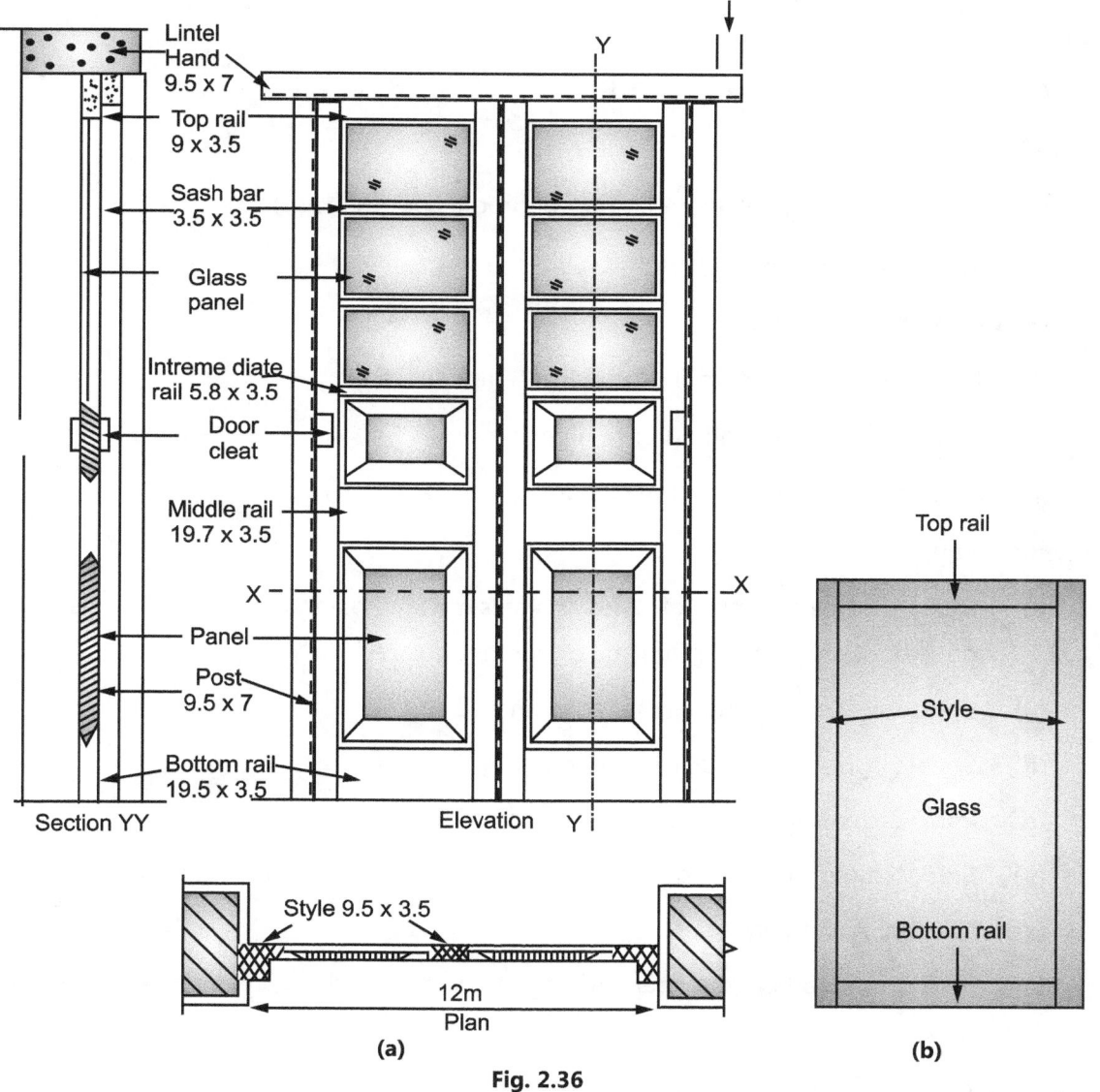

Fig. 2.36

2.14.4 Windows

Depending upon various natural agencies deciding the climatic pattern at a particular place the window area in % of floor area will vary with a minimum of $1/10^{th}$ (10%) of floor area.

Continuous sash or one large window in a room gives better light distribution, than separated narrow windows.

The selection of size, shape, location and the number of windows in a room depends upon the following factors:

(a) Area to be ventilated and lighted.

(b) Location of the room.

(c) Utility of the room (Kitchen - Living - Bedrooms or otherwise).

(d) Direction to which window fronts.

(e) Direction of the wind.

(f) Other natural parameters like humidity, temperature etc.

(g) Exterior views (to be sighted or to hide).

(h) Architectural treatment for the exterior.

Terminology:

(i) **Sash:** A single assembly of styles and rails made into a frame for holding glass, with or without dividing bars, may be glazed or unglazed.

(ii) **Window:** Sash and the glass that fill an opening.

(iii) **Styles:** Upright - vertical or border pieces.

(iv) **Rails:** Cross-horizontal pieces.

(v) **Bar:** Member that extends in height and width of an opening to be ventilated.

(vi) **Muntin:** A short light bar.

(vii) **Mullion:** A vertical member dividing the window (Please refer other details with door section.)

(viii) **Transom:** A horizontal dividing member.

Types of Window:
1. Casement Windows:

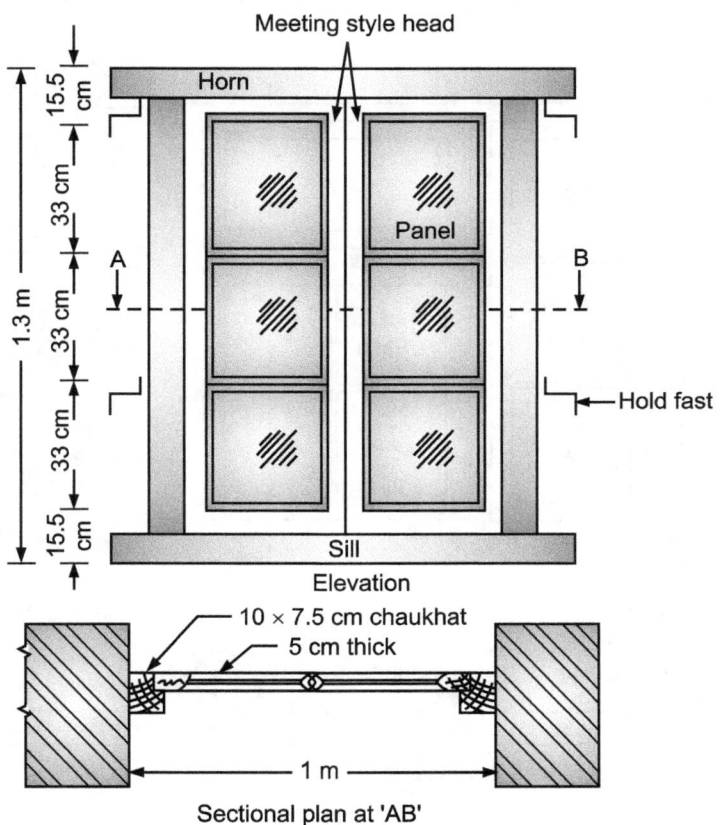

Fig. 2.37: Casement window

Members: Shutter with styles, rails, sash bars, panels (glazed, unglazed or partially glazed). Frame with jambs, head, sill and sometimes with mullion and transomes.

Material: Timber, metal.

Sometimes a combination of door, window and ventilator is also provided specially at the entrance to enhance appearance and to check for unwanted entries.

Construction Method: Construction method is same as door, side hinged opening part of window with glass panes is known as casement and hence the name.

2.15 SASH OR GLAZED WINDOWS

A sash window is a type of casement window in which the panels are fully glazed. The frame of each shutter consists of two vertical styles, top rail and a bottom rail. The space between the top and bottom rails is divided into small panels by means of small timber members placed horizontally and vertically. These timber members, known as sash bars or glazing bars are rebated to receive glass panes. Glass-panes are fixed to these sash bars either by means of putty or by timber beads commonly known as glazing beads secured to the sash bars by means of nails.

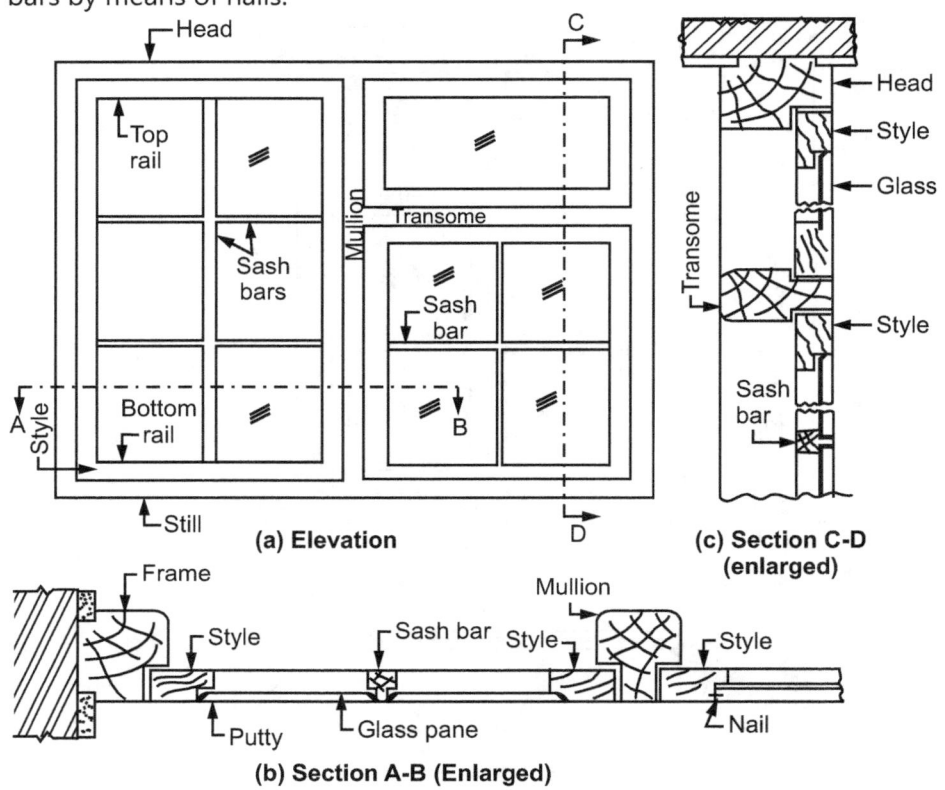

Fig. 2.38: Sash windows

If the window opening is wide, the window frame may have central vertical member known as mullion. Similarly, if the height of window opening is more (or if a ventilator is combined with the window) the window frame may have horizontal member called transome.

2.16 STAIRS

A successful functioning of a multistorey building needs circulation of traffic in normal use and in emergency requirement. For proper appreciation of building design, a due care should be required for selection of type of vertical circulation, their location, number of units required and design and arrangement. Vertical circulation between the various floors is possible by different structures such as stairs, lifts, escalators, ladders and ramps.

A stair is a set of steps arranged for the purpose of connecting various floors and to provide means of ascent and descent between various floors of a building. Stairs can be made up of various materials such as wood, stones, bricks, steel, P.C.C., R.C.C. etc.

The location of staircase in a building is very important. It should be located in such a way that, it should give maximum benefit to its user. In public building, it should located near the main entrance and in residential building it should provided centrally. So as to provide easy access from all the rooms and to maintain privacy.

2.17 DEFINITION AND TECHNICAL TERMS

1. **Baluster:** It is vertical member of wood or any metal supporting the hand rail.
2. **Balustrade:** The combined frame work of hand rail and baluster is known as balustrade.
3. **Flight:** A series of steps without any platform, break or landing in their direction.
4. **Step:** It is the portion of a stair which consists of riser and tread. This allows ascent and descent from one floor to another.
5. **Tread:** It is the upper horizontal portion of each step on which the foot is placed while ascending or descending.
6. **Rise:** This is a vertical distance between the upper surface of the two successive treads.
7. **Going:** It is the width of the tread between two successive risers.
8. **Landing:** It is the platform provided between two flights. It allows facility for change of direction and provides a resting place in between ascends and descends.
9. **Nosing:** It is the projecting part of the tread beyond the face of the riser. It is generally rounded to give pleasing appearance.
10. **Scotia:** It is a moulding provided under the nosing to improve the beauty of the step.
11. **Soffit:** It is the under surface of a stair.
12. **Winders:** These are tapering steps used for providing for change of the direction of a stair.
13. **String:** It is the sloping member which supports the steps in a stair.
14. **Newel Post:** It is the vertical post provided at the top and bottom ends of flights supporting the hand rails.
15. **Head Room:** This is the minimum clear height from a tread to overhead construction.

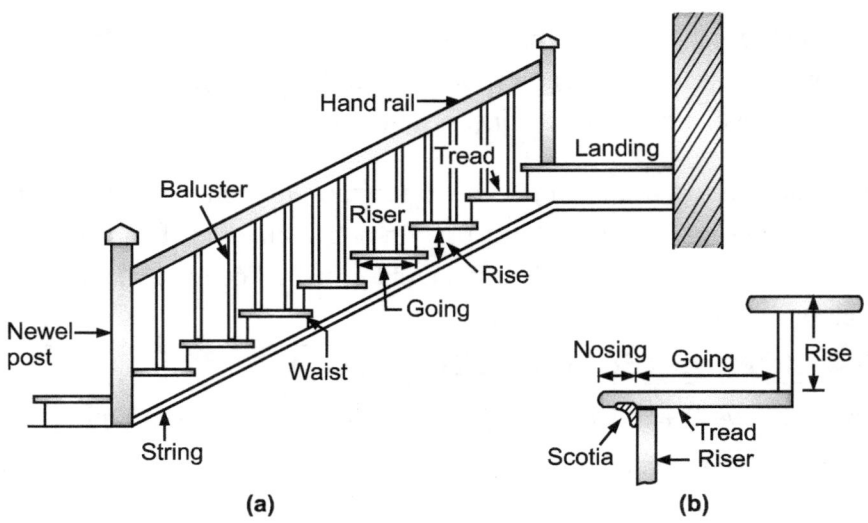

Fig. 2.39: Terms used in stairs

2.18 REQUIREMENTS OF A GOOD STAIRCASE

1. Stair should be so located as to provide easy access to the occupants, there should be proper light and ventilation directly from the exterior and it should be so located as to have approaches convenient and spacious approaches.

2. It should have sufficient stair width to accommodate number of persons in peak hours. In residential building 90 cm wide stair is sufficient. While in public building 1.5 to 1.8 m width may be provided.

3. The number of steps in a flight should generally be, maximum of 12 and minimum of 3 from comfort point of view.

4. Sufficient head room should be provided to avoid head injury to tall people. At the same time it should give a feeling of spaciousness. Vertical clearance should not be less than 2.15 m.

5. Risers and treads should generally be proportioned from comfort point of view. Treads should be 25 to 30 cm wide and rise should be 17.5 to 18.5 cm in height. Generally, the following thumb rules are used.

    (i) (2 × Rise in cm) + (Tread in cm) = 60.

    (ii) (Rise in cm) + (Tread in cm) = 40 to 45.

    (iii) (Rise in cm) × (Tread in cm) = 400 to 450.

6. The minimum width of landing should be equal to the width of the stairs.

7. The pitch of stair or slope of the stair should never exceed 45° and should not be flatter than 25°.

8. The material used for the construction of stair should have sufficient strength and should be fire resistant.

2.19 TYPES OF STAIRS

Generally, stairs are of the following types:
(1) Straight stairs,
(2) Dog legged stairs,
(3) Open newel stairs,
(4) Geometrical stairs,
(5) Circular stairs,
(6) Bifurcated stairs,
(7) Open well stairs,
(8) Half turn stair,
(9) Quarter turn stair.

1. **Dog Legged Stair:** It consists of two straight flights of steps with abrupt 180° turn between them. In this type, a level landing is placed between the two flights at the change of direction. This type of stair is useful where the width of the staircase hall is sufficient to accommodate two widths of stairs.

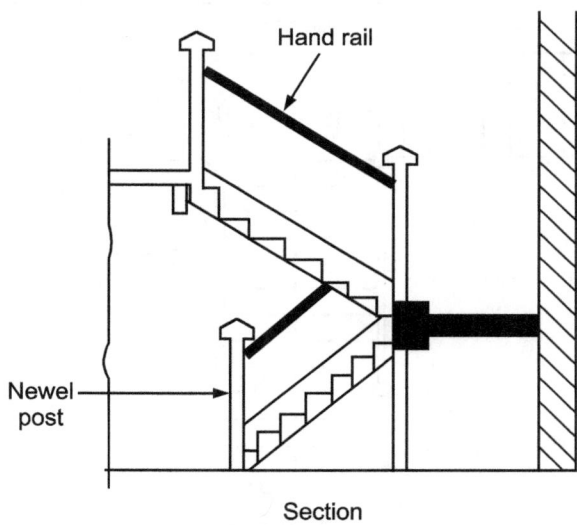

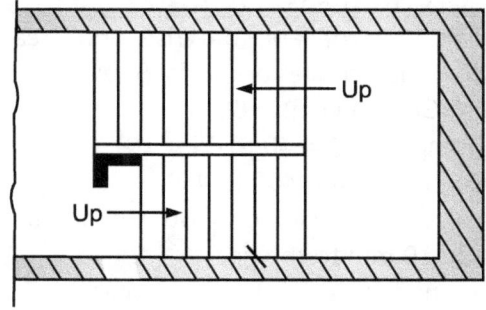

Fig. 2.40: Dog legged

2. **Bifurcated Stair:** These stairs are so arranged that there is wide flight at the start which is sub-divided into narrow flights at the mid-landing. The two narrow flights start from either side of the mid-landing. This type of stair is commonly used in public building at the entrance.

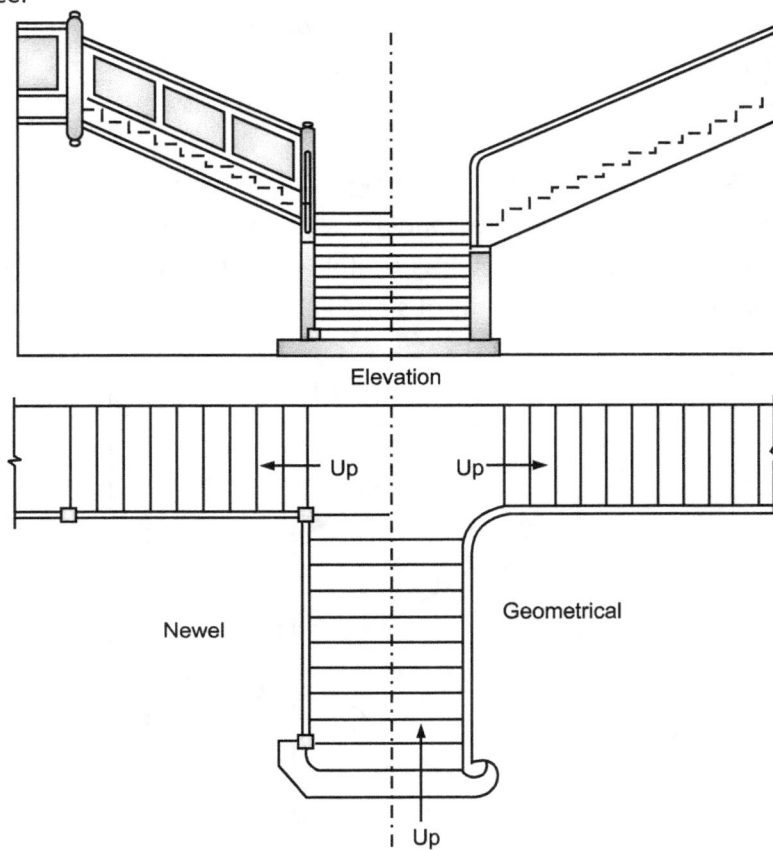

Fig. 2.41: Bifurcated stair

2.20 THUMB RISE FOR RISE AND TREAD

For comfortable ascent and decent, the rise and tread of a step should be well-proportioned. The following thumb rules are as follows:

(i) (2 × Rise in cm) + (Going in cm) = 60.
(ii) (Rise in cm) + (Going in cm) = 40 to 45.
(iii) (Rise in cm) × (Going in cm) = 400 to 450.
(iv) Adopt Rise = 14 cm and Going = 30 cm as standard; then for every 20 mm subtracted from going, add 10 mm to the rise.

Thus, other combinations for rise and going would be 15 cm × 28 cm; 16 cm × 26 cm; 17 cm × 24 cm.

For residential buildings, the common size of the steps is 16 cm × 26 cm. In hospital etc., the comfortable size of the steps is 10 cm × 30 cm.

2.21 FLOORS

The horizontal members of the building which divide vertical space into different parts at different level are called as **floors**. Floor supports the occupants, furniture and equipments. A building may be single storeyed or multi storeyed. Single storeyed building has only one floor which is called as ground floor. In multi-storeyed structures, there are additional floors which are called as upper floors. The floors which are constructed below ground floor are called as **basement floor**. A floor consists of two components:

(1) Sub-floor or base course or sub-grade which imparts strength, stability and support floor covering and all other super imposed loads.
(2) Floor covering which provides a hard, durable, clean, smooth, impervious and beautiful surface to the floor.

2.22 REQUIREMENT OF FLOORING MATERIAL

The floor is intended to serve the following functions:

1. It should be strong though to sustain safely the intended to the applied.
2. It should resist wear and tear.
3. It should sustain impact load.
4. It should be easy to clean and maintain.
5. It should have pleasing appearance.
6. It should be impermeable.
7. It should take polish.
8. It should not be slippery.
9. It should be easily available and economical.

2.23 SELECTION OF A FLOORING MATERIAL

Following factors are to be carefully considered before selecting the material for flooring of a particular building:

(1) Appearance (7) Fire resistance
(2) Cleaning   (8) Hardness
(3) Comfort   (9) Maintenance
(4) Cost   (10) Noise
(5) Damp resistance (11) Slipperiness
(6) Durability.

1. **Appearance:** The flooring material should be desired appearance and it should produce the colour effect in conformity with the use of building.
2. **Cleaning:** The flooring material should be such that it can be easily and effectively cleaned. It should have effective resistance against absorption of oil, grease, etc.

3. **Comfort:** The flooring material should be such that it gives comfort when used. If the flooring material possesses reasonably good thermal insulation, it imparts comfort to the residents of the building to a great extent.
4. **Cost:** The cost of flooring material should be reasonable as compared to the utility of the building.
5. **Damp resistance:** The flooring material should offer sufficient resistance against dampness so that healthy environment prevails in the building.
6. **Durability:** The flooring material should be durable and it should be strong enough to impart resistance to wear, tear, chemical action, temperature changes, etc.
7. **Fire resistance:** This quality of flooring material is of more importance for upper floors. It should offer sufficient fire resistance so that the fire barriers are obtained between different levels of a buildings.
8. **Hardness:** The flooring material should be sufficiently hard so as to have resistance to make or signs caused by the shifting or rubbing of furniture, equipment etc.
9. **Maintenance:** The flooring material should be such that minimum maintenance is required. However, when repairs are required, it should be possible to carry out them speedily, easily and with minimum cost.
10. **Noise:** If noise is created by the use of flooring material, it leads to discomfort and hence, at places where silence is required, such flooring material giving less noise should only be preferred.
11. **Slipperiness:** The surface of floor should be smooth but at the same time, it should not be too slippery. It is dangerous for old people, children and pregnant women.

2.24 FLAG STONE FLOORING

Flag stone is any laminated sand stone available in 2 cm to 4 cm thickness, in the form of stone slabs of square (30 cm × 30 cm, 45 cm × 45 cm or 60 cm × 60 cm) or rectangular size (45 × 60 cm). This type of work is also called paving. The stone slabs are laid on concrete base. The sub-soil is properly compacted, over which 10 to 15 cm thick lime concrete or lean cement concrete is laid. This forms the base course of the floor. The flag stones (stone slabs) are then laid over 20 to 25 mm thick layer or bed mortar (Fig. 2.42). In laying the slabs, work is started from two diagonally opposite corners and brought up from both sides. A string is stretched between two corner slabs laid first to correct level. Other slabs are then so laid that their tops tough the string. If any particular slab falls lower than the string level, it is re-laid by putting fresh layer of stiff mortar. When the stone slabs are properly set, mortar in the joints is raked out to a depth of about 15 to 20 mm and then flush pointed with 1: 3 cement mortar. Proper slope is given to the surface for drainage. The work is properly cured.

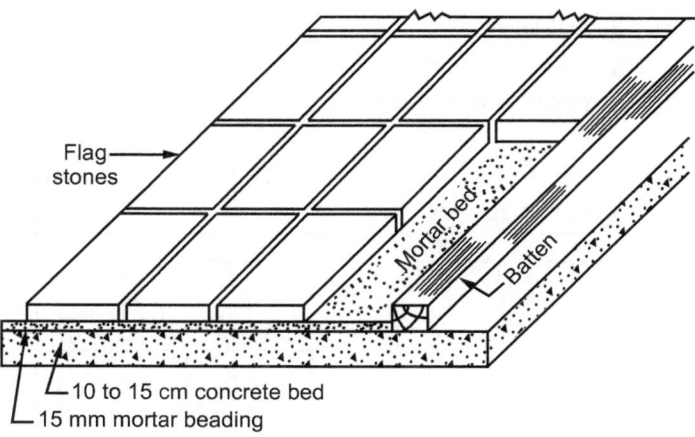

Fig. 2.42: Flag stone flooring

2.25 CONSTRUCTION DETAILS OF CONCRETE FLOOR

This flooring is called as artificial stone flooring. It's constructional details are explained as follows:

(i) Preparation of Ground: It should be well compacted. It should be watered properly to gain considerable strength to offer support. It should not contain pockets of loose soil.

(ii) Preparation of Sub-grade: If sub-grade is of concrete it's proportion will be 1: 2: 4. It should be mixed thoroughly by any means i.e. manually or mechanically. It should be provided with proper slope. It should be coated with cement slurry to get a good bond between the sub-grade and concrete floor. The surface of subgrade should be roughened with steel wire brushes without disturbing the concrete. The sub-grade may be R.C.C. slab.

(iii) Laying of Flooring: The concrete should be placed gently and evenly spread within the panel of area 2 m². The panel should be of uniform size. It's dimension should not exceed 2 m. The operation of laying of concrete for each panel should be finished within half an hour.

To ensure uniformity of colours and straightens in all the panels it should be laid in one operation using plain asbestos sheet stripes at the junction of the panels. The panels should be bounded by wooden battens. The depth of the battens should be same as that of the concrete flooring surface of the flooring which should be smoothed with wooden floats.

The battens should be removed after 24 hours once laying of concrete is finished.

If ends are damaged, it should be repaired with cement mortar 1: 2.

(iv) Finishing of Flooring: Once moisture is varnished cement slurry should be prepared. It should spread over flooring. It should be properly pressed and finished smooth.

(v) Curing: Once the top layer has hardened, curing should be done for minimum ten days.

Casting Large Floors:

For large industrial and commercial buildings it is not feasible to cast floor of the size required in one section. There are two methods of casting large floors to remove this difficulty.

These are explained as follows:

(1) The Chequer Board Method: In this method, floor can be subdivided into a series of sections of restricted width and length. Alternate sections of the floor can cast in a chequer board arrangement.

This method is not easy. It requires to put many structural joints running along and across the floor. It does not offer speedy construction.

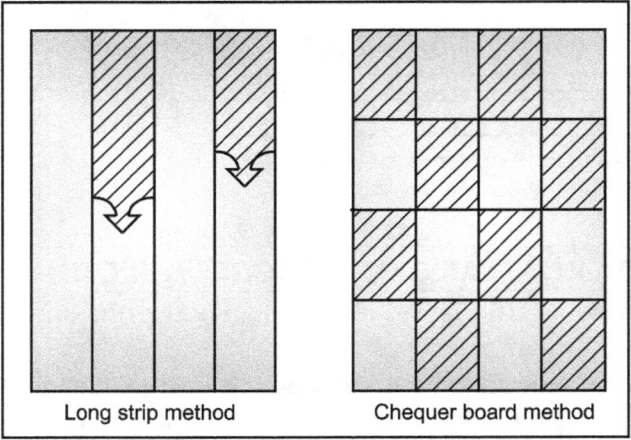

Fig. 2.43: Long strip and chequer boad options

(2) The Long Strip Method: It is based on the division of floor into a series of long strips. It is around 4.5 m in width, running the full length of the building or upto a selected movement joint. The strips can be cast in two phases, initially with alternate strips and the in-fill joints cast after some days.

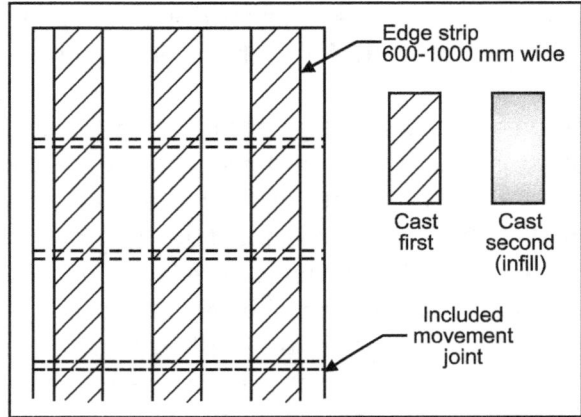

Fig. 2.44: Long strip floor layout

Narrow edge strips (630 – 1000 mm wide) are formed near the walls to allow ready access for the compacting beam across full width strips. There is possibility of development of cracks. To control it strips are normally divided into bays. The need of the joints is related to the length of the strips and the presence of reinforcement.

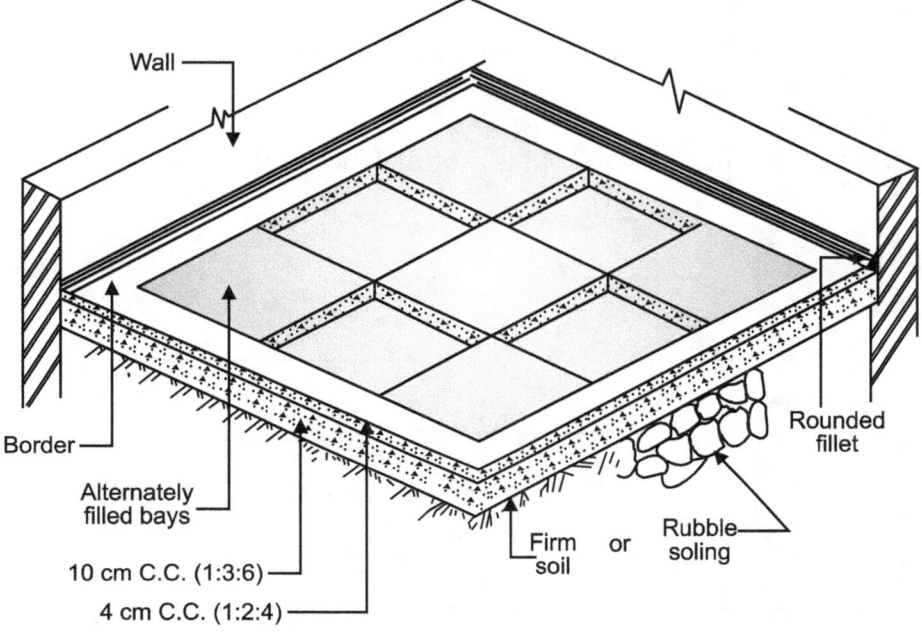

Fig. 2.45: Laying of concrete flooring

2.26 ROOFS

Roofs form important part of superstructure and serves the following functions:
(1) It should offer adequate protection against natural forces like heat, sound, rain, etc.
(2) It should sustain various stresses due to dead load, wind load, etc.
(3) It should also enhance aesthetic sense of building.
(4) It should be easy to maintain and durable.
(5) It should be economical.
(6) Roofs constructed out of materials of inferior quality, bad workmanship and inadequate attention to safety practices often leads to permanent source of nuisance and maintenance. Hence, it is essential that adequate steps are taken to guard against the same.

This chapter deals with these aspects.

2.27 TYPES OF ROOF AND THEIR SUITABILITY

2.27.1 Requirements of a Good Roof

The design and choice of roof is also as important as its foundation. The former protects the building from the damaging forces starting from its top and the latter takes its care from the likely damages at its bottom. Following are the requirements of a well planned roof:

(i) It should be durable against the adverse effects of various agencies such as wind, rain, sun, etc.
(ii) It should grant the desirable insulation against sound and heat.

(iii) It should be structurally stable and sound and it should be capable of taking the loads likely to come over it.
(iv) It should be well-drained.
(v) It should have efficient water-proofing arrangement.
(vi) It should be fire resistant.

2.27.2 Types of Roof

Roof types are governed by slope of the roof, material used for roof, span of it etc.

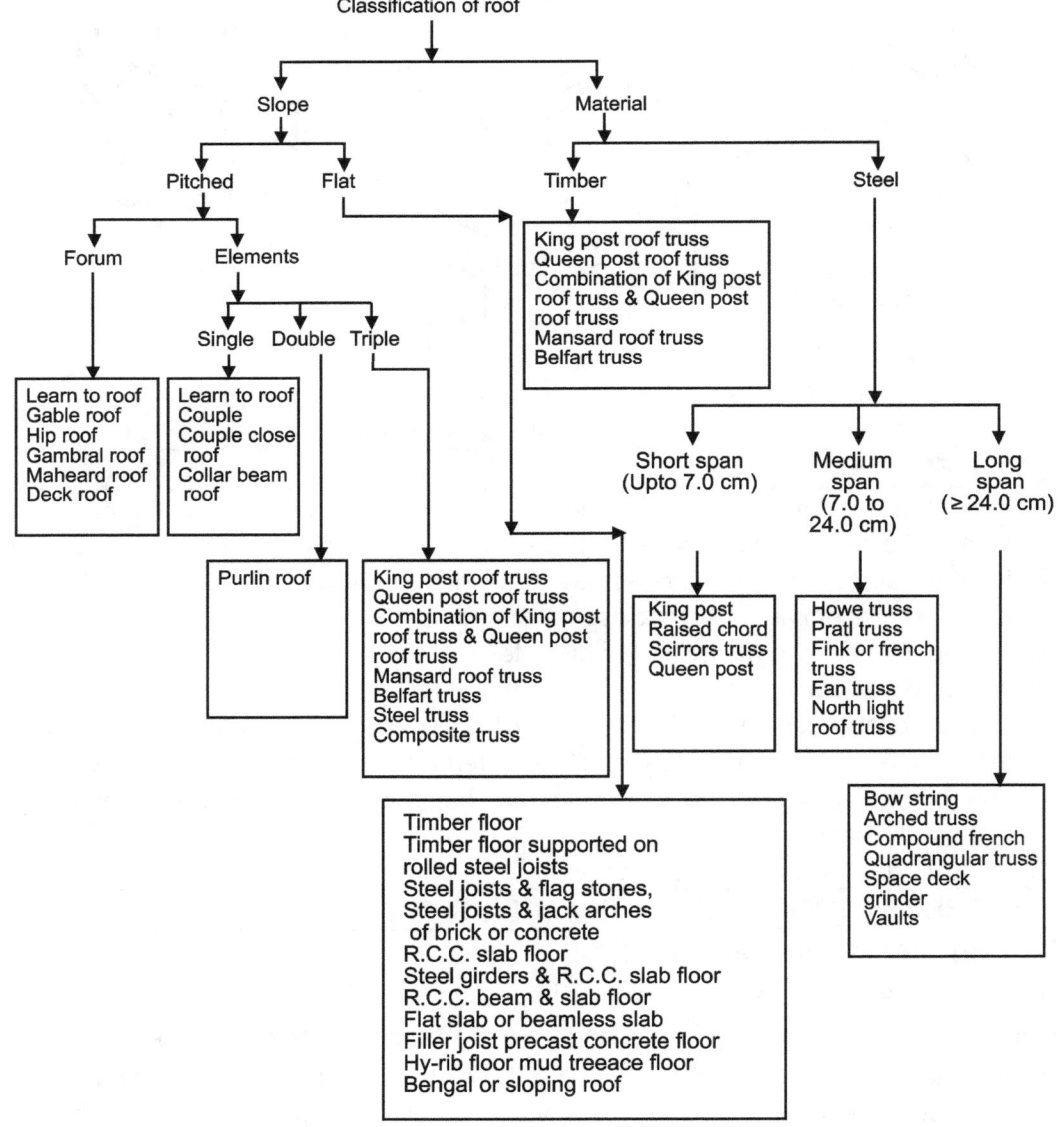

Chart: Classification of Roof

2.27.3 Technical Terms in Sloping Roof and Roof Trusses

Fig. 2.46 and shows various elements of sloping roof and roof trusses. These elements are defined below.

1. **Ridge:** It is the apex line of the sloping roof.
2. **Span:** It is the clear distance between the supports of an arch, beam or roof truss.
3. **Pitch of roof:** It is the inclination of sides of a roof to the horizontal plane. The pitch of the roof is usually expressed either in terms of degrees (angle) or as a ratio of rise to span.

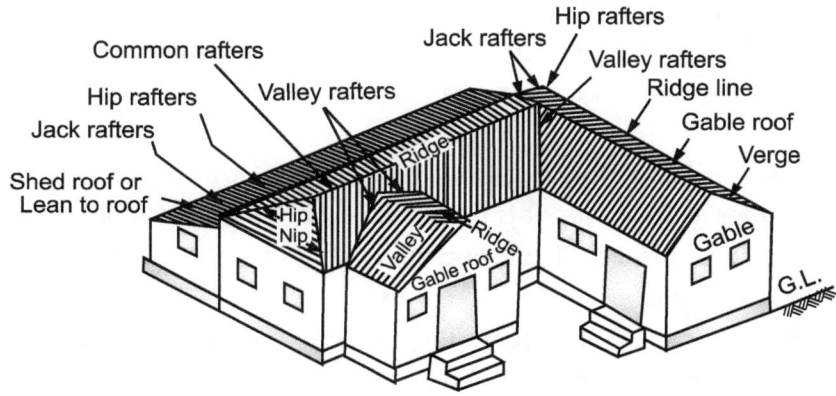

Fig. 2.46: View of a building with basic sloping roofs.

4. **Rise:** It is the vertical distance between the top of the ridge and the wall plate.
5. **Eaves:** The lower edge of the inclined roof surface is called eaves. From eaves, the rain water from the roof surface drops down.
6. **Hip:** It is the ridge formed by the intersection of two sloping surfaces, when the exterior angle is greater than 180°.
7. **Valley:** A valley is the reverse of a hip. It is formed by the intersection of two roof surfaces having external angle, which is less than 180 degrees.
8. **Hip Rafters:** These are the wooden members which form the hip of a pitched roof. These rafters run diagonally from the ridge to the corners of the walls to support roof covering. They receive the ends of purlins and ends of jack rafters.
9. **Jack Rafters:** These are common rafters shorter in length which run from a hip to the eaves or from a ridge to a valley. A hip or valley is formed by the meeting of jack rafters.
10. **Common Rafters or Spars:** These are the inclined wooden members supporting the battens or boarding to support roof coverings. They run from a ridge to the eaves. They are normally spaced at 30 to 45 cm centre to centre, depending upon the roof covering material.

11. **Valley Rafters:** These are sloping rafters which run diagonally from the ridge to the eaves for supporting valley gutters. They receive the ends of the purlins and ends of jack rafters on both sides.
12. **Hipped End:** It is the sloped triangular surface formed at the end of a roof.
13. **Verge:** This is the edge of sheets, slates or tiles which projects beyond the gable end of the sloped roof.
14. **Ridge Piece, Ridge Beam or Ridge Board:** It is the horizontal wooden member, in the form of a beam or board, which is provided at the apex of a roof truss. It supports the common rafter fixed to it.
15. **Purlins:** These are the horizontal wooden or steel members, used to support common rafters of a roof when span is large. Purlins are supported on trusses or walls.
16. **Eaves Board or Facia Board:** It is a wooden plank or board fixed to the feet of the common rafter at the eaves. It is usually 20 - 25 mm thick and 20 - 25 cm wide. The ends of the lower most roof covering material rest upon it. The eaves gutter can also be secured against it.
17. **Barge Board:** It is the timber board used to hold the common rafter forming verge.
18. **Wall Plates:** These are long wooden members which are provided on the top of stone or brick wall, for the purpose of fixing the feet of the common rafters. These are embedded from sides and bottom in masonry of walls, almost at the centre of their thickness. Wall plates actually connect the walls to the roof.
19. **Post Plate:** This is similar to wall plate except that they run continuous, parallel to the face of wall, over the tops of the posts and support rafters at their feet.
20. **Battens:** These are thin strips of wood, called scantlings which are nailed to the rafters for lying roof materials above.
21. **Boardings, Sheeting or Sarking:** This consists of boards which are nailed to the upper edges of common rafters and to which tiles and other roofing materials are secured.
22. **Truss:** A roof truss is a frame work of triangles designed to support the roof covering or ceiling over rooms.
23. **Template:** This is a square or rectangular block, about 10 to 15 cm thick, which is placed below a beam or a truss, so as to spread the load over a larger area. It may be made of fine dressed flat stone, squared wood, concrete block or R.C.C. block.
24. **Cleats:** These are short sections of wood or steel [angle iron], which are fixed on the principal rafters or trusses to support the purlins.

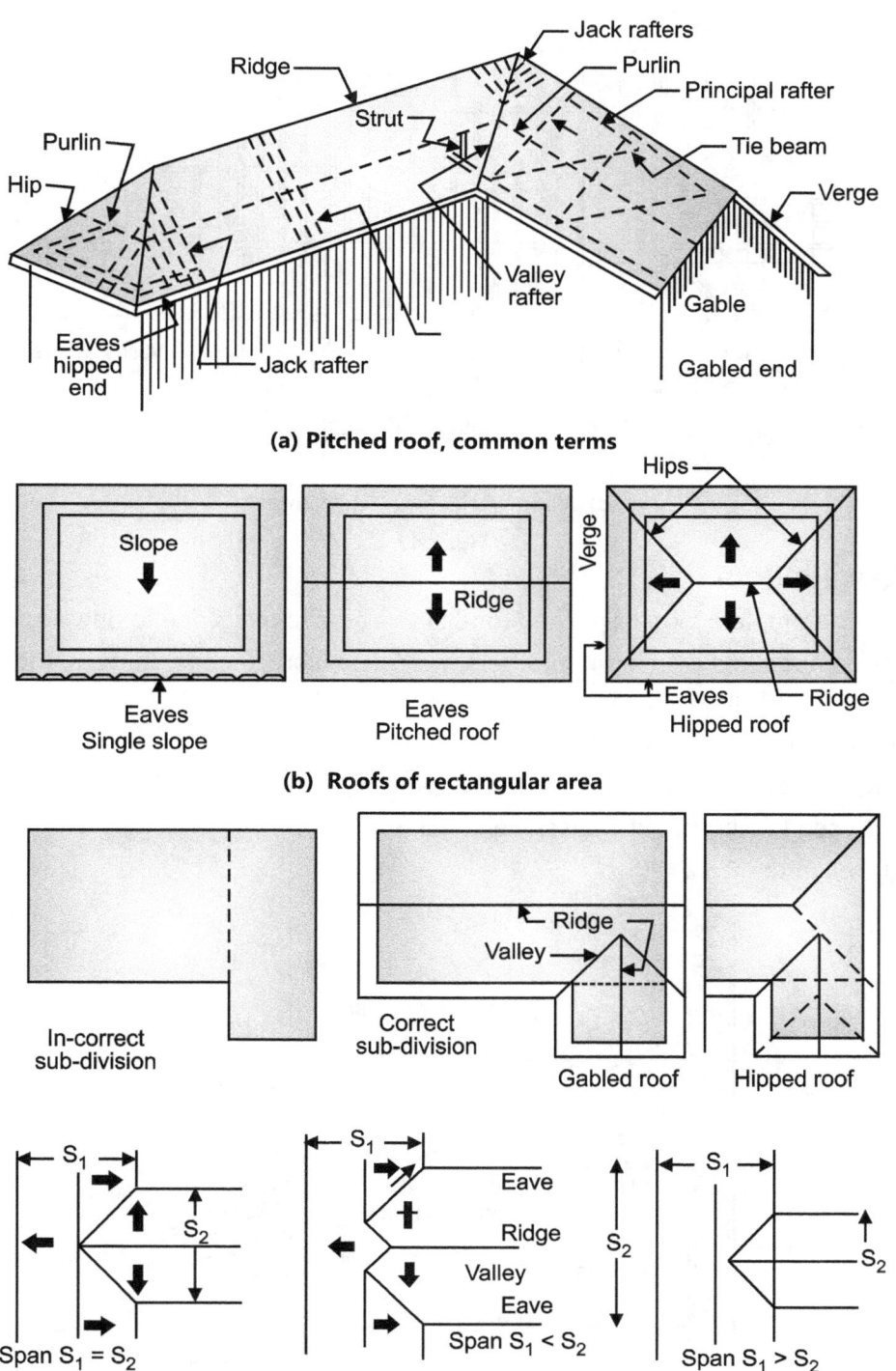

(a) Pitched roof, common terms

(b) Roofs of rectangular area

(c) Junctions of roofs of different spans

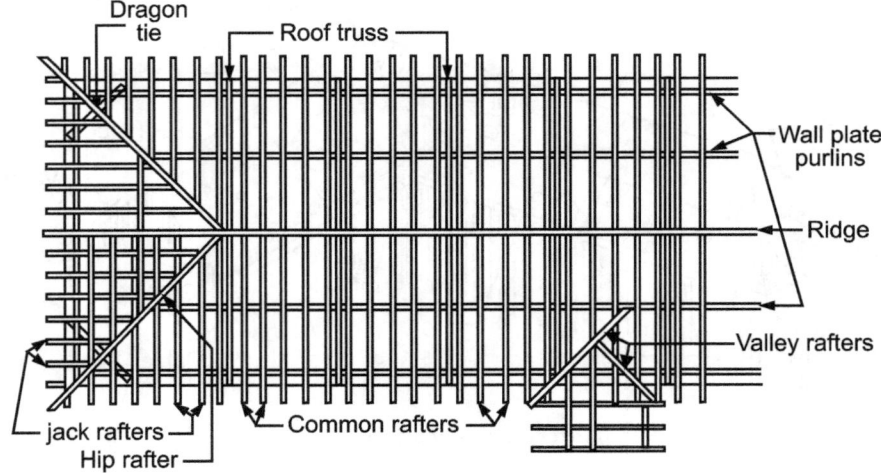

(d) Wood works for pitched roof

Fig. 2.47

2.27.4 Lean to Roof

(i) It is the simplest form of pitched roof. In this type rafters slope to one side only.

(ii) It's components are common rafters, wall plate, corbel stone, battens, roof covering, eaves board, string course etc.

(iii) Inclination of common rafter is limited to 30°.

(iv) The knee straps and bolts are used to connect the rafters with the posts.

(v) It is used for sheds, out-houses, verandah etc.

It is shown in the Fig. 2.48.

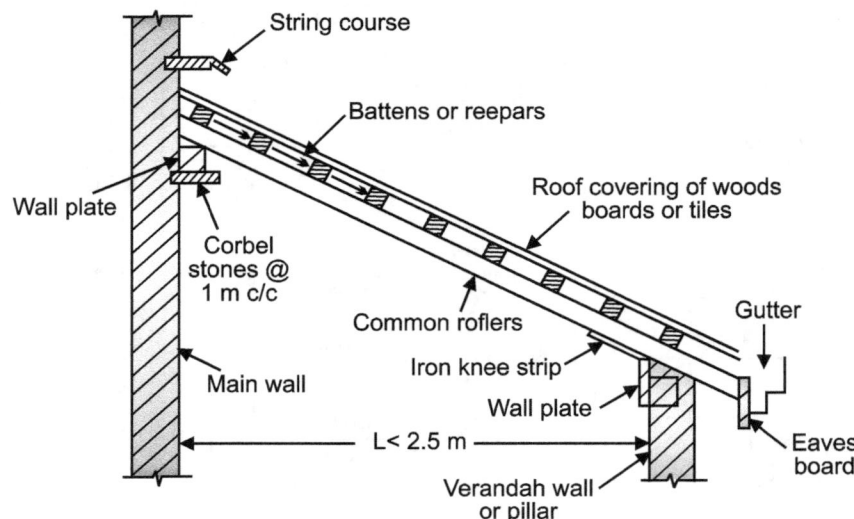

Fig. 2.48: Lean to roof or verandah roof

2.27.5 Reinforced Concrete or Reinforced Brick Flat Roofs

These R.C.C. or R.B. flat roofs are constructed in a similar way as R.C.C. or R.B. floors, except that they are required to be protected against weather elements, i.e., rain, snow, heat, etc. A protective covering, consisting of 10 cm thick layer of lime concrete terracing with some waterproofing compound is provided over the R.C.C. or R.B. slab. This layer makes the roof leak-proof. The layer of lime concrete is thoroughly beaten by hand beaters to make it hard, impervious and compact. A the junction of wall, the L.C. terracing is taken inside the wall for a depth of 10-15 cm and the corner is given a round smooth finish. This is done to prevent the accumulation and leakage of water at junctions. The construction details are illustrated in Fig. 2.49.

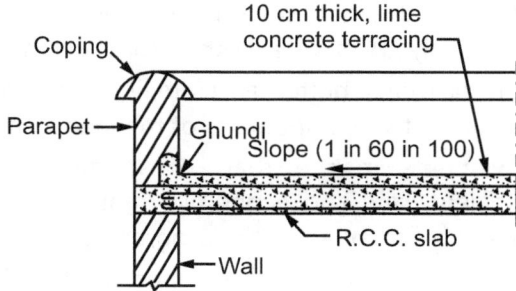

Fig. 2.49: Reinforced concrete slab roof

The lime terracing is provided with a little slope, usually 1 in 60 to 1 in 100, to drain off the rain water rapidly and easily.

Lime concrete terracing in flat roofs: The lime concrete terracing in case of flat roofs, such as R.C.C. flat roofs, R.B. flat roofs, jack arch flat roofs, etc. should be laid as below:

The surface meant for receiving the L.C. terracing should be first thoroughly cleaned with a rag soaked in kerosene oil and then treated with two coats of bitumen.

Lime concrete terracing of the following mix should be laid in single layer in thickness of 7.5 cm to 12.5 cm or average 10 cm.

(i) For Mumabi and Kolkata regions, the L.C. mix should consist of 2 parts of lime, 2 parts of surkhi and 7 parts of brick ballast of 25 mm gauge.

(ii) For chemical region, the L.C. mix should consist of 2 parts of lime and $2\frac{1}{2}$ parts of bricks ballast of 20 mm gauge.

(iii) For Delhi, Punjab, U.P. and Rajasthan regions, the L.C. mix should consists of 1 part of lime, 2 parts surkhi and 4 parts of 25 mm gauge bricks ballast. Lime used in this is slaked lime, i.e., lime putty.

While laying L.C. terracing, the following points should be remembered:

(i) Porous or defective brick ballast should not be used. Moreover, the brick ballast should be thoroughly soaked in water for not less than 6 hours before mixing.

(ii) For water-proofing, 12 kg of bar soap and 4 kg of alum dissolved in water should be added for every one m^3 of concrete.

(iii) The thickness of concrete after compaction by hand beaters must not be less than 7.5 cm. Adequate slope, varying from 1 to 40 to 1 in 100, should be given to the surface to drain off the rain water.

2.28 ROAD CONSTRUCTION

Transportation System:
- The transportation system essentially had two components to begin with: (i) the Water transportation and (ii) the Land transportation.
- The land transportation is the most suitable type for short haul passenger and goods transport. Especially in hilly areas, where other transport modes cannot reach.
- Land transportation provides better accessibility and door to door service. The railways and the roads are two components of the land transportation.
- Continuous improvements in the road construction have contributed to the development of efficient, safe and economic transportation system. This has been considered as a parameter to measure the progress of a country.
- India, being an agricultural country, has planned the development of road network, keeping in mind the social and economic needs of the people. For example,
   (i) Development of roads in rural areas develops transport of agricultural produce to the market.
   (ii) Development in planning of urban roads, flyovers, expressways takes care of ever increasing urban traffic.
- New method like BOT (Built, Operate and Transfer) has attracted the participation of private agencies into the implementation of development programmes.
- In this way, the land transportation has become an integral part of infrastructure development of any country.

2.29 CLASSIFICATION OF ROADS

Roads of different types:

(a) All-weather roads: The roads, which are negotiable during all the weathers, are called 'all-weather roads'.

(b) Fair-weather roads: The roads, which are negotiable during fair weather only, are called 'fair-weather roads'.

Roads based on the type of carriage way or road pavement:

(a) Paved roads: The roads provided with a hard pavement course such as Water Bound Macadam layer are called 'paved roads'.

(b) Unpaved roads: The roads, which are not provided with a hard course, are called 'unpaved roads'. Earth and gravel roads are the examples of unpaved roads.

Roads based on the type of the pavement surfacing provided:

(a) **Surface roads:** The roads, which are provided with cement or bituminous surfacing, are called 'surface roads'. The roads with bituminous surfacing are also called 'black topped roads'.

(b) **Unsurfaced roads:** The roads, which are not provided with cement or bituminous surfacing, are called 'unsurfaced roads'.

Methods of Classification:

The roads are classified on the following three basis:

1. Location and function (Classification of roads according to Nagpur Plan),
2. Classification of roads according to traffic, and
3. Classification of roads according to tonnage.

2.19.1 Classification of Roads According to Nagpur Plan

In the year 1943, the conference of Chief Engineers of Central and State Governments, at Nagpur, convened by the Central Government, formulated a balanced system of road development plan for the country popularly called 'Nagpur Plan'. It is finalized by Indian Road Congress (IRC). Therefore, this classification of roads is also known as 'IRC classification of roads'. According to this plan, the roads were classified into the five categories as follows:

(a) National Highways (NH),
(b) State Highways (SH),
(c) Major District Roads (MDR),
(d) Other District Roads (ODR),
(e) Village Roads (VR).

(a) National Highway (NH):

- National highways are the principal roads, which run through the length and breadth of the country connecting capitals of states, major ports, foreign highways and the places of strategic importance.
- Generally, the national highway should have two lanes of atleast 8 m width and atleast 2 m wide shoulders on both sides.

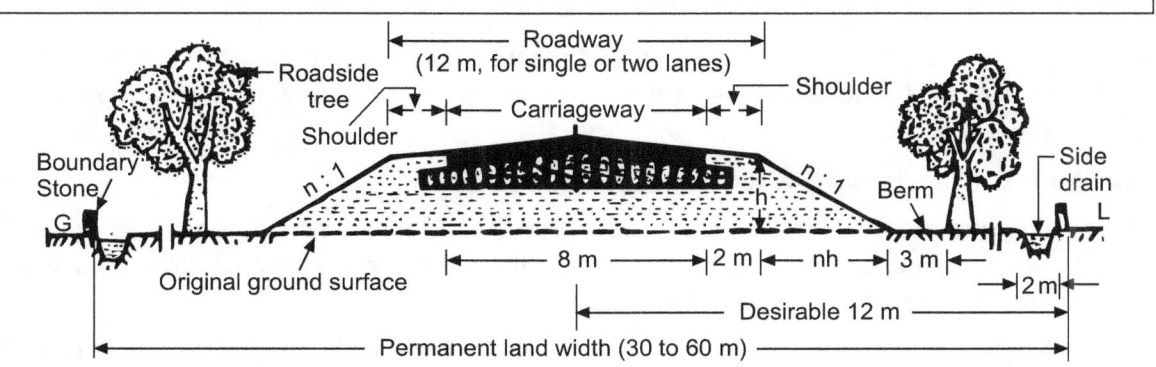

Fig. 2.50: Typical cross-section of National or State Highway

All National Highways are assigned respective numbers. Some of the Important National Highways in our country are given in Table 2.2.

Table 2.2: Important National highways in India

Sr. No.	Destination of the road	Number
1.	Delhi-Chandigarh-Amritsar Road	NH-1
2.	Delhi-Agra-Kanpur-Kolkata Road	NH-2
3.	Mumbai-Nasik-Agra Road	NH-3
4.	Mumbai-Bengaluru-Chennai Road	NH-4
5.	Chennai-Kolkata Road	NH-5
6.	Mumbai-Kolkata-Nagpur Road	NH-6
7.	Benaras-Nagpur-Hyderabad-Kanyakumari Road	NH-7
8.	Mumbai-Ahmedabad-Delhi Road	NH-8

- The responsibility of construction and maintenance of these roads is of the Central Government Departments such as Central Public Works Department (C.P.W.D.) and Military Engineering Services (M.E.S.) etc.

(b) State Highway (SH):

- The highways, which link the capital of the state to important cities within the state and connect them with National Highways, are known as *State Highways* (SH).

- State Highways are arterial roads of state, connecting up with the national highway's adjacent states, district head quarters and important cities within the state are serving as the main arteries of traffic to and from district roads. (Refer Fig. 2.50)

- These highways were considered as main arteries of commerce by road within a state or a similar geographical unit. It was thought that in some places they may carry heavier traffic than many of the national highways but this will not alter their destination or function.

- State Highways should preferably be of two-lane width. They should have modern type of surfacing.

- The responsibility of construction and maintenance of state highways lies with state governments. However, the central government gives grants for the development of these roads.

(c) Major District Roads (MDR):

- The important roads within the district, which connects market centers to areas of production and also carry the traffic into the interior areas serving rural population, are known as 'Major District Roads' (MDR).

- Major district roads should be capable of taking road traffic into the heart of the rural areas throughout the year without any interruption due to unabridged crossing.

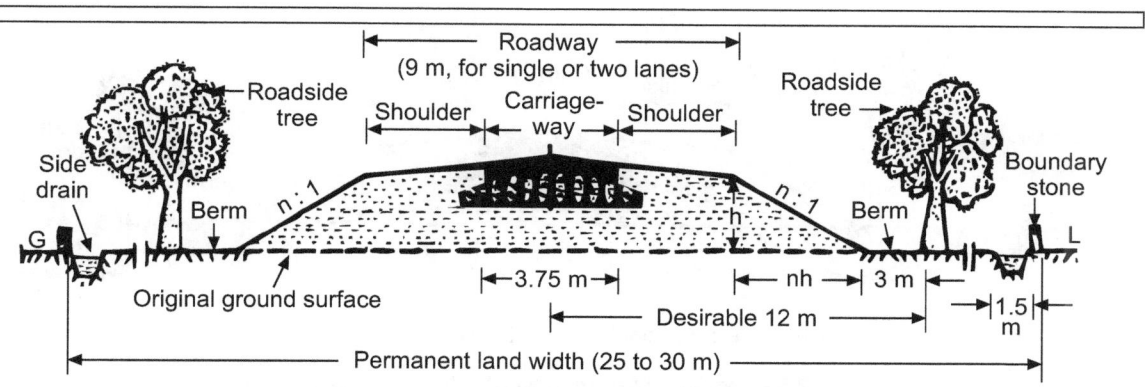

Fig. 2.51: Typical cross-section of Major District Roads (MDR)

- These roads should have at least metalled single lane carriage-way. The responsibility of construction and maintenance of these roads lies with District Authorities. However, the state governments give grants for the development of these roads.

(d) Other District Roads (ODR):

- Major district roads having lower specifications serving areas of production, Thehsil headquarters, Market centers, railway stations or block development headquarters are known as Other District Roads.
- These roads should have single lane width of atleast stabilized soil, gravel or Water-Bound-Macadam surface.

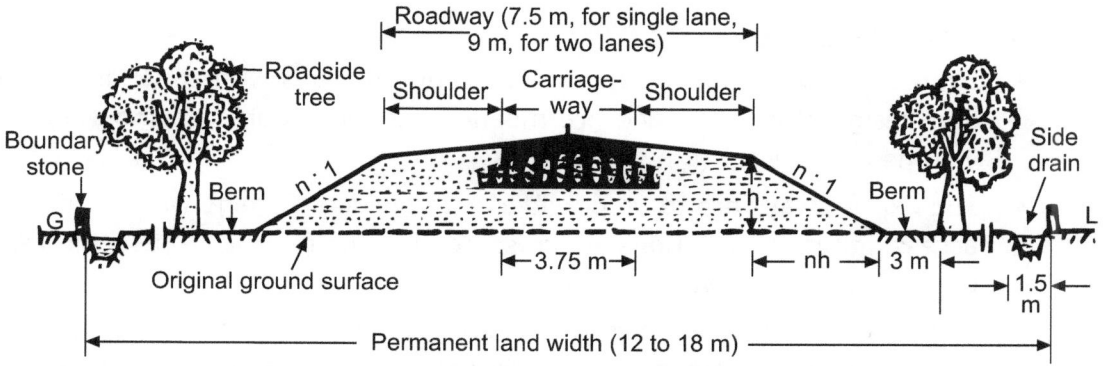

Fig. 2.52: Typical cross-section of Other District Roads (ODR)

(e) Village Roads (VR):

- Roads connecting villages or a group of villages to the next important roads are known as 'village roads'. These roads are very important from the rural development point of view. They are generally unmetalled and should have single lane width of stabilized soil or gravel.
- The responsibility of construction and maintenance of these roads lies with Local District Authorities.

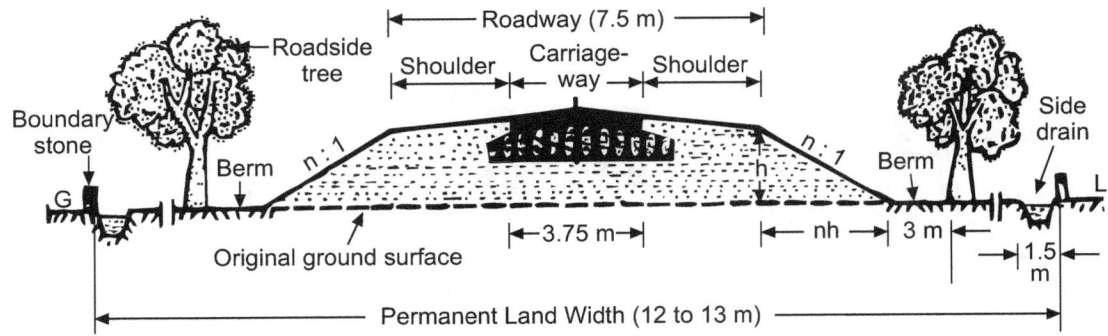

Fig. 2.53: Typical cross-section of Village Roads (VR)

2.29.2 Modified Classification of Road System by the Third Road Development Plan (1981-2001)

The roads in the country are now classified into three classes according to Third Development plan, viz.;

1. Primary System.
2. Secondary System.
3. Tertiary System or rural roads, for the purpose of transport planning, functional identification, earmarking administrative jurisdictions and assigning priorities on a road network.

1. **Primary System:** This system consist of two categories of roads:

   (a) Express Highways:
   - Express highways are a separate class of highways with superior facilities and design standards, and are meant as though routes having very high volume of traffic.
   - The expressways are to be provided with divided carriage ways, controlled access, grade separations at cross roads and fencing. These highways permit only fast moving vehicles.
   - Expressways may be owned by the Central Government or a State Governments, depending on whether the route is a National Highway or State Highway.

   (b) National Highways (NH):
   - These are the principal roads, which run through the length and breadth of the country connecting capitals of state, major ports, foreign highways and the places of strategic importance.
   - Generally, the national highway should have two lanes of at least 8 m width and the least 2 wide shoulders and both sides. All National Highways

are assigned respective numbers. For example, NH-3 – Mumbai-Nasik-Agra Road.
2. **Secondary System:** This system consists of two categories of roads:
   (a) State Highways (SH) and
   (b) Major District Roads (MDR).
3. **Tertiary System or Rural Roads:**
   This system consists of two categories of roads:
   (a) Other District Roads (ODR) and
   (b) Village Roads (VR).

2.29.3 Classification of Roads According to Traffic

According to intensity of traffic, roads are classified into the following categories:
1. **Very Heavy Traffic Road:** The road, which carries above 600 vehicles per day, is called 'Very Heavy Traffic Road'.
2. **Heavy Traffic Road:** The road, which carries 251 to 600 vehicles per day, is called 'Heavy Traffic Road'.
3. **Medium Traffic Road:** The road, which carries 70 to 250 vehicles per day, is called 'Medium Traffic Road'.
4. **Light Traffic Road:** The road, which carries below 70 vehicles per day, is called 'Light Traffic Road'.

2.29.4 Classification of Roads According to Tonnage or Load Transported

According to total tonnage per day, roads are classified into the following categories:
1. **Very Heavy Traffic Road:** The road, which carries over 1524 metric tonne vehicles per day, is called 'Very Heavy Traffic Road'.
2. **Heavy Traffic Road:** The road, which carries 1017 to 1524 metric tonne vehicles per day, is called 'Heavy Traffic Road'.
3. **Medium Traffic Road:** The road, which carries 508 to 1016 metric tonne vehicles per day, is called 'Medium Traffic Road'.
4. **Light Traffic Road:** The road, which carries below 508 metric tonne vehicles per day, is called 'Light Traffic Road'.

2.30 IMPORTANTCE OF ROAD IN INDIA

Roads, in India, perform a variety of roles in achieving speedy economic development. The importance of roads in India can be easily judged from the following purpose or advantages of roads:
1. **Connection to villages:** Accessibility to villages is possible only with a good system of roads. Roads facilitate conveyance of people, goods, raw materials, manufactured articles etc. speedily and easily in the different parts of a country. Thus, social uplift, health and education of the village population are aided by roads.

2. **Communication in hilly terrain:** For the hill states located along the Himalayan Range, communication facility is possible only by roads because of the steep terrain involved. Jammu and Kashmir, Himachal Pradesh, Sikkim, Assam, Meghalaya, Manipur, Mizoram, Tripura and Arunachal Pradesh depend heavily on roads for their very survival.
3. **Strategic Importance:** The defense of the northern, north-eastern and western borders of the country is dependent to a large extent on the road system.
4. **Helps agricultural development:** Roads have fostered quicker agricultural development facilitating movement of modern inputs such as fertilizers and high yielding seeds. Haryana and Punjab, which have connected all their villages by a road, are examples of agricultural prosperity aided by roads.
5. **Helps dairy development:** Since the cattle wealth of the nation is concentrated in innumerable small villages, the collection and processing of surplus milk is possible only because of roads.
6. **Fisheries development:** The development of fisheries along the coast-line has been rendered possible because of the construction of link roads leading of the coast.
7. **Forestry development:** The forest wealth of the country is being exploited mainly because of the roads, which penetrate into the thick jungles.
8. **Administrative convenience:** Roads have helped the effective administration of this large country. Maintenance of law and order and dispensation of justice have been aided by roads.
9. **Employment:** Since road construction employs still labour intensive techniques in India, the large unemployed labour force gets gainful employment.
10. **Tourism development:** Some of the ancient monuments, religious places, national parks and sanctuaries are accessible only by roads. Tourism, both domestic and international, has been greatly aided by roads serving such places of interest.
11. **Flood and famine relief:** Roads have helped operations pertaining to flood and famine relief. The affected people are frequently employed on road construction to build durable assets.

Thus, the importance of road can be summarized as follows:

1. It helps in development of natural resources of the area.
2. It helps in development of agriculture of the area.
3. The improvement of highway system of a region increases the land value.
4. It helps in development of the commerce of the area.
5. It helps in better fire and police protections.

6. It facilitates conveyance of people, goods, raw materials, manufactured articles etc. speedily and easily from one place to another in the different parts of country.
7. It increases mail facilities.
8. It helps in medical and education facilities.
9. It is essential in case of national defense.
10. It helps in maintaining the better law and order in a country.
11. It serves as feeders for Airways, Waterways and Railways.
12. A new road shortens the distance and improves the speed.
13. It opens up new avenues for exchange of goods and services uptill now unconnected to markets.
14. The highways provide facilities of transporting rural products such as vegetables, fruits etc. in a very short period to the cities.
15. The improvement in highway system helps in development of social, cultural and intellectual life of the people and also increases political activities.
16. The improvement in highway system helps in the development of the industry and promotes regional specialization.
17. The improvement or openings of new road helps in the development of recreational facilities.

2.31 RIGID AND FLEXIBLE PAVEMENT

2.31.1 Pavement

Pavement can be defined as a structured having several layers bound together and placed on top of the soil sub-grade so that it provides a smooth riding surface for the vehicles. A pavement also protects the sub-grade from surface water. A pavement for example be of cement concrete or several soil layers bound by the action of water or thin layer of bituminous material. Pavements should have good flexural strength and rigidity.

2.31.2 Objective of Pavement

A road pavement is a structure consisting of one or more layers of materials which may be in the natural form or it may be processed. The main function of the pavement is to distribute the loads coming on to it in such a way that the bearing capacity of sub-grade on which the pavement rests is into exceeded. The traffic load transmitted through the wheels decreases with depth and hence the thickness of the pavement is so designed that stress is reduced to the desired limit.

2.31.3 Structure of Pavement

Road pavement is generally designed to have more than one layer with each layer made up of suitable material. Each layer is properly treated, compacted and placed on above the other Fig. 2.54 shows layers which are generally provided to form a road pavement.

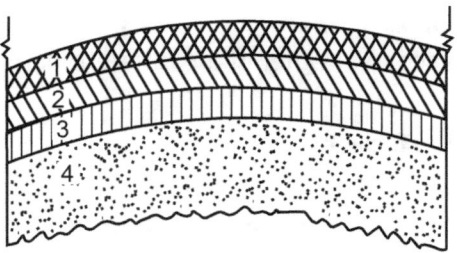

1. Wearing surface
2. Base
3. Sub-base
4. Subgrade

Fig. 2.54: Road pavement

Requisites of Good Pavement:

A good road pavement should:

1. Be cheap and easy in construction.
2. Be strong and durable.
3. Provide an impervious and sanitary surface.
4. Be smooth enough to provide low *tractive resistance but* not so smooth which may becomes slippery.
5. Not develop *corrugations.*
6. Not cause *glare* in the sun.
7. Provide good visibility at night.
8. Be suitable for all types of traffic.
9. Provide a safe and comfortable riding surface under all weather conditions.
10. Have long life.
11. Have low maintenance cost.

2.31.4 Types of Pavements

Road pavements are basically classified under two heads:

(a) Flexible pavement.

(b) Non-flexible or rigid pavement.

(a) Flexible pavements: Bituminous pavements, W. B. Macadam roads, Stabilized soil bases are the examples of flexible pavements. The pavement assumes the shape of underlying base course layers on application of load. The strength and rigidity of flexible pavement is much less than that of rigid pavement. See Fig. 2.55 for flexible pavement.

(b) Rigid pavements: It is a concrete slab laid on subgrade. It has considerable strength and rigidity. Rigid pavement is not deformed to the shape of lower surface as it can bridge the gaps in the lower layer. See Fig. 2.56 i.e. section of a concrete road which is the example of rigid pavement.

The following figures show the section of a bituminous road and concrete road.

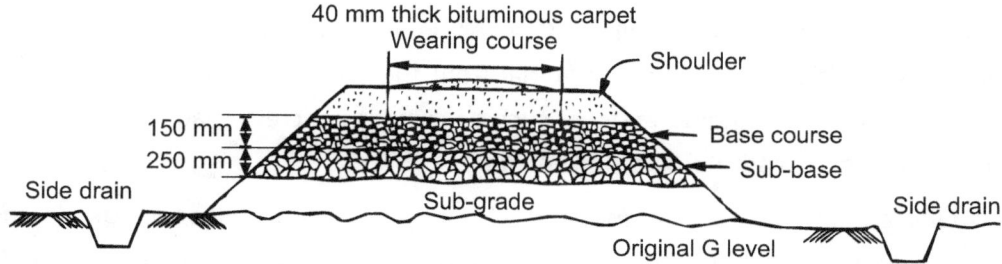

Fig. 2.55: Section of a bituminous road (i.e. Flexible pavement)

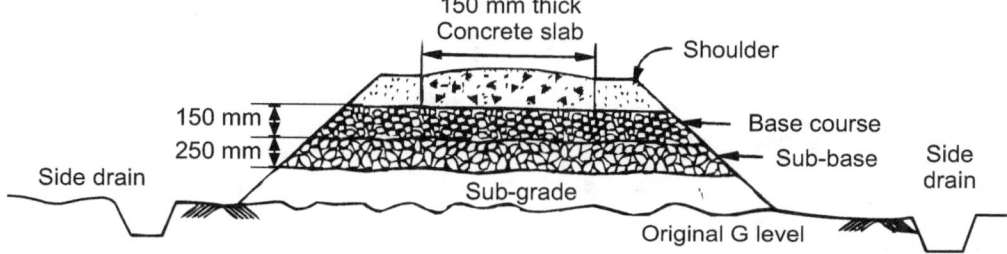

Fig. 2.56: Section of concrete road (i.e. Rigid pavement)

The points of difference between the flexible and rigid pavements are summarized in Table 2.3.

Table 2.3: Comparison between flexible and Rigid pavements

Flexible pavement	Rigid pavement
1. Yields under excessive stresses due to wheel loads.	1. Does not yield. It may rupture and result into cracking of the pavement.
2. Variations in the surrounding temperature does not produce stresses.	2. The temperature variations may induce stresses.
3. When a deformation occurs due to heavy loads it may be recovered after removal of load, if the deformation is within limits.	3. No recovery is possible, on the contrary the pavement may crack.
4. Traffic load is distributed through the series of layers. The stress therefore goes on reducing at the lower depths.	4. This pavement distributed the load over a wider area. The topmost layer contributes major portion of the structural strength.
5. In case the sub-grade is of varying strength the components above it will adjust to the irregularities and differential settlement.	5. No such adjustment is possible and the component above acts like a beam if there is differential settlement.
6. Comparatively cheaper is construction but maintenance cost is high.	6. Involves high cost. Maintenance cost is low.

Natural earth road stabilized soil road, water bound macadam roads and road surface consisting of asphaltic or bituminous material from the flexible pavements while the roads where cement is used as binding material such as cement concrete road or stone pavement set in cement mortar constitute rigid pavements.

Material used in the various components of the road pavement depends on whether the pavement is rigid or flexible. Some of the materials used in components are mentioned below:

1. **Wearing surface:** Natural soil or stabilized soil, crushed stone, bituminous material;i cement etc.
2. **Base:** Gravel, broken stone (oversize aggregate).
3. **Sub-base:** Natural gravel, boulders, rubble, etc.
4. **Sub-grade:** Natural soil in embankment or in cutting. It will be compacted to improve its performance.

Function of Pavement Components:

From top to bottom the different components and their functions are explained below:

1. **Wearing surface:** This is the topmost layer. It comes in direct contact with the traffic. Its functions are: (i) to resist wear and tear, (ii) to provide adequate foot hold and avoid slipping or skidding of vehicles. It must also be sufficiently water tight so as to prevent seepage of surface water to the components down below.

2. **Base:** Base forms a support to the wearing surface. Base may be made up of untreated or treated material. This layer distributes the concentrated loads from the upper layer to the lower layers and withstand high shearing stress. It also provides some degree of flexibility to the pavement.

3. **Sub-base:** This layer is laid on the natural layer down below and supports wearing surface and base. It is an intermediate layer and performs more or less the same function as the base. At times the two layers base and sub-base may be combined.

4. **Sub-grade:** Sub-grade is the last layer forming the foundation for the road pavement. It is the natural soil and carries the entire load of the traffic and the pavement which rests on the sub-grade. Depending on the gradient of the road it may be in cutting, in the embankment or at the ground level. It is formed into proper shape and treated if necessary to improve its properties.

2.32 TYPICAL ROAD SECTION

The road formation or width formation includes the width of pavement, shoulders, and separators if any. In the case of embankment, the formation width is equal to the top width of embankment and in case of cutting; it is taken as the bottom width of cutting minus the side drains.

Fig. 2.57 (a) shows formation width in embankment and Fig. 2.57 (b) shows the cutting.

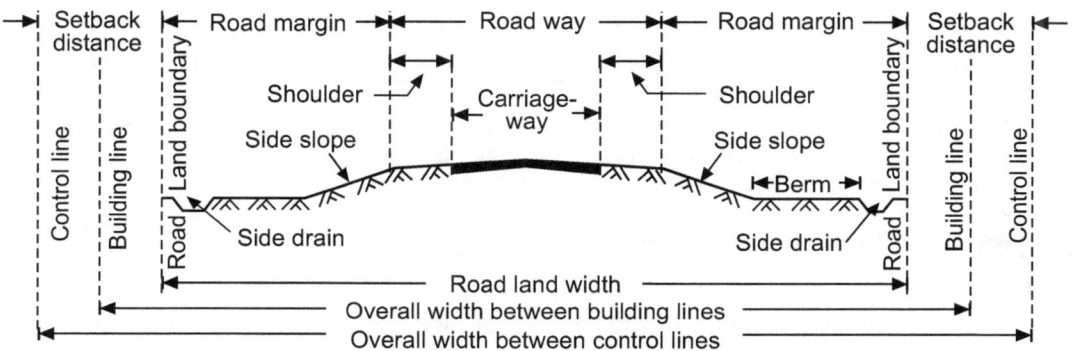

(a) Formation width in embankment

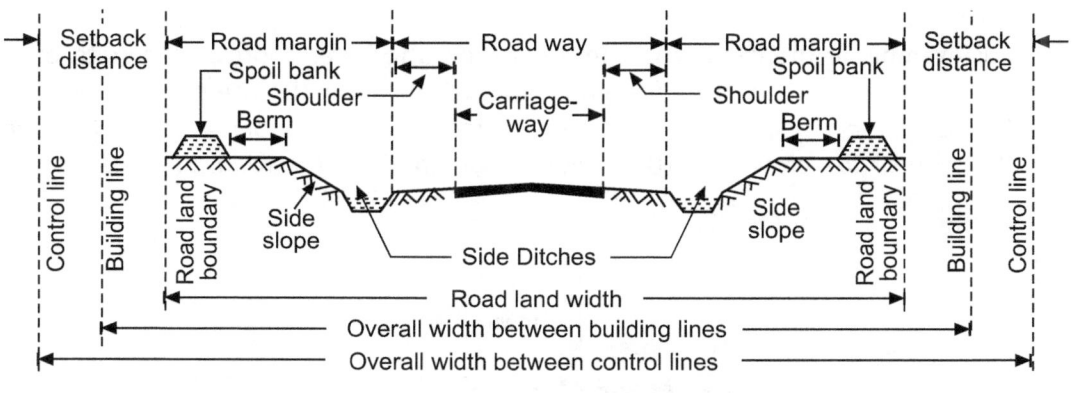

(b) Formation width in cutting

Fig. 2.57: Formation width of road in embankment and in cutting

The formation width and road width recommended by IRC for single lane and two lanes are given in table 2.4.

Table 2.4: Roadway widths as per Recommendations of IRC

Sr. No.	Category of roads	Roadway width in metres	
		Plain and rolling terrain	Mountainous and steep terrain
1.	National and State Highways	12 m (Single or two lanes)	(a) Two lanes = 6.25 m (b) Two lanes = 8.8 m
2.	Major District Roads	9.0 m (Single or two lanes)	4.75 m (Single lane)
3.	Other District Roads	(a) Single lane = 7.5 m (b) Two lanes = 9 m	4.75 m (Single lane)
4.	Village Roads	7.5 m (Single lane)	4.0 m (Single lane)

Note:
(i) The roadways widths in mountainous and steep terrain given in this table are exclusive of the parapets (usual width 0.6 m) and side drains (usual width 0.6 m) which should be provided in addition to these dimensions.
(ii) In case of State Highways having single lane pavement, the width of roadway might be reduced to 9 m, if the possibility of widening the carriageway to two lanes is considered remote.

2.33 CAMBER AND FUNCTIONS OF CAMBER

3.33.1 Camber

- Study of the cross-section of the road on straight alignment shows that the centre of the road is raised above its edges.
- The centre is known as the crown of the road and slope of the road surface joining the crown to the edges is known as camber or cross slope.
- Camber is defined as 'the slope provided to the cross-section of the road'. It is expressed as the ratio of the crown height to half the horizontal width of the carriageway.
- For example, if the camber is 1 in 45, it means for every horizontal length of 45 m measured from the centre of the road towards its edge, the rise of the crown is 1 m. It is also expressed as percentage. A camber of 2% means 2 m rise of the crown for 100 m horizontal length of the road. In other words, 2% camber = $\frac{2}{100}$, i.e. 1 in 50.

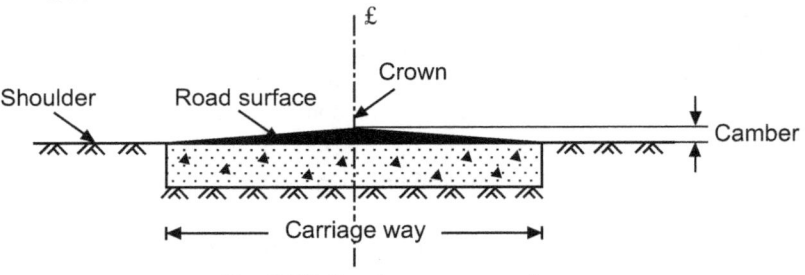

Fig. 2.58: Camber or cross-slope

- It is expressed as the slope of line or the ratio C: $\frac{b}{2}$. It is also expressed as a percentage.

2.33.2 Purpose of Providing Camber

- Camber is provided mainly to drain-off water from the road surface as quickly as possible. Incidentally, it may also help the vehicles moving in opposite directions to restrict to half of the road.

- Poor drainage will result in water percolating to the sub-strata and standing water on the road surface may cause inconvenience to the traffic.

These points can be summarized as:

(a) To drain-off rainwater from the surface of carriageway towards the roadside gutters as quickly as possible.

(b) To regularize the vehicles to their proper lanes.

(c) To improve aesthetic appearance of the road.

2.33.3 Types of Camber

The road cambers can have four shapes as mentioned below:

(a) Straight camber: Joining the crown of the road to its edges by straight lines forms this camber. The straight camber can also be obtained by two straights of different slopes. This shape is easy to construct. Fig. 2.59 shows the straight camber.

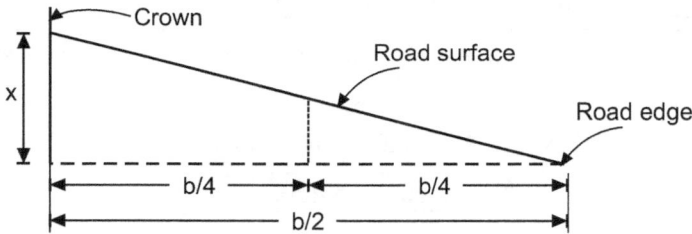

Fig. 2.59: Straight camber in one or two straights

(b) Parabolic or Elliptical camber: The camber is given a continuous curve of parabolic or elliptical shape from the edge to crown. Fig. 3.3 shows the parabolic and elliptical camber.

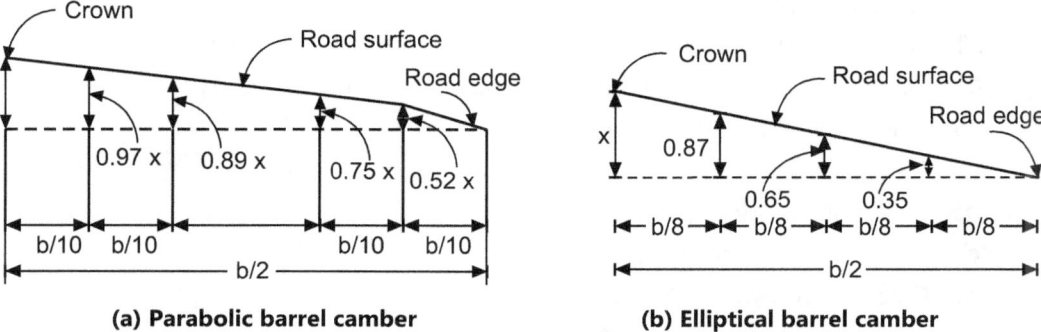

(a) Parabolic barrel camber (b) Elliptical barrel camber

Fig. 2.60

(c) Composite camber: This camber is a combination of parabolic or elliptical and straight camber. Central portion of the road is formed by curve-parabolic or elliptical and edges are straight lines. Curved camber is difficult to construct for WBM road surface. Due to curved camber road cross-section is rather flat and vehicles find this cross-section more convenient. Fig. 3.4 shows the composite camber.

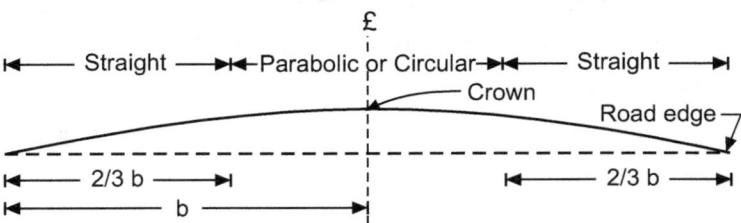

Fig. 2.61: Composite camber

(d) Barrel camber: This camber consists of a continuous curve that may be either parabolic or elliptical. Fig. 3.5 shows the barrel camber.

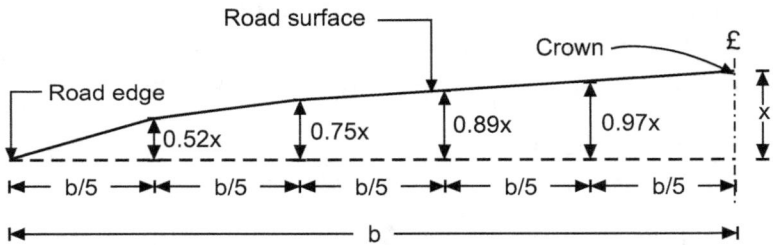

Fig. 2.62: Barrel camber

EXERCISE

1. Explain the various loads coming on the structure.
2. Differentiate between load bearing structure and framed structure.
3. Define foundation and explain the functions of foundation.
4. Draw a typical cross-section through load bearing wall.
5. Differentiate between English and Flemish bond.
6. What are the various precautions to be taken for brick masonry ?
7. What are the various precautions to be taken for stone masonry ?
8. Draw the sketch of the following:
   (a) Glazed doors.
   (b) Casement windows
   (c) Framed and panelled door
   (d) Glazed window.
9. Explain the various requirements of a stair.

10. Short note on: Thumb rule for rise and tread.
11. What are the requirements of floors ?
12. Explain the flag stone in flooring.
13. Explain the cement concrete flooring.
14. Define: (a) Roof, (b) Stairs, (c) Door, (d) Window, (e) Lintel, (f) Rigid pavement, (g) Flexible pavement, (h) Camber.
15. Explain the various requirements of a roof.
16. Explain with neat sketch lean to roof.
17. Explain with neat sketch flat R.C.C. roof.
18. Differentiate between rigid and flexible pavement.
19. Classify the roads according to the materials used.
20. Define camber and functions of camber.
21. Classify the road according to the importance.

❏❏❏

UNIT 3

EARTHQUAKE ENGINEERING

3.1 INTRODUCTION

A study of earthquake engineering is a understanding of geophysical process that causes earthquakes and various effects of earthquakes. Seismology is the study of the generation, propagation and measurement of seismic waves through earth and the sources that generate them. The word seismology originated from Greek words, 'seismos' meaning earthquake and 'logos' meaning science. The study of seismic wave propagation through earth provides the maximum input to the understanding of internal structure of earth.

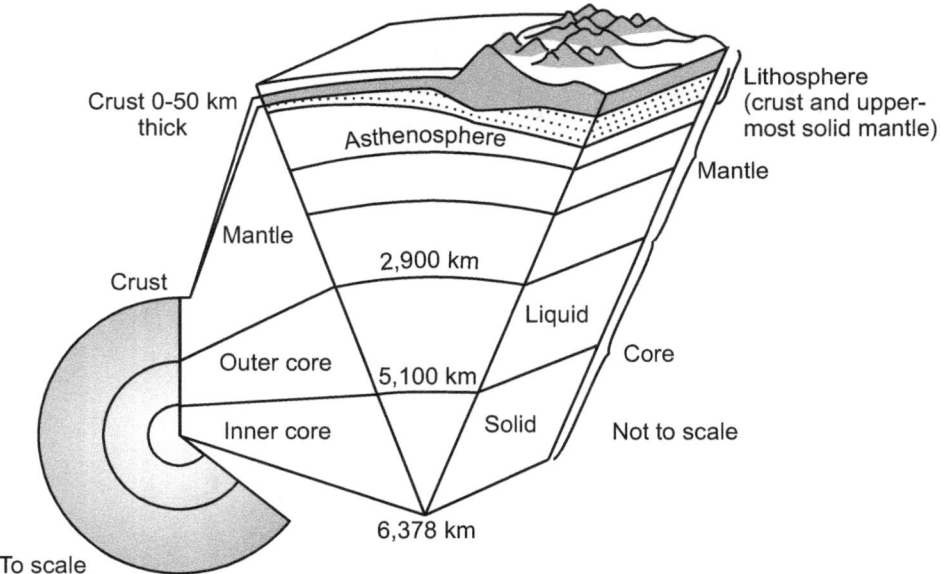

Fig. 3.1: The interior of the Earth

The earth's shape is an oblate spheroid with a diameter along the equator of about 12,740 km with the polar diameter as 12,700 km. The higher diameter along equator is caused by the higher centrifugal forces generated along the equator due to rotation of earth. Though the specific gravity of materials that constitute the surface of earth is only about 2.8, the average specific gravity of earth is about 5.5 indicating presence of very heavy materials towards interior of earth. The interior of the earth can be classified into three major categories as Crust, Mantle and Core.

1. Crust:

It is also called as lithosphere; the outer part of the earth is where the life exist. The average thickness of crust beneath continents is about 40 km where as it decreases to as much as 5 km beneath oceans. The oceanic crust is constituted by basaltic rocks and continental part by granitic rocks overlying the basaltic rocks. Compared to the layers below, this layer has high rigidity and anisotropy.

2. Mantle:

It is a 2900 km thick layer below crust. The mantle consists of;

(1) Upper Mantle reaching a depth of about 400 km made of olivine and pyroxene and

(2) Lower Mantle made of more homogeneous mass of magnesium and iron oxide and quartz.

No earthquakes are recorded in the lower mantle. The specific gravity of mantle is about 5. The mantle has an average temperature of about 2200°C and the material is in a viscous semi-molten state. The mantle act like fluid in response to slowly acting stresses and creeps under slow loads. But it behaves like as solid in presence of rapidly acting stresses, which are caused due to earthquake waves.

3. Core:

It has a radius of 3470 km and consists of:

(1) Inner core of radius 1370 km and

(2) Outer core (1370 km < R < 3470 km).

The core is composed of molten iron, probably mixed with small quantities of other elements such as nickel and sulphur or silicon. The inner solid core is very dense nickel-iron material and is subjected to very high pressures. The maximum temperature in the core is estimated to be about 3000°C. The specific gravity of outer core is about 9 - 12 whereas of inner core is 15.

Earthquakes are measured using observations from seismometer. The magnitude of an earthquake is measured with two scales, which are as follows:

(1) Numerical scale: The scale, 3 or less is scarcely noticeable, and magnitude 7 (or more) causes damage over a wide area. The moment magnitude is the most common scale on which earthquakes larger than approximately 5 are reported for the entire globe.

(2) Richter scale: The more numerous earthquakes smaller than magnitude 5 reported by national seismological observatories are measured mostly on the local magnitude scale, also referred to as the ***Richter scale***.

These two scales are numerically similar over their range of validity. Magnitude 3 or lower earthquakes are mostly almost imperceptible or weak and magnitude 7 and over potentially causes serious damage over larger areas, depending on their depth. The largest earthquakes in historic times have been of magnitude slightly over 9, although there is no limit to the possible magnitude. The most recent large earthquake of magnitude 9.0 or larger was a 9.0 magnitude earthquake in Japan in 2011 (October 2012), and it was the largest Japanese earthquake since records began. Intensity of shaking is measured on the modified Mercalli scale. The shallower an earthquake, the more damage to structures it causes, all else being equal.

At the Earth's surface, earthquakes manifest themselves by shaking and sometimes displacement of the ground. When the epicenter of a large earthquake is located offshore, the seabed may be displaced sufficiently to cause a tsunami. Earthquakes can also trigger landslides, and occasionally volcanic activity.

In its most general sense, the word Earthquakes is used to describe any seismic event - whether natural or caused by humans - that generates seismic waves. Earthquakes are caused mostly by rupture of geological faults, but also by other events such as volcanic activity, landslides, mine blasts, and nuclear tests. An earthquake's point of initial rupture is called its focus or hypocenter. The epicenter is the point at ground level directly above the hypocenter

One of the most frightening and destructive phenomena of nature is a severe earthquake and its terrible aftereffects. An earthquake is a sudden movement of the Earth, caused by the abrupt release of strain that has accumulated over a long time. For hundreds of millions of years, the forces of plate tectonics have shaped the Earth as the huge plates that form the Earth's surface slowly move over, under, and past each other. Sometimes the movement is gradual. At other times, the plates are locked together, unable to release the accumulating energy. When the accumulated energy grows strong enough, the plates break free. If the earthquake occurs in a populated area, it may cause many deaths and injuries and extensive property damage.

3.2 DEFINATION

An earthquake is a violent movement of the rocks in the Earthcrust. Earthquakes are usually quite brief, but may repeat over a long period of time. They are the result of a sudden release of energy in the Earthcrust. This creates seismic waves, waves of energy that travel through the Earth.

There are large earthquakes and small earthquakes. Large earthquakes can take down buildings and cause death and injury. The study of earthquakes is called Seismology. Seismology studies the frequency, type and size of earthquakes over a period of time.

When the earth moves offshore in the ocean, it can cause a tsunami. A tsunami can cause just as much death and destruction. Landslide can happen, too. This is an important part of the Earth's cycle.

Earthquakes are measured using observations from seismometer. The magnitude of an earthquake, and the intensity of shaking, is measured on a numerical scale. On the scale, 3 or less is scarcely noticeable, and magnitude 7 (or more) causes damage over a wide area.

Therefore, an earthquake is the result of a sudden release of energy in the Earthcrust that creates sesmic waves. The seismicity, seismism or seismic activity of an area refers to the frequency, type and size of earthquakes experienced over a period of time.

3.3 CAUSES OF EARTHQUAKES

Most earthquakes are occur due to compression or tensile stresses built up at the margins of the huge moving lithospheric plates that is **plate tectonics** that make up the earth's surface (see lithosphere). The immediate cause of most shallow earthquakes is the sudden release of stress along a **fault**, or fracture in the earth's crust, resulting in movement of the opposing blocks of rock past one another. These movements cause vibrations to pass through and around the earth in wave form, just as ripples are generated when a pebble is dropped into water. *Volcanic eruptions, rock falls, landslides* and *explosions* can also cause a earthquake, but most of these are of only local extent. Shock waves from a powerful earthquake can trigger smaller earthquakes in a distant location hundreds of miles away if the geologic conditions are favorable.

1. **Plate Tectonics:**

First presented in 1967, the theory of plate tectonics postulates that the earth once was covered by a single crust, or plate, with no oceans.

   1. We could think of the earth at this time like a hard-boiled egg, with a thin hard shell extending over the entire surface of the earth.
   2. Over time, this single shell, or plate, started to split and drift into separate plates of land or ocean crusts.
   3. Now the earth's surface looks much like a spherical jigsaw puzzle; all the plates fit together.
   4. The plates over the earth are in constant slow motion. The plates generally move in one of three ways - **colliding, spreading or sliding**.
   5. Plates experience convergent plate movement when they collide or bump into one another. When they spread or move away from one another, they experience divergent plate movement.
   6. Plates also can slide by one another with lateral plate movement. Any one of these plate movements can cause an earthquake.

7. Constant movement of the plates puts a tremendous stress on the earth's rock. Earthquakes tend to occur at the boundaries of plates.

8. ***Convergent, divergent*** and ***lateral movement*** all can cause earthquake activity.

9. Convergent plates experience the movement of one plate below the edge of another. As plates collide, the edge of the heavier ocean plate is pushed down into the earth's interior by the lighter continental plate, and a trench forms between the plates. As this occurs, material from the lower plate is "recycled" by melting into the earth's interior. This whole process is called subduction.

10. Where plates diverge (move away from each other), molten rock from beneath the earth's crust rushes up to fill in the resulting rift and forms a ridge. These ridges add even more pressure on the divergent plates as they continue to push adjacent plates away from one another. The Mid-Atlantic Ridge, located in the middle of the Atlantic Ocean, is a good example of a ridge formed by the divergent movement of plates.

11. Sometimes tectonic plates neither move towards or away from each other, but side by side each other. This is known as lateral slipping and forms transform faults. The movement of the lateral slipping of tectonic plates is rigid and so the plates stick until the pressure and friction (stored energy) builds up to a level which forces the plates to slip. This slip releases the immense stored energy and forms energy waves, known as earthquakes.

2. Fault:

Faults occur when brittle rocks fracture and there is an offset along the fracture. When the offset is small, the displacement can be easily measured, but sometimes the displacement is so large that it is difficult to measure.

Types of Fault:

Faults can be divided into several different types depending on the direction of relative displacement. Since, faults are planar features, the concept of strike and dip also applies, and thus the strike and dip of a fault plane can be measured. One division of faults is between dip-slip faults, where the displacement is measured along the dip direction of the fault, and strike-slip faults where the displacement is horizontal, parallel to the strike of the fault.

(a) Dip Slip Faults:

Dip slip faults are faults that have an inclined fault plane and along which the relative displacement or offset has occurred along the dip direction. Note that in looking at the displacement on any fault we do not know which side actually moved or if both sides moved, all we can determine is the relative sense of motion.

For any inclined fault plane we define the block above the fault as the **hanging wall block** and the block below the fault as the **footwall block**.

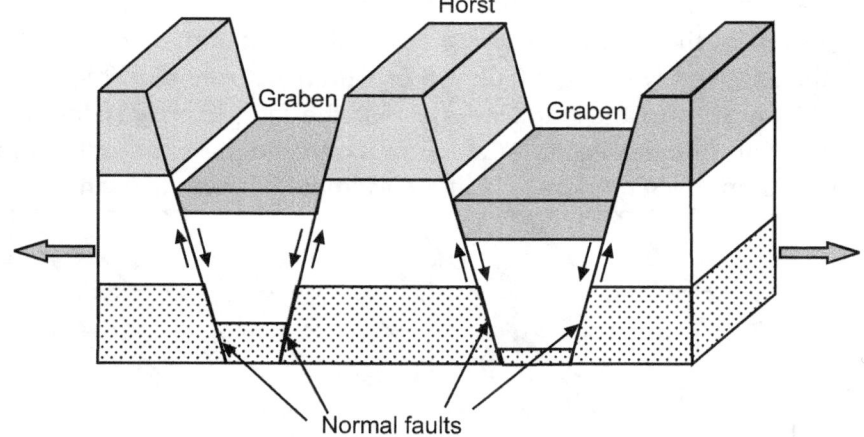

Fig. 3.2

(b) Reverse Faults:

These are the result from horizontal compression stresses in brittle rocks, where the hanging-wall block has moved up relative the footwall block.

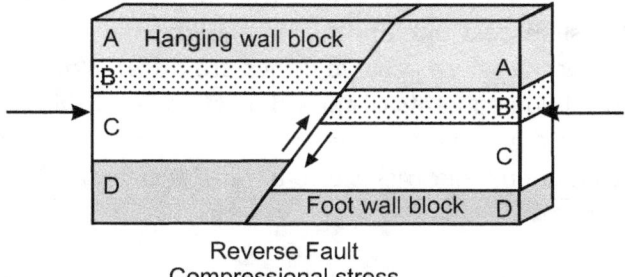

Reverse Fault
Compressional stress

Fig. 3.3

(c) Thrust Fault is a special case of a reverse fault where the dip of the fault is less than 45°. Thrust faults can have considerable displacement, measuring hundreds of kilometres, and can result in older strata overlying younger strata

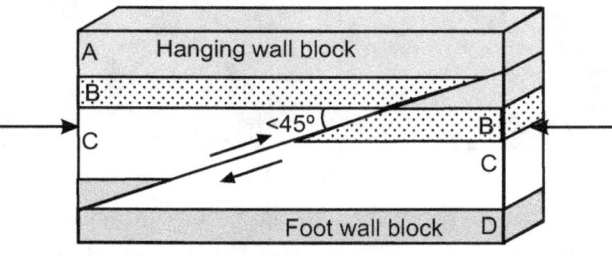

Thrust fault
Compressional stress

Fig. 3.4

(d) Strike Slip Faults – are faults where the relative motion on the fault has taken place along a horizontal direction. Such faults result from shear stresses acting in the crust. Strike slip faults can be of two varieties, depending on the sense of displacement. To an observer standing on one side of the fault and looking across the fault, if the block on the other side has moved to the left, we say that the fault is **a left-lateral strike slip fault**. If the block on the other side has moved to the right, we say that the fault is a **right-lateral strike slip fault**. The famous San Andreas Fault in California is an example of a right-lateral strike slip fault. Displacements on the San Andreas fault are estimated at over 600 km.

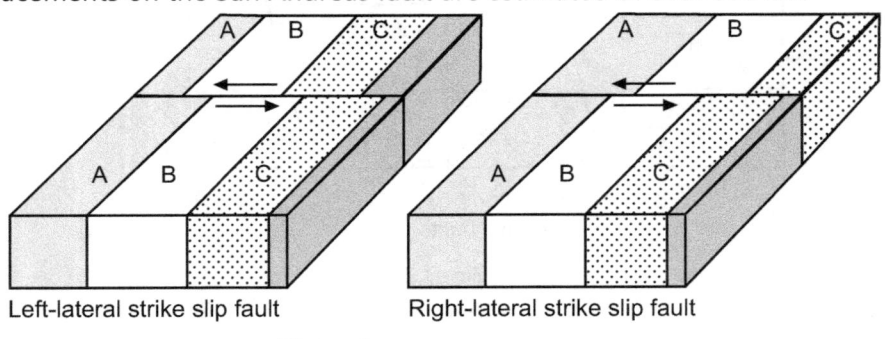

Left-lateral strike slip fault   Right-lateral strike slip fault
Shear stress
Fig. 3.5   **Fig. 3.6**

(e) Transform-Faults are a special class of strike-slip faults. These are plate boundaries along which two plates slide past one another in a horizontal manner. The most common type of transform faults occur where oceanic ridges are offset. Note that the transform fault only occurs between the two segments of the ridge. Outside of this area there is no relative movement because blocks are moving in the same direction. These areas are called fracture zones. The San Andreas fault in California is also a transform fault.

Fig. 3.7

Major earthquakes, such as the 1964 Alaskan earthquake, can occur in areas where subduction has occurred. Fig. 3.7 illustrates the formation of an ocean ridge caused by divergent plates and a subduction trench caused by convergent plates. Plates also can grind past each other laterally, causing the edges to lock and release. This is happening along the San Andreas fault, which runs most of the length of California.

The second example is the 1993 Killari earthquake in central peninsular India is the latest intracratonic event to be responsible for a large disaster. It measured 6.4 on the Richter Scale. The earthquake's focus was around 12 km deep relatively shallow causing shock waves to cause more damage. It is possible that this pressure is released along fault lines. Another argument is that reservoir construction along the Terna River was responsible for increasing pressure on fault lines.

3. Change in Earth Crust during Earthquakes:

Weathering and erosion usually change the earth's crust very slowly. Sometimes, however, The crust changes very quickly. An earthquake is a shaking or sliding of the earth's crust. Earthquakes happen when rocks inside the earth move. As the rocks move; they may form new cracks in the crust. Sometimes, the movement of rocks makes the land move up, down or sideways.

During an earthquake, it is observed that the mass distribution in the Earth's crust changes. This changes the Earth's moment of inertia, which is the sum of the moments of inertia of each point. The moment of inertia of a point mass is the product of its mass and the square of its distance to the axis of rotation. Meanwhile the angular momentum is preserved, this angular momentum is the sum of the moments of inertia of each point mass times its angular velocity. Hence, if the moment of inertia of the earth decreases (increases), the angular velocity of the Earth increases (decreases). The simple physical principle of conservation of angular momentum thus allows us to explain disparate phenomena such as the Earth's changing rotation rate, figure skaters spinning, spinning tops and gyroscopic compasses.

Earthquakes produce several effects that cause damage and destruction. Some of these effects are the direct result of the ground shaking produced by the arrival of seismic waves and others are secondary effects.

Among these effects are the following:

(i) Ground Shaking:

Shaking of the ground caused by the passage of seismic waves near the epicenter of the earthquake is responsible for the collapse of most structures. The intensity of ground shaking depends on distance from the epicenter and on the type of bedrock underlying the area.

(a) In general, loose unconsolidated sediment is subject to more intense shaking than solid bedrock.

(b) Damage to structures from shaking depends on the type of construction. Concrete and masonry structures, because they are brittle are more susceptible to damage than wood and steel structures, which are more flexible.

Different kinds of shaking occur due to passage of different kinds of waves. As the P-waves arrive the ground will move up and down. The S-waves produce waves that both move the ground up and down and back and forth in the direction of wave motion. The Love waves shake the ground from side to side, and the Rayleigh waves create a rolling up and down motion.

(ii) Ground Rupture:

Ground rupture only occurs along the fault zone that moves during the earthquake. Thus, structures that are built across fault zones may collapse, whereas structures built adjacent to, but not crossing the fault may survive.

(iii) Fire:

Fire is a secondary effect of earthquakes. Because power lines may be knocked down and because natural gas lines may rupture due to an earthquake, fires are often started closely following an earthquake. The problem is compounded if water lines are also broken during the earthquake since there will not be a supply of water to extinguish the fires once they have started. In the 1906, earthquake in San Francisco more than 90% of the damage to buildings was caused by fire.

(iv) Landslides and Debris/Rock Falls:

In mountainous regions subjected to earthquakes ground shaking may trigger rapid mass-wasting events like landslides, rock and debris falls, slumps, and debris avalanches.

(v) Liquefaction:

It is a process that occurs in water-saturated unconsolidated sediment due to shaking. In areas underlain by such material, the ground shaking causes the grains to loose grain to grain contact, and thus the material tends to flow.

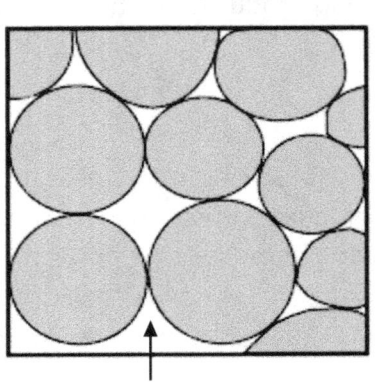
Water saturated sediment

Water fills in the pore space between grains. Friction between grains holds sediment together.

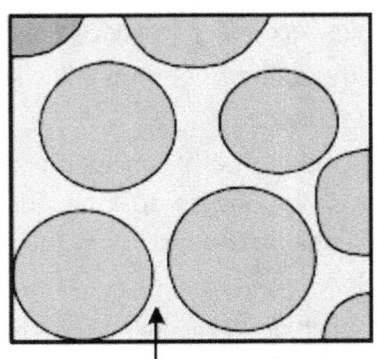
Liquefaction

Water completely surrounds all grains and eliminates all grain to grain contact. Sediment flow like a fluid.

Fig. 3.8

3.4 TECHNICAL TERMS RELATED TO EARTHQUAKES.

3.4.1 Focus

The originating source of the elastic waves inside the earth which cause shakings of ground due to earthquake. The point of maximum shock/stress release during an earthquake. Deeper focus earthquakes are often less damaging because the rocks absorb more energy before the waves hit the surface.

(1) Focal Distance:

The straight-line distance between the places of recording/observation to the hypocenter is called the focal distance.

(2) Intermediate Focus Earthquake:

The focus is between 70 to 300 km deep.

(3) Shallow Focus Earthquake:

Earthquakes of focus less than 70 km deep from ground surface are called shallow focus earthquakes.

3.4.2 Epicenter

The geographical point on the surface of earth vertically above the focus of the earthquake.

(i) Epicentral Distance:

Distance between epicenter and recording station in km.

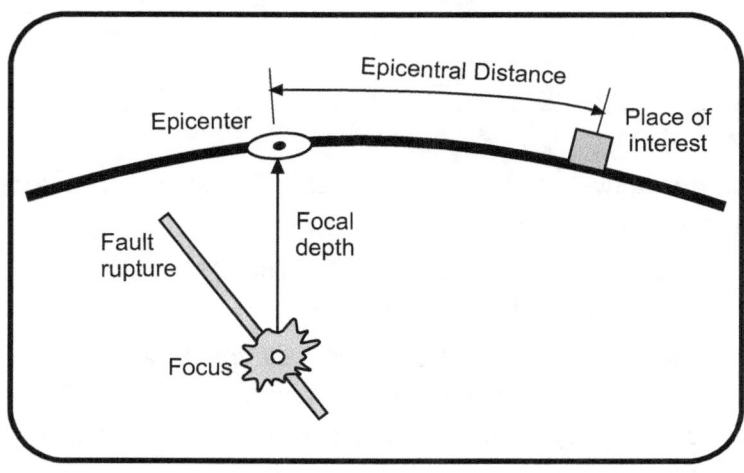

Fig. 3.9 : Basic terminology

3.4.3 Magnitude

Measure of the amount of energy released during an earthquake. It is usually expressed using Richter scale.

Professor Charles Richter noticed that at a constant distance, seismograms records of earthquake ground vibration of larger earthquake have bigger wave amplitude than those of smaller earthquakes, and for given earthquake, seismograms at farther distances have smaller wave amplitude than those at close distances. Now commonly used magnitude scale, the Richter scale.

There are other magnitude scales viz,
1. Body wave magnitude
2. Surface wave magnitude and
3. Wave energy magnitude.

It is defined as logarithm to the base 10 of the maximum trace amplitude, expressed in microns, which the standard short-period torsion seismometer would register due to the earthquake at an epicenter distance of 100 km.

Earthquakes are often classified into different groups based on their magnitude.

Table 3.1

Group	Magnitude
Great	8 and Higher
Major	7-7.9
Strong	6-6.9
Moderate	5-5.9
Light	4-4.9
Minor	3-3.9
Very Minor	< 3.0

3.4.4 Intensity

Intensity is a qualitative measure of the actual shaking at a location during an earthquake, and is assigned in Roman Capital Numeric.

It refers to the effects of earthquakes. Modified Mercalli scale is the standard measurement. There are many intensity scales.

Two commonly used ones are the *Modified Mercalli Intensity (MMI) scale* and *MSK* scale. Both are quite similar and range from I to XII. These intensity scale are based on the features of shaking perception by people and animals, performance of buildings, and changes to natural surroundings.

Table 3.2: For Ressi-Forrel scale of earthquake Intensity

Class	Name	Effects
1.	Imperceptible	Recorded by sensitive seismograph
2.	Feeble	Recorded by seismograph difference may be felt by number of person at rest.
3.	Very slight	Felt by several persons at rest, is strong enough for the duration and direction to be recorded.
4.	Slight	Disturbs persons in motion, movable objectes distributed, creaking of doors and windows.
5.	Weak	Disturbances of furniture and ringing of bells.
6.	Moderate	General awakening of those asleep, stopping of clocks, visible disturbances of trees.
7.	Strong	Overthrow of movable objects, fall of plaster, general panic without serious damage to building.
8.	Very strong	Fall of chimneys, cracks in the walls.
9.	Severe	Partial or total destruction of some buildings.
10.	Destructive	All structures distributed.

(1) Shaking Intensity as per MSK Scale:

Intensity VIII- Destruction of buildings

1. Fright and panic. Also, persons driving motorcars are disturbed. Here and there branches of trees break off. Even heavy furniture moves and partly overturns. Hanging lamps are damaged in part.

2. Most buildings of type C suffer damage of Grade 2, and few of grade 3. Most buildings of Type B suffer damage of Grade 3, and most buildings of Type A suffer damage of Grade 4. Occasional breaking of pipe seams occurs. Memorials and monuments move and twist. Stone walls collapse.

3. Small landslips occur in hollows and on banked roads on steep slopes, cracks develop in ground up to widths of several centimeters. Water in lakes becomes turbid. New reservoirs come into existences. Dry wells refill and existing wells become dry. In many cases, changes in flow and level of water are observed.

Note:

    Type A – structures - rural constructions.

    Type B – Ordinary masonry constructions.

    Type C – Well-built structures

    Single Few - about 5%

    Many – about 50%

    Most – about 75%

    Grade 1 Damage – Slight damage

    Grade 2 moderate damage

    Grade 3 Heavy damage

    Grade 4 Destruction

    Grade 5 Total damage.

3.4.5 Richter Scale

A measure of earthquake magnitude allowing an estimate of energy levels involved.

3.4.6 Rossi-Forrel Scale

An observational scale for measuring earthquake intensity. This was improved and expanded by Mercalli to produce the "Modified Mercalli Scale".

3.4.7 Seismograph

A printout from a seismometer. Studies of seismograph traces can be used to pinpoint both the epicenter of an earthquake and the nature of the fault movement.

3.4.8 Seismometer

Seismic waves travel through the earth as elastic vibrations. A seismometer is an instrument used to record these vibrations and the resulting graph that shows the vibrations is called a seismogram.

The seismometer must be able to move with the vibrations, yet part of it must remain nearly stationary. This is accomplished by isolating the recording device (like a pen) from the rest of the Earth using the principal of inertia. For example, if the pen is attached to a large mass suspended by a spring, the spring and the large mass move less than the paper which is attached to the Earth, and on which the record of the vibrations is made.

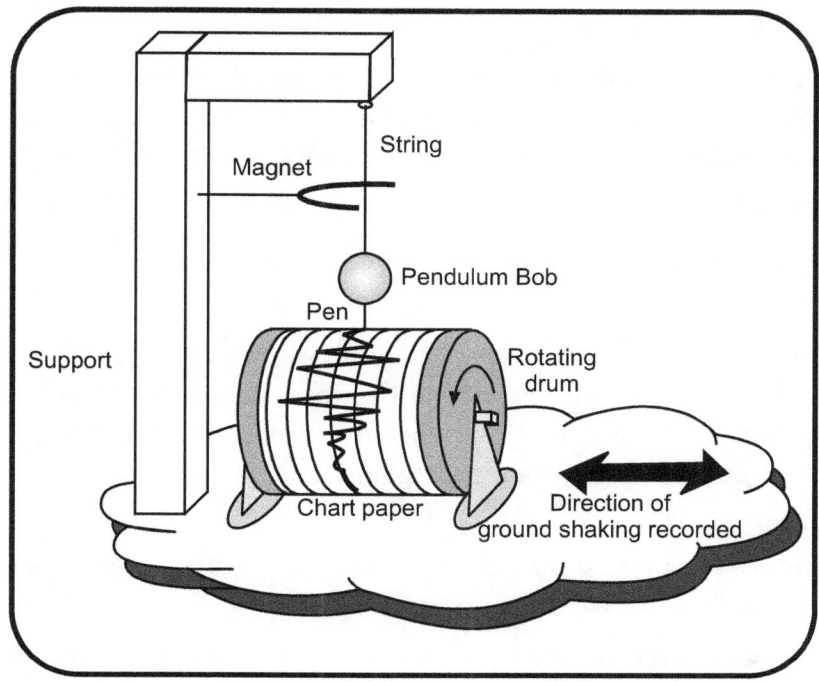

Fig. 3.10: Schematic of early seismograph

The record of an earthquake, a seismogram, as recorded by a seismometer, will be a plot of vibrations versus time. On the seismogram time is marked at regular intervals, so that we can determine the time of arrival of the first P-wave and the time of arrival of the first S-wave.

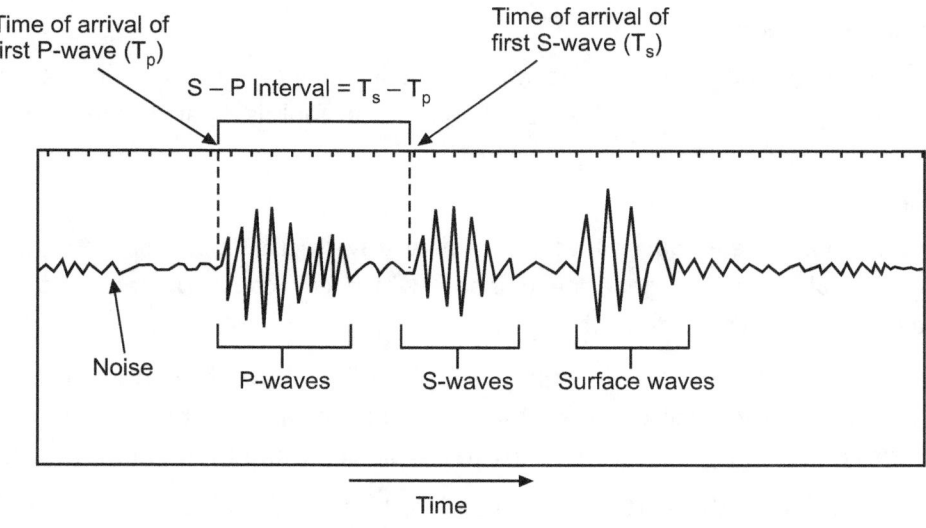

Fig. 3.11

(Note again, that because P-waves have a higher velocity than S-waves, the P-waves arrive at the seismographic station before the S-waves).

3.4.9 Teleseism

A teleseism is an earthquake recorded by a seismograph at a distance. By international convention the distance is over 1000 kilometers from the epicenter. Earthquake originating near the recording station are termed as near earthquake or local earthquake.

3.4.10 Microseism

These are more or less continuous disturbances in the ground recorded by seismographs.

(1) Micro-earthquake:

Very small earthquake having magnitude less than measurable than three on Richter scale are called Micro-earthquake. Highly sensitive seismographs are employed to monitor these for seismological and engineering applications.

(2) Accelerogram:

The ground acceleration record produced by accelerograph is called Accelerogram.

(3) Accelerograph:

This is an earthquake recording device designed to measure the ground motion in terms of acceleration in the epicentral region of strong shaking. It writes the time wise history of ground acceleration at a particular site.

(4) Seduction zone:

A narrow region along a destructive plate boundary where one plate is consumed underneath another.

(5) Transform boundary:

A plate boundary where the relative movement is sideways. The classic example of a transform boundary is in California where the San Andreas fault is a part of a transform plate boundary.

(6) Tsunami:

Tsunami are giant ocean waves that can rapidly travel across oceans. Earthquakes that occur along coastal areas can generate tsunami, which can cause damage thousands of kilometers away on the other side of the ocean.

Tsunami can be generated by anything that disturbs a body of water. This includes earthquakes that cause vertical offset of the sea floor, volcanic eruptions into a body of water, landslides into a body of water, underwater explosions, and meteorite impacts.

In general, the larger the earthquake, eruption, landslide, explosion or meteorite, the more likely it will be able to travel across an ocean. Smaller events may, however cause a tsunami that affect areas in the vicinity of the triggering event.

Tsunami waves have wavelengths and velocities much higher that wind driven ocean waves. Velocities are on the order of several hundred km/hr, similar to a jet aeroplane. They usually are more than one wave, that hit the coastline tens of minutes to hours apart. Although wave heights are barely perceptible in the open ocean, the waves become amplified as the approach the shore and may build to several tens of metres. Thus, when the come ashore, they can flood areas far away from the coast. Often the trough of a tsunami wave arrives before the crest; this produces a phenomenon called drawdown where the ocean recedes from the normal shoreline by as much as a kilometre.

Tsunami warning systems have been developed for the Pacific Ocean basin and, recently, the Indian Ocean where a tsunami killed over 250,000 people in 2004. But, such warning systems depend on the ability to detect and forecast a tsunami after an earthquake occurs and may take several hours to come up with an accurate forecast of wave heights and travel time.

3.5 FACTORS AFFECTING DAMAGE

One of the most frightening and destructive phenomena of nature is a severe earthquake and it's terrible after effects. Earthquakes strike suddenly, violently and without warning at any time of the day or night. If an earthquake occurs in a populated area, it may cause many deaths and injuries and extensive property damage.

There are two types of factors affecting of damage i.e. direct and indirect factors.

3.5.1 Direct Factor of Damage

Direct factors cause damages directly and include ground motion and faulting.

- **Location:** An earthquake that hits in a more populated area is more damage than one that hits a lower populated area.

- **Magnitude:** Scientists assign intensity of a number to represent the amount of seismic energy released by an earthquake. The Richter magnitude scale 6 is more powerful than one of intensity of 4 magnitude scale. The more energy in an earthquake, the more destructive.

- **Depth:** Earthquakes can happen anywhere from at the surface to 700 kilometers below. In general, deeper earthquakes are less damaging because their energy dissipates before it reaches the surface. The recent New Zealand earthquake is thought to have occurred at a more shallow depth than the one last year.

- **Distance from the epicenter:** The epicenter is the point at the surface above where the origin of earthquake. It is near to the place where the earthquake's intensity is the greatest. So that more damage is done.

- **Time of Day:** An earthquake during a busy time, such as rush hour, may cause more deaths than an earthquake at a quiet time. When there are fewer people in industrial and commercial areas on Sundays; there are more people in homes at night.

- **Local geological conditions:** The nature of the ground at the surface of an earthquake can have a profound influence on the level of damage. When the shaking is strong and long enough of liquefying of Loose, sandy, soggy soil. That doesn't bode well for any structures on the surface. Buildings should be built on flat areas formed of solid rock.

    Geological Conditions involved are as per following:

- **Seismic waves:** Seismic waves through surface of rock layers result in ground motion that motion can be done more damage or completely destroy of buildings. And strong surface seismic waves make the ground heave and lurch then damage the total structure.

- **Landslides:** In region of hills and steep slopes. An earthquake vibration may cause landslides and mudslides and cliffs to collapse. This can damage buildings and lead to loss of human life.

Fig. 3.12: Earthquake-induced landslide – Kobe, Japan

- **Shaking of ground:** Soil vibration can either shake a building of its foundations modify its supports or cause its foundation to disintegrate.

Fig. 3.13: Bhuj Earthquake India 2001

- **Liquefaction:** The area of high water table may cause problem of liquefaction. The liquefied cohesion less soil has no strength to support the structure. Lose their bearing capacity of foundation. i.e. fluid due to sudden reduction in shear resistance. When this happen buildings start to lean (slope over the one side) or partially sink.

Fig. 3.14

3.5.2 Indirect Factors of Damage

Indirect factors cause damages indirectly as a result of the processes set in motion by an earthquake.

- **Secondary effects:** Earthquakes can trigger landslides, fires, floods or tsunamis more damages are done. In 2004 Sumatran-Andaman earthquake that caused so much damage in 2004 but the Indian Ocean tsunami it triggered. Nearly a quarter of a million people in 14 countries were killed when coastal communities were inundated by the water.

(a) Tsunami:

In open sea tsunamis i.e. series of sea waves with extremely long time periods occur due to earthquake or sudden settlement of large bed strata near the shore of sea the energy of waves due to tsunami gets concentrated in the vertically due to reduction of water depth. And as well as in horizontally in direction. Tsunami can travel very quickly at speed of 1000 kmph. Similar to small tsunami occur as a result of the slashing of enclosed water in reservoirs, lakes and harbors shaken by earthquake.

Fig. 3.15: Open sea tsunamis

(b) Fire:

Earthquake can fire by damaging of gas pipelines and snapping electric wires or towers.

Fig. 3.16: Damage caused by fire (2009 West Sumatra Earthquake, Indonesia)

(c) Flood:

Earthquakes can rupture dams and raised river embankments causing floods. Resulting in damage to structures and considerable loss of life.

(d) Architecture of Structure:

The strongest buildings may not or less damage by a bad earthquake. Architecture plays a huge role in construction of earthquake resisting structures. But poor construction, weak cement and unenforced building codes more damages are done.

3.6 CONSIDERATIONS OF EARTHQUAKE FORCES IN DESIGN

In motion of ground caused by inertia forces of structure is horizontally and vertically. These are the following:

1. Design horizontal earthquake force:

Lateral loads resisting elements are in orthogonal horizontal directions. Structure Design should be that full design earthquake load act in one horizontal direction at a time. When this load not oriented along horizontally. The load takes of 30% of the design earthquake load in other directions.

2. Design vertical earthquake force:

The structure vibrating due to earthquake ground motions. It resolving in three perpendicular directions. Stronger direction of vibration of ground is horizontally. All vibrating forces depend on direction of ground motion due to under gravity. Factor of safety for gravity force is sufficient to cover the earthquake induced vertical acceleration. In the effect of vertical earthquake loads are to be considered for design of vertical force it calculated by due to vertical acceleration as two thirds of the horizontal acceleration.

3. Other Forces:

(a) The structures are generally subjected to two types of loads statics and dynamics. Statics loads are constant with time while dynamic loads are time varying. In effect of dynamic load is not considered because the structure is rarely subjected to dynamic loading. Its consideration in the analysis of structure makes the analysis more complicated and time consuming. But negligence sometime when causes of great disaster i.e. earthquake which is one of dynamic load.

(b) The Earthquake causes motion in the structure which includes vertical and horizontal oscillations in structures. It results in acceleration, velocity and displacements of structure. The induced acceleration generates inertial forces which are proportional to acceleration of mass and acts opposite to ground motion.

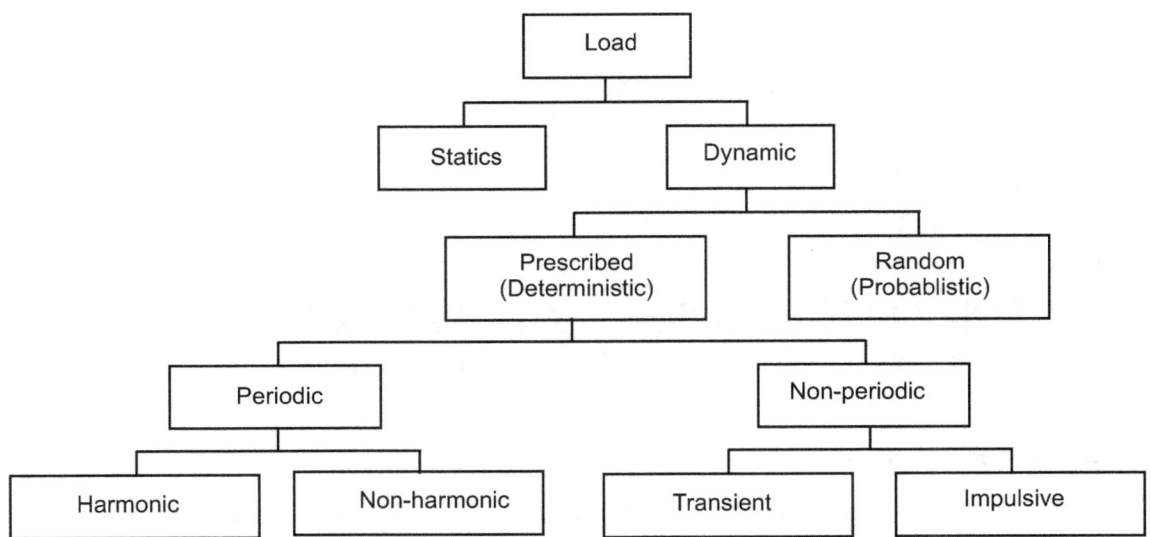

(c) The energy produced in structure by ground motion is dissipated through internal friction within the structural and non-structural element. This dissipation of energy is called damping. These damping forces are proportional to velocity induced in structure.

(d) The displacement in the structure causes restoring forces in structure due to stiffness. On the basis of Stiffness the structure may be classified as brittle or ductile. The greater stiffness proves to be less durable during earthquake while ductile structures performs well in earthquake.

Therefore, the equation of dynamic equilibrium of an earthquake has the form in which inertia damping and restoring forces balance the applied force.

$$F(t) = m\ddot{y}(t) + c\dot{y}(t) + ky(t)$$

Where,

(i) $m\ddot{y}(t)$ is inertia force which depend on characteristics of ground motion and Structure.

(ii) $c\dot{y}(t)$ is damping force acting opposite to seismic motion. It is depend on its components.

(iii) $k\,y(t)$ is restoring force.

3.7 GENERAL CONSTRUCTION ASPECTS

Following are the certain points taken to the accounts for construction of earthquake resisting structures.

1. **Plan of Building:**

    The building should neither be slender in plan nor should have redundant corners. Building should be separated into simple rectangular box type. The building should not be excessively long relative to its width and the length to width ratio should not exceed 4.

    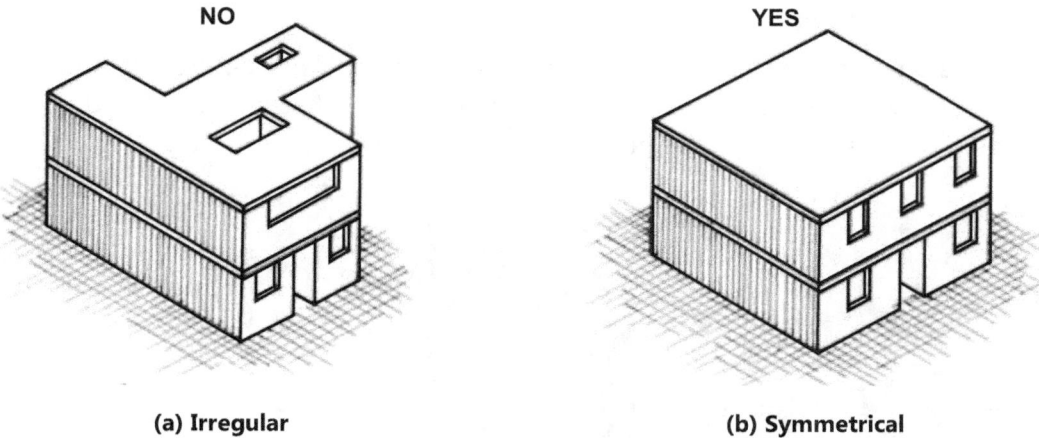

    (a) Irregular (b) Symmetrical

    Fig. 3.17

2. **Masonry Wall:**

    (a) The earthquake response of a masonry wall depends on the relative strength of bricks and mortar. The bricks must be stronger than the mortar. These should have a compressive strength not less than 35 N/mm^2.

    (b) Good interlocking of masonry courses at the junction. Should be ensured as the wall transfers loads to each other at the junction. To obtain full bond between perpendicular walls.

    (c) For single storey construction of wall thickness should not be less than one brick.

    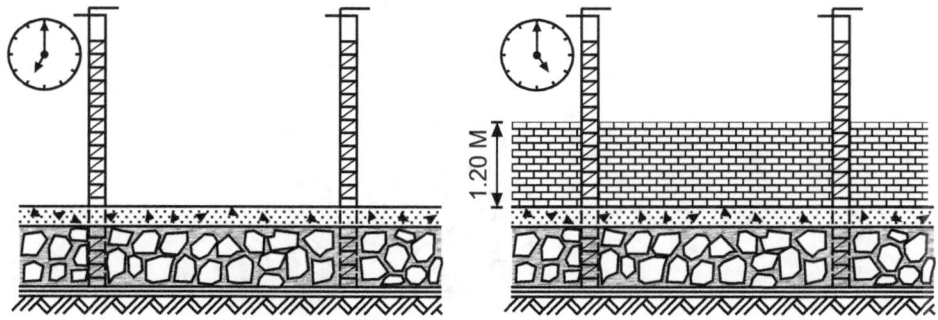

    Fig. 3.18: Masonry wall construction

    (d) Horizontal reinforcements should be provided in walls to strength them against in horizontal in plane bending. This is also helps to walls perpendicularly tie together.

(e) The lintel band ties the walls together and creates a support to the loaded in the weak direction. This bond also reduces unsupported height of the walls and improves their stability in weaker direction.

(f) As a supplement to the bands above steel dowel bars may be used at corner and T-junctions to integrate the box action of walls.

(g) Tensions occur in the jambs of opening, at corners and junctions of walls. Therefore, vertical bars should be provided. Amount of vertical steel will depend upon the number of storey and their height.

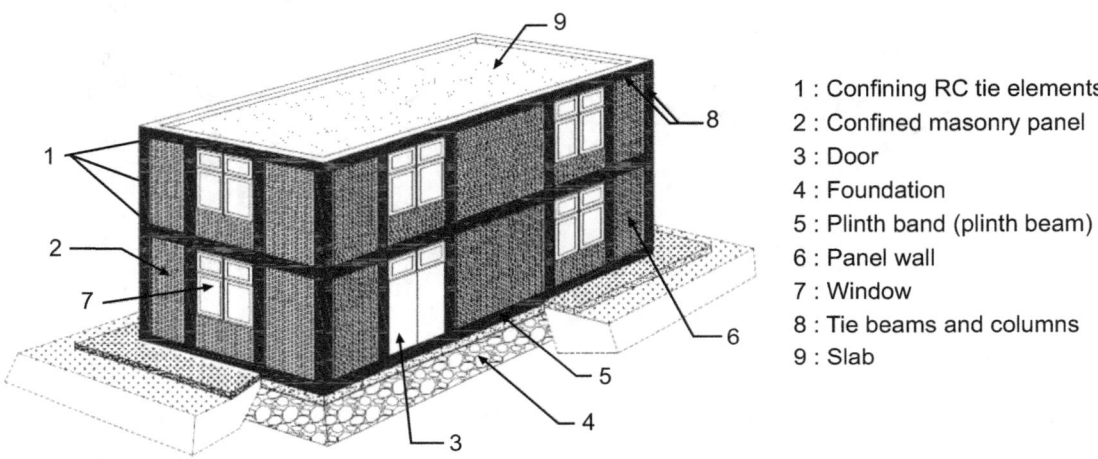

1 : Confining RC tie elements
2 : Confined masonry panel
3 : Door
4 : Foundation
5 : Plinth band (plinth beam)
6 : Panel wall
7 : Window
8 : Tie beams and columns
9 : Slab

Fig. 3.19: Features of earthquake resistant buildings

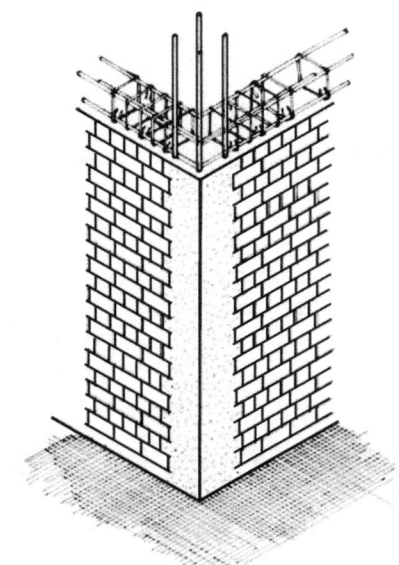

Fig. 3.20: Wall intersections

3. Reinforcement:

(a) Vertical reinforcement should be properly embedded in the plinth of masonry of the foundation and roof of slab or roof and lintel band. So to develop its tensile strength in band all storey.

(b) Shear reinforcement should be providing in walls to ensure their ductile behavior.

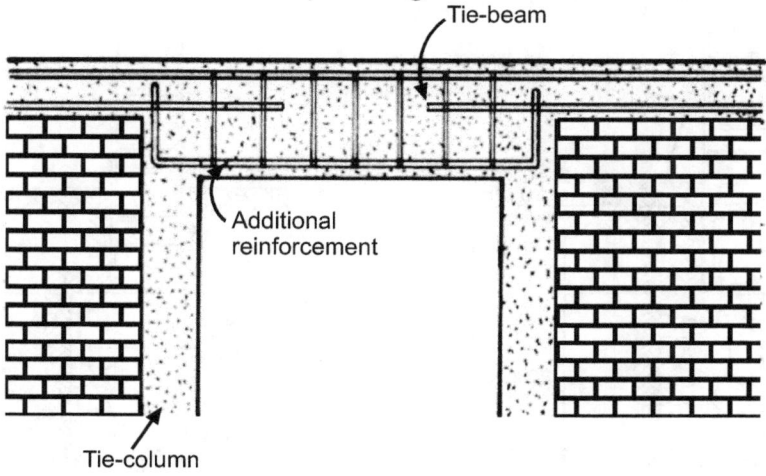

Fig. 3.21: Lintel beam reinforcement

4. Opening Size:

Location and size of opening is deciding the performance of masonry building subjected to earthquake force. Size of doors and windows to keep in smaller provided at the central. Tie-columns should be placed at both sides of any opening having an areaof more than 1.5 m².

(a) Poor location of window and door opening (b) Good location of window and door opening

Fig. 3.22

5. Stair Case:

Inclined of stair flights joining different floor level will act like a cross brace between various floors. They transfer the large horizontal forces at the roof level and lower levels and cause damage during earthquake. Staircase should be provided completely separately from whole structure.

6. Footing:

Steep and strong continuous footing should be used for the foundation. The foundation should be constructed as in brick or an uncoursed random rubble stone masonry footing. Or a RC strip footing can be used in foundation. In masonry construction, plinth band provide on top of foundation is essential for preventing building settlements in soft soil.

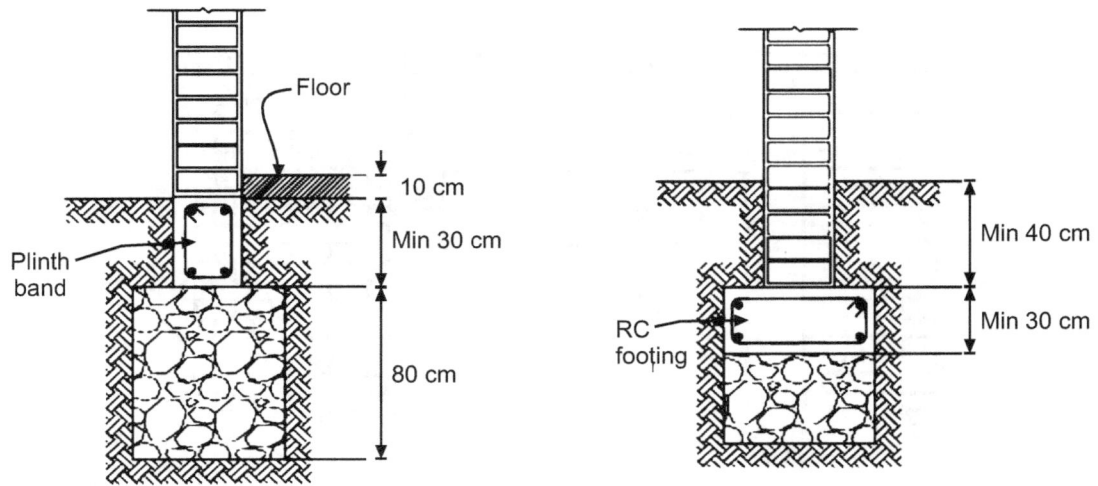

(a) RC plinth band and stone masonry foundation   (b) RC strip footing

Fig. 3.23

3.8 EARTHQUAKE RESISTANT LOW COST BUILDINGS

Approximately 20% of the world population lives in or near earthquake zones, more than that of 70% population is low income or poverty level socio-economic classes. The statistics show that countries with high population density and lower standards of living countries situated in seismically active regions. That is like Indonesia, India, China, Asia, and portions of the South America. A large majority of the population in these areas is live in low income housing constructed of earth, stone, hollow block, and other types of low cost materials.

3.8.1 Need of Low Cost Earthquake Resistant Building

In seismic building design, a certain type of construction material can be use an earthquake is a function not only of the material's resilience and strength, but also how it is incorporated into the structure. A long, straight stone wall, for example, using only friction and geometry to keep stones in place, will almost certainly collapse in an earthquake. This is because the mass, or inertia, of the wall tends to keep its motion lagging behind the motion of the earth during a quake. This not only begins to dislodge stones from their initial resting position, but without lateral support can shift the weight of the wall so far out of the stable load line that the top of the wall begins to topple over.

General aspects of the building indicated below can be used in construction of walls and their joint with roof in low cost buildings for improving stability walls:

1. Changing the course of the wall from a straight line to a zigzag line for improving its stability wall.

2. Modifying the geometry of the individual stones to incorporate interlocking grooves, diagonal faces can improve the base to top integrity of the wall. Conforming to one or more s-curves provides almost continuous lateral support along the entire length.

3. Providing a wall cap or lintel helps ensure the integrity of the top course of the wall stones, tying them together without benefit of the weight of the wall.

4. If a house is rectangular in shape, without adequate ties between roof and walls, the walls will become unstable near the top and topple or collapse in the direction of least lateral support.

5. Changing the footprint to a more compact therefore square geometry with internal cross walls will improve this stability. Changing the footprint to a round or oval geometry will improve the stability even more, as example of the Bhongas structures in India.

6. Providing a plate or rim band at the top of the walls helps for the ensure integrity is maintained at that location.

7. Incorporating a light weight structural roof with positive connection to the top plates and wall rims will also more improving the structure's resist due to an earthquake, therefore providing almost continuous lateral support at the top of the walls.

8. In addition, if ties to properly foundation are not sufficient, the structure stands a good chance of sliding off the foundation during a earthquake effectively destroying the structure from the bottom to top.

3.8.2 Improved Quincha Techniques for Low Cost Housing

Improved quincha techniques had the following characteristics over and above traditional quincha:

1. Concrete foundations for greater stability.

2. Wooden columns treated with tar or pitch to protect against humidity, concreted into the ground with nails embedded in the wood at the base to give extra anchorage.

3. Using concrete wall bases to prevent humidity affecting the wood and the canes in the walls.

4. Careful jointing between columns and beams to improve structural stability. Canes woven in a vertical fashion to provide greater stability.

5. Light weight metal sheet roofing to reduce danger of falling tiles. Nailing roofing material to roof beams; tying of beams and columns by roof wires.

6. Incorporating roof eaves of sufficient width to ensure protection of walls from heavy rains.

Fig. 3.24: Quincha Technique

3.8.3 Materials of Construction of Low Cost Building

The development of cost effective solutions for improving the seismic resistance of structures are an important and challenging issue for earthquake engineers to reduce the earthquake hazard of poor people in developing countries. Natural fibres (straw and jute) and cementing materials (cement and gypsum) were used to improve the block and mortar properties.

1. Straw: Straw is effective for improving the ductility of block. The strength of adobe block prepared with crushed straw is higher than that of the specimens prepared with whole straw. Straw in the shear band transfers the stress across the crack and prevents the crack from opening. Hence, straw improves the ductility. Reduction in the friction between soil to soil due to the replacement of the soil-sand part by straw and micro-cracks that were cause by straw are responsible for the reduction of strength. Since the cracks in the adobe block increase with the increase of both the straw content and length, strength decreases with the increase of both the straw content and length. The reason behind the better performance of crushed straw might be its higher flexibility, which helps to prevent the shrinkage cracks in the adobe block.

Fig. 3.25

2. **Jute:** Jute is also effective for improving the ductility. Jute is to be the most effective among the selected fibers. Since jute improves both the ductility and toughness of adobe material with slight decreases in compressive strength. There are also an optimal jute content and jute length, which are 2.0% by weight and 2 cm, respectively. The higher flexibility, friction to soil, and the tensile strength of the jute fiber in comparison with those of straw and hemp might be the reason for its best performance among the selected fibers.

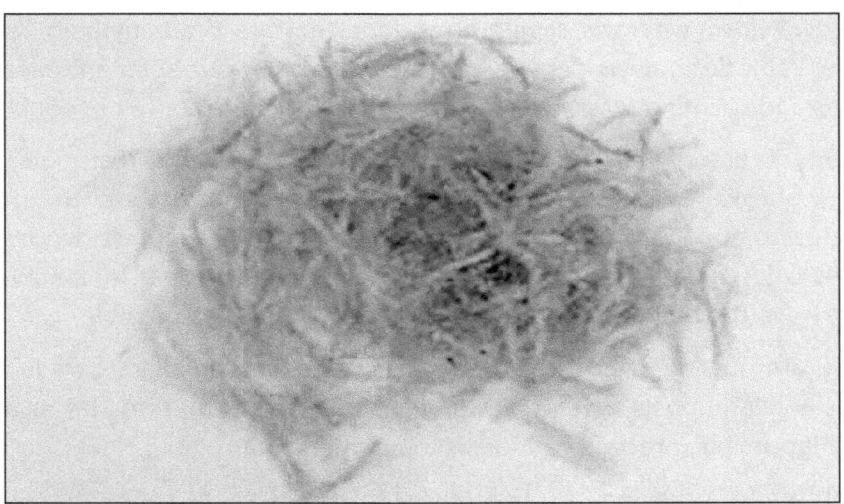

Fig. 3.26

3. **Gypsum:** Gypsum improves the strength of the block. Gypsum gives cohesion to the matrix and thus the strength increases. Soil composition also plays a significant role in the seismic resistance of block. Both the compressive strength and failure strain are dependent on the soil composition.

3.9 PRECAUTIONS TO BE TAKEN BEFORE OCCURRENCE OF AN EARTHQUAKE

Although there are no guarantees of safety during an earthquake, identifying potential hazards ahead of time and advance planning can save lives and signicantly reduce injuries and property damage. Repairing deep plaster cracks in ceilings and foundations, anchoring overhead lighting factures to the ceiling, and following local seismic building standards, will help reduce the impact of earthquakes.

1. If you are indoors, stay there: You get under a sturdy table, desk or bed. Brace yourself in an inside corner away from windows. Move to an inner wall or corridor. Because a door frame or the structural frame or inner core of the building are its strongest points and least likely to collapse. They will also break the impact of any falling objects.

2. In an apartment building the safest place is by the central reinforced core of the building. This is usually located by the elevator well; if it collapses choose shelter which will provide airspace. If your furniture shelter moves, stay under it and follow it around the apartment.

3. Watch for falling objects like plaster, bricks, light fixtures, pots and pans, etc. Stay away from tall shelves, china cabinets and other furniture, which might slide or topple over.

4. Stay away from windows, sliding glass doors, mirrors. Grab anything handy (blanket, pillow, tablecloth, news papers, box, etc.) to shield your head and face from failing debris and splinting glass. Do not be alarmed if the fire alarm or sprinklers go off.

5. When you are on the floor stay on the same floor do not rush outside. Stairways may be broken and exits jammed with people. Do not use elevators as the power for elevators may go out and leave you trapped. The greatest danger from falling debris is just outside door-ways and close to outer walls. If for safety reasons you must leave the building, choose your exits as carefully as possible.

6. If you are outside, stay there. Move away from the building, garage, walls, power poles and lampposts. Electric power lines are a serious hazard stay away from fallen lines. If possible, proceed cautiously to an open area.

7. If you are in a moving car. Then car stop as quickly as safety permits in the best available space. Stay in your car. Don't stop where buildings can topple down on top of you. A car is an excellent shock absorber and will shake a lot on its springs during an earthquake, but it's a fairly safe shelter from which to assess your situation.

8. Avoid fallen power lines. The possibility of encountering fallen live wires is great during and after an earthquake. If you are on foot, make a wide path around the wires. If you are in the car and live wires have fallen across the car, remain where you are. Your car is usually well insulated and will protect you from electric shock. Never assume that downed power lines are dead.

EXERCISE

1. What are the causes of earthquake ?
2. Explain change in earth crust during earthquake.
3. Explain consideration of earthquake forces in design.
4. Explain precautions to be taken before occurrence of an earthquake.
5. Write in brief general construction aspects.
6. Write short notes on the following :

   (a) Focus, (b) Epicenter, (c) Seismograph, (d) General construction aspects, (e) Earthquake.

SURVEYING AND LEVELLING

4.1 INTRODUCTION

Surveying is an important branch of Civil Engineering which includes linear and angular measurements.

Vertical measurements are made in the vertical plane and are grouped under the term 'Levelling'.

Surveying is carried out to obtain information about the piece of a land or a plot or features in a particular locality. Surveying is the preliminary and very important work in all of the civil engineering projects like buildings, roads, railways, tunnels, dams, canal etc.

These measurements enable the surveyor to locate the boundaries of the plot or features of an area and to show to them on paper by drawing a plan of these features.

In this chapter, we have dealt with objects, principles of surveying and study of modern survey methods.

4.1.1 Importance of Surveying to Civil Engineers

Planning and design of all civil engineering projects such as highways, tunnels, dams, bridges etc. are based upon surveying measurements.

Other principal works in which surveying is primary utilized are:

- To fix national and state boundaries.
- To chart coastlines, navigable streams and lakes.
- To establish control points.
- To execute hydrographic and oceanographic charting and mapping.
- To prepare topographic map of land surface of the earth.

4.1.2 Objectives of Surveying

- To collect field data.
- To prepare plan or map of the area surveyed.

- To analyse and to calculate the field parameters for setting out the operation of actual engineering works.
- To set out field parameters at the site for further engineering works.

Classification of Surveying:

Most of the civil engineering works are concerned only with a small portion of the earth which seems to be the plane surface. Thus based upon the consideration of the shape of the earth, surveying is broadly classified as:

1. Plane Surveying.
2. Geodetic Surveying.

4.1.3 Principles of Surveying

Surveying involves different operations and techniques, but all of these are based on the following principles such as:

1. To work from whole to part.
2. To locate a point by at least two independent processes:
   (a) Linear measurements.
   (b) Angular measurements.
   (c) Both linear and angular measurements.

1. To work from whole to part:

For any particular survey, whether it is an entire town or field, the main framework for the entire area to be surveyed consists of polygons or triangles and is set out by fixing control points. The main framework is then divided suitably for detailed surveying. **This principle prevents accumulation of errors in the surveying and localises the errors of measurement.**

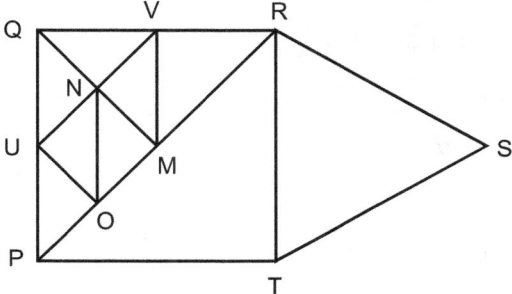

Fig. 4.1

Suppose a big piece of land PQRST is to be surveyed. Then control points i.e. stations P, Q, R, S and T are established at each of the corners of land. Then the rectangular area is subdivided into two triangles PQR and RPT by joining stations P and R. Further subdivision of ΔPQR can be done by selecting another station M on the line PR and framing triangles PQM and QMR. For surveying purpose by selecting stations M, O, U and V on different sides, the bigger area can be divided into smaller triangles as shown in Fig. 4.1. This process is called as working from whole to the part.

However, if the work is started from part to whole i.e. from ΔMNO and the survey is completed by extending the sides of the ΔMNO, then the errors in the measurement of length will accumulate and will result in wrong calculation of area. Thus, it can be stated that if we adopt the method of working from part to whole, small errors increase and thus become uncontrollable at the end. This will have an adverse effect on the precision of survey.

2. To Locate a point by at least two Independent Measurements (Fig. 4.2.):

Here, two points are selected in the field and distance between them is measured. The relative positions of the other points in the field can be located from these two reference points.

To locate a point D with respect to given points of reference A and B, the following methods can be employed.

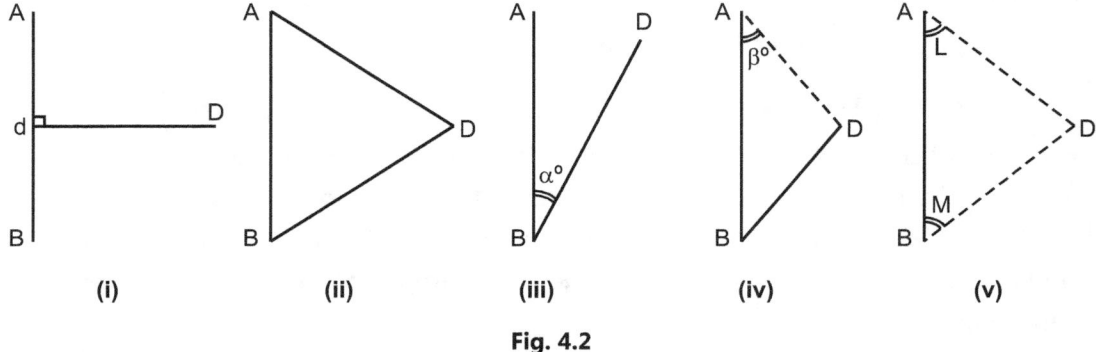

Fig. 4.2

(i) Distance Ad and perpendicular dD.

(ii) Lengths AD and BD.

(iii) Length BD and angle $\alpha°$.

(iv) Length BD and angle $\beta°$.

(v) Angles L and M (∠DAB and ∠DBA).

Similarly position of a new point with reference to three known points can also be fixed.

4.2 LINEAR MEASUREMENTS

The distances on the ground are measured either with a metric chain or tape.

Different methods can be adopted for making linear measurements depending on the degree of precision required. These methods can be broadly divided into three groups:
1. Direct measurement.
2. Measurement by optical distance measuring instrument.
3. Electronic devices.

In direct measurement, distances are actually measured on the ground with the help of a tape. Measurements by optical instruments means which involve the use of instruments like tacheometer, subtence bar, telemeter, etc. The electronic distance measuring instruments rely on propagation, reflection and reception of radio or light waves. These include instruments like Geodimeter, Tellurometer, and Distomat. i.e. Electronic Distance meter or Total station.

4.2.1 Direct Measurement of Distances

The most commonly adopted method for measurement of distances is by using chain or tape known as 'chaining' or 'taping'.

4.2.2 Instruments for Chaining

Following instruments are used for determining the length of a given line.

A. (i) Chain or (ii) tape   E. Offset rods
B. Arrows   F. Plumb bob
C. Pegs   G. Line ranger
D. Ranging rods.

A. (i) Chain:

The chains are available in lengths of 20 m and 30 m. The chain consists of 100 links for 20 m. chain and 150 links for 30 m chain. Link is made of galvanised mild steel wire 4 mm in diameter. Length of each link is the distance between the centres of two consecutive middle rings. Each link is bent into loop at the ends and joined to each other by three small circular or oval shaped rings. These rings offer flexibility to the chain. The ends of the chain are provided with brass handle at each end with a swivel joint, so that the chain can be turned without twisting. A semicircular groove is provided in the centre on the outer periphery of handle for fixing the m.s. arrow at the end of one chain length. Brass tags or tallies are inserted at every 5 m length to make out the part length of chain. The length of chain is measured from the outside of one handle to the outside of the other handle.

The commonly used chain is the metric chain.

(i) Metric chain: These are available in lengths of 20 m and 30 m. The details for 30 m chain are shown in Fig. 4.3.

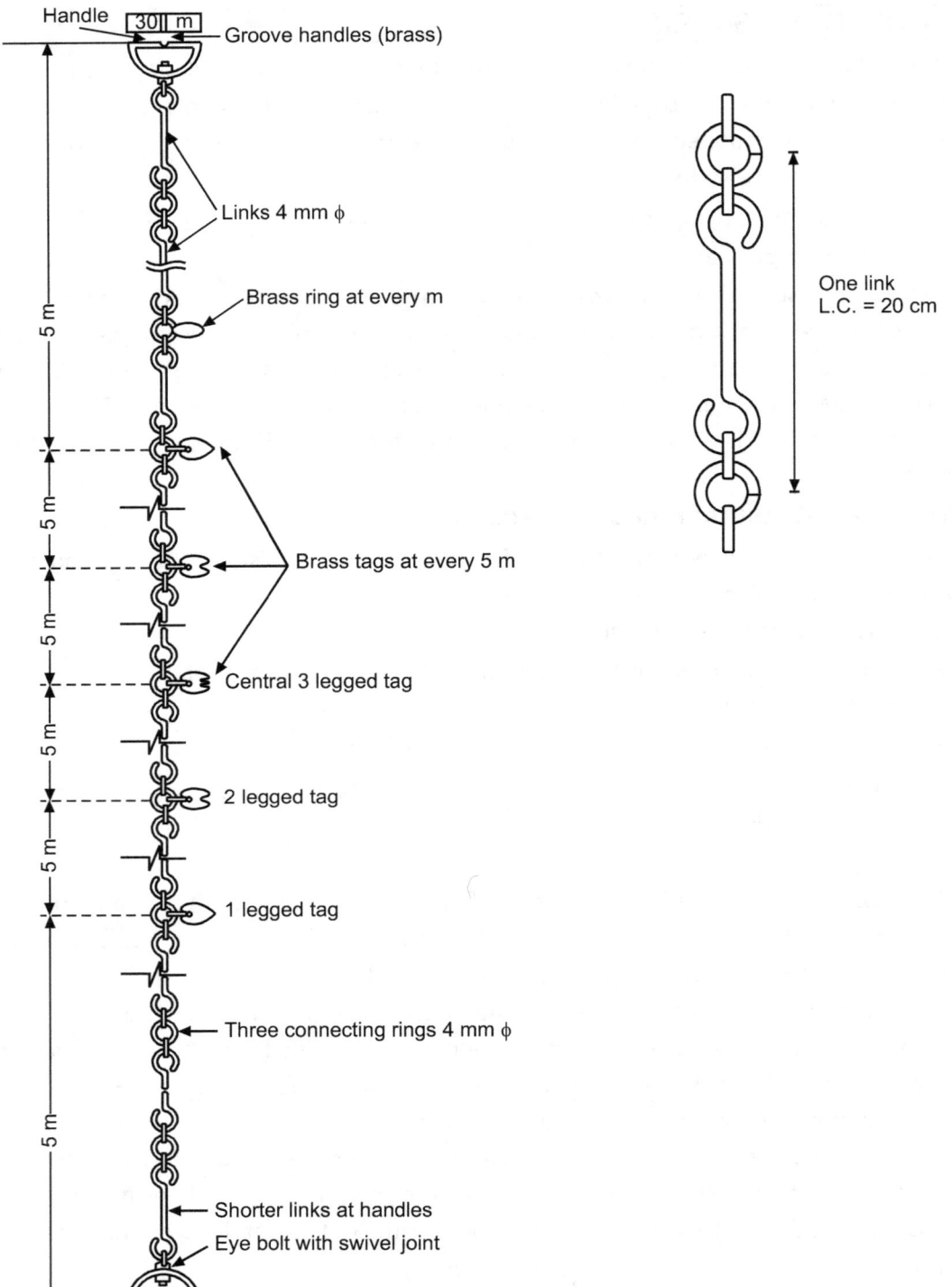

Fig. 4.3 : 30 m metric chain

(ii) Tapes:

Tapes are used for more accurate measurements of length and are classified as per the material of which they are made.

1. Cloth or linen tape,
2. Metallic tape,
3. Steel tape,
4. Invar tape and
5. Fibre glass tape.

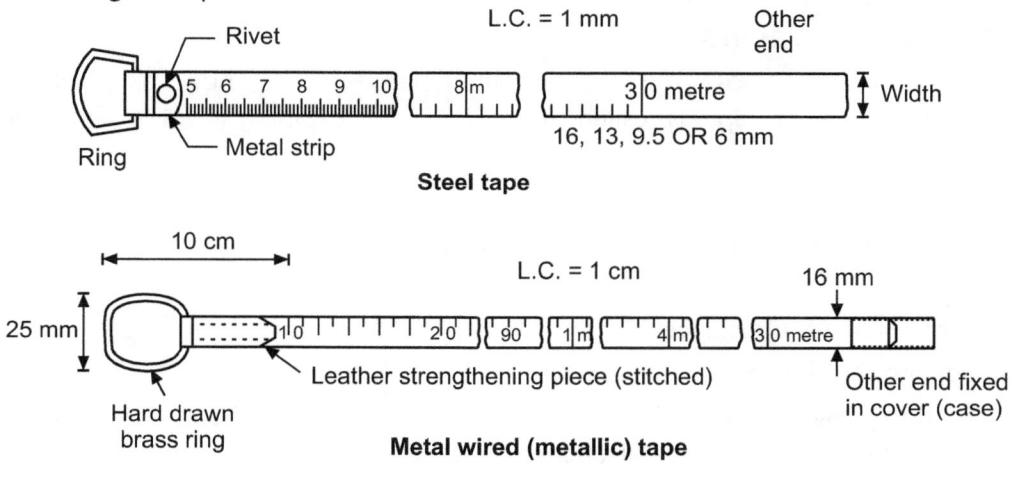

Fig. 4.4: Types of tape

1. **Cloth or Linen Tape:** It is made up of closely woven linen, 12 to 15 mm wide and varnished to resist moisture. It is light and flexible. It is commonly available in lengths of 10 m, 20 m, 25 m and 30 m. This tape is rarely used for accurate measurements due to its shrinkage when wet, twisting and weakness.

2. **Metallic Tape:** It is made up of varnished strip of waterproof linen interwoven with small brass, copper or bronze wires and does not stretch as easily as cloth tapes. It is available in lengths of 2, 5, 10, 20, 30 and 50 m. Tapes of 10, 20, 30 and 50 m lengths are supplied in metal or leather case fitted with winding device.

3. **Steel Tape:** A steel tape consists of a light strip of steel of width 6 to 10 mm and is more accurately graduated. Steel tape is available in lengths of 2, 10, 30, 50 metres. It is delicate and very light type and therefore it's rough use should be avoided. The tape should be wiped clean and dry after using, to avoid rusting.

4. **Invar Tape:** Invar tape is made up of an alloy of nickel (36%) and steel and has very low coefficient of thermal expansion. It is used mainly for linear measurements of a very high degree of precision. It is more expensive, and more easily deformed than steel tapes.

5. Fibre-glass Tape: Fibre glass tape is now-a-days extensively used in the field. This tape has very low coefficient of thermal expansion, and it is strong and durable. It is cheap and gives fairly good degree of precision. The tape is available in 5 m, 10 m, 20 m and 30 m lengths. The least count of measurement may be 1 cm or 1 mm.

Precautions in using the tape for measurement of distance:
1. While laying the tape on the ground, it should be laid straight (without twist).
2. The tape should not be allowed to get wet and smeared with soil.
3. While winding back in the case, it should be wound dry (if wetted) and straight after cleaning or wiping out properly.

4.2.3 Chaining or Taping

Measurement of distance on ground with the help of chain is known as *"Chaining"* and done with the help of tape is called 'Taping'. Chaining/taping involves the following operations:
1. Marking the stations.
2. Unfolding the chain/unwinding the tape.
3. Ranging.
4. Measurement of distance.
5. Folding the chain/winding the tape.

1. Marking the stations: The stations along the direction of survey line are marked with ranging rods so that these are distinctly visible.

2. Unfolding the chain: Two persons are required for measuring the length of a line which is greater than a chain length. The person staying at the zero end of chain or starting station is called *'follower'*, while the other person holding the forward handle is called 'leader'. The leader also carries few arrows and a ranging rod. To unfold the chain, both handles are kept in one hand and the rest of the bundle of chain is thrown in the forward direction with the other hand. The chain is laid straight.

3. Ranging: If the distance between two stations is less than one chain/tape length, then after stretching the chain/tape, the distance can be directly measured. When the length of a survey line is more than one chain length, intermediate points are to be located in order that the chain/tape is pulled along the proper survey line in a straight direction. This operation is known as Ranging a Line.

4. Measurement of distance: After setting up of each intermediate point and stretching the chain/tape between two points, the leader fixes up arrow at the end of one chain/tape length, touching the groove of handle. The chain is dragged forward upto the last station point. The follower goes on collecting the arrows. The length of the line is determined from the arrows collected by the follower. Each arrow represents one chain/tape length. Any fractional distance at the end is measured by stretching the chain/tape and counting the length upto the end station. The total length of line is, thus, determined.

5. Folding the chain: Starting from the middle of the chain, it is folded, holding pair of links at a time. If a metallic tape is used for measurement of distance, winding back in the case is very simple.

4.2.4 Ranging

It is the process of establishing some intermediate points on a survey line, between the two terminal stations; when the length of line exceeds the length of chain. There are two methods of ranging: (a) Direct ranging, (b) Indirect ranging.

(a) Direct ranging:

Direct ranging is possible when the ends of survey line i.e. end survey stations are intervisible. It can be done by eye or by an instrument called line ranger.

(i) Ranging by eye: After the chain/tape is stretched and laid approximately on line AB, the follower stands behind ranging rod at A and the leader stands at such a distance not greater than one chain/tape length from A, with ranging rod in his hand at an arm's length sideways from his body.

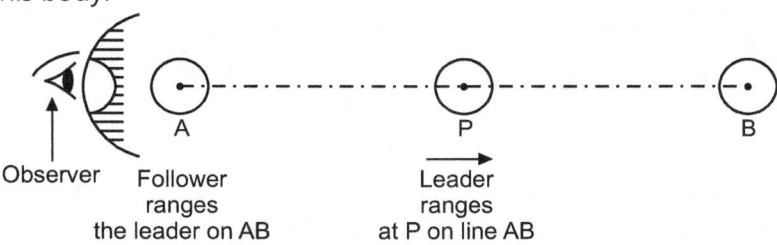

Fig. 4.5: Ranging by eye

The follower positions himself behind A in line with AB. Then he directs the leader by means of signals, to move his ranging rod to the desired direction so that the leader is brought in line with AB at point P. The code of signals used for this purpose are tabulated as follows:

Code for Ranging by hand signals:

Signal by Follower	Action of Leader
1. Rapid sweep with right/left hand.	1. Move considerably to right/left.
2. Slow sweep with right/left hand.	2. Move slowly to right/left.
3. Right/left arm extended.	3. Continue to move to right/left.
4. Right/left arm up and moved to right/left.	4. Plumb the rod to right/left.
5. Both hands above head and brought down.	5. Correct position; no movement.
6. Both arms extended forward horizontally and depressed briskly.	6. Fix the rod.

(ii) Ranging by Line Ranger: The line ranger consists of either two plane mirrors or two right-angled isosceles prisms, placed one above the other, as shown in Fig. 4.6. In case the prisms are used, the diagonals of both prisms are silvered so as to reflect the incident rays.

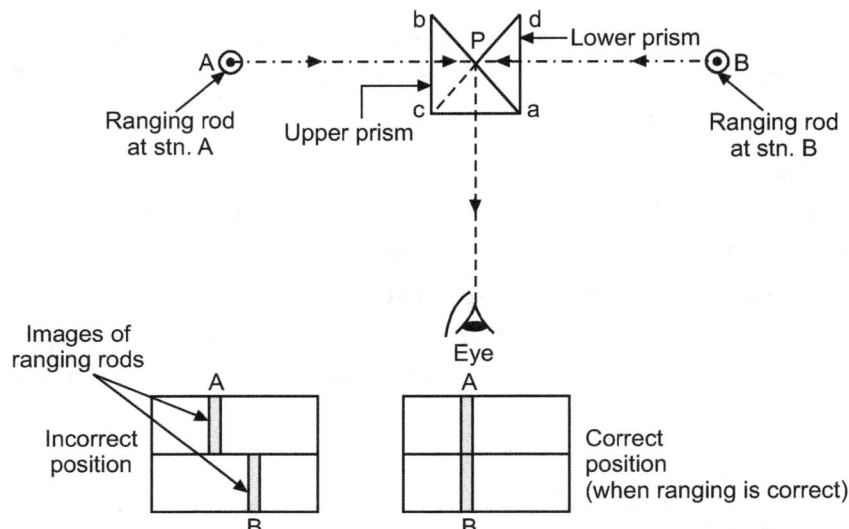

Fig. 4.6: Line ranger

Line ranger is provided with a handle at the bottom, to hold the instrument in hand. From the handle, required point can be transferred to the ground.

Two ranging rods are fixed at A and B. To obtain a point P on survey line AB, the surveyor holds the line ranger approximately very near to the line AB. Upper prism abc receives rays from A which are reflected by diagonal ab towards the observer. The lower prism cda receives rays from B that are reflected by diagonal cd to the observer. Thus, observer can see both ranging rods at A and B. The images of these two ranging rods may not be coinciding indicating that the instrument is not on line AB [as shown in Fig. 4.6]. To remove the parallax, the observer moves the instrument sideways till the two images are in the same vertical line, as shown in Fig. 4.6. Now the point P is transferred to the ground.

Thus use of line ranger proves to be advantageous from the point of view of requirement of only one person to do the ranging. Line ranger can also be used for setting out right angle.

(b) Indirect Ranging or Reciprocal Ranging:

This process of ranging is adopted when both the ends of survey line are not visible either due to high intervening ground or due to long distance between them. In such a case, ranging is done indirectly. Two intermediate points M_1 and N_1 are selected approximately in line such that from M_1, both N_1 and B are visible and from N_1 both M_1 and A are visible.

Two persons stand at M_1 and N_1 with ranging rods. Person at M_1 directs person at N_1 to move to N_2 in line with M_1 B. Then person at N_2 directs person at M_2 to move to a new position M_2 in line with N_2 A. Thus, the two persons continue to range each other alternately till both of them at M and N are on line AB. From M and N, other points can be established by direct ranging.

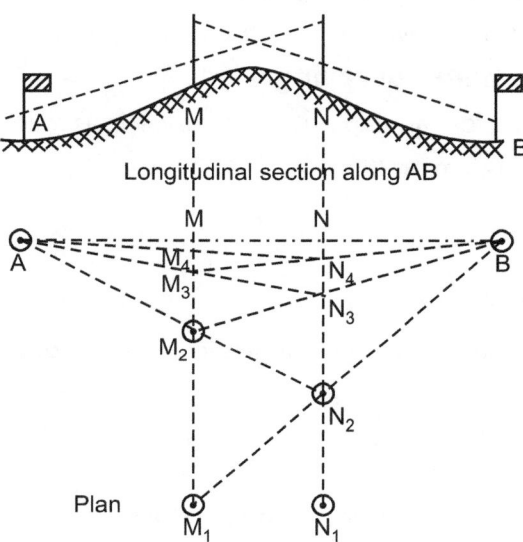

Fig. 4.7: Reciprocal ranging

4.3 SURVEY LINES

The survey lines joining the main survey stations are called **Main Survey Lines** or **Chain lines**. The longest of main survey lines is called the **'Base Line'**.

Base Line: It should run roughly through the middle of the area to be surveyed. It should be laid on a fairly level ground. The framework of survey is built on the base line. It fixes up the directions of all the survey lines. It should be measured very accurately.

Tie Line: A line which joins the tie or subsidiary stations on main line is known as **Tie line**. Tie lines are run to locate the interior details such as buildings, fences, hedges, etc., when they are distant from the main survey lines. A framework may have one or more tie lines, depending on the field requirements.

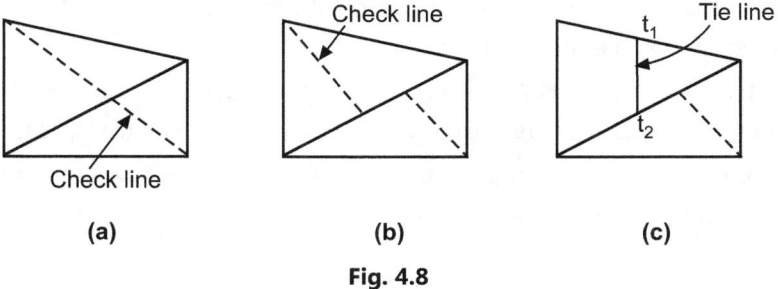

Fig. 4.8

Check Line: Apart from subsidiary lines, other types of lines are run in the field to check the accuracy of the work. Such lines which are laid in the field to check the accuracy of the framework are known as **check lines** or **proof lines**. The length of check line measured in the field should agree with its length on the plan. A check line may join the apex of triangle to any point on the opposite side or join two points on two sides of a triangle. Each triangle must have a check line. Fig. 4.8 shows various arrangements of check lines for the framework.

4.3.1 Equipment for Chain Surveying

The equipment required for carrying out chain survey is as follows:

1. One chain or tape (20 m or 30 m.)
2. Ten arrows.
3. Metallic tape.
4. Ranging rods and offset rod.
5. Instruments for setting out right angles-cross staff, optical square, Indian optical square.
6. Plumb bob.
7. Pegs, hammer, axe, etc.
8. Survey field book, pencil, eraser, set square, chalks, etc.

4.3.2 Steps in Chain Surveying

As has been explained earlier, chain surveying is carried out by the following principle of working from whole to the part. The chain surveying is conducted in the following steps:

1. Reconnaissance.
2. Marking the stations.
3. Preparing location sketches.
4. Running the survey lines.

1. Reconnaissance:

It is the preliminary inspection of the area to be surveyed. In reconnaissance, the area that is to be surveyed, is observed by walking to every nook and corner. The main features and the boundaries of the area are observed from the point of view of choosing the best locations of survey stations and thus fixing the positions of survey lines. The survey stations selected should be intervisible among each other.

An index sketch or key plan is prepared, showing the plan of ground, boundaries of the land and prominent features such as buildings, roads, nallas, poles, trees, etc.

A thoughtfully carried out reconnaissance gives the surveyor a fair idea of the shape and extent of the area, difficulties in the work and also the time required for the completion of survey.

2. Marking the Stations :

The positions of stations determined in reconnaissance, are marked on the ground in such a way that these can be readily located if required in future. The survey stations can be marked by adopting the following methods:

(a) By driving a wooden peg in the ground with 8 small projection of 2.5 cm to 4 cm above ground.
(b) By fixing a ranging rod temporarily.
(c) In case of hard surfaces such as roads, pavement or rocks, by using nails or spikes or by cutting a cross on the surface.
(d) For permanent marking, a stone can be embedded in the ground and a cross-mark made on its top.

3. Preparation of Location Sketches (Reference sketch):

The location sketch of a station indicates the position of the station with reference to two or three permanent and prominent features in the vicinity of the station. These features may be a building corner, tree, electric pole, etc. The location sketches of the stations are necessary to retrace the positions of stations if required in future.

The location sketch is drawn, facing the North at every station. North-line has to be shown on the location sketch as shown in Fig. 4.9.

4. Running the Survey Lines:

Chaining operation is started from the base line and carried through all the lines of the framework. The work consists of:

(i) Laying the chain line/tape line.
(ii) Locating the adjacent details along the chain line by means of offsets.

The record of chaining and offsetting is made in the field-book.

The details of chain lines in chain surveying are shown in Fig. 4.9.

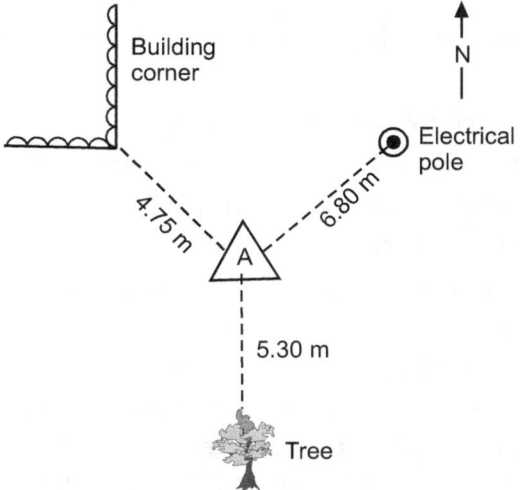

Fig. 4.9 : Typical location sketch of station A

4.3.3 Offsets

For locating the details on ground, with reference to survey lines, it is necessary to measure lateral distance of the features or ground points from survey lines. Such lateral distances which are measured from the chain line to the objects are called **offsets**.

The offsets can be measured either to the right or left of chain line.

Thus, there are two **types** of offsets:

(1) Perpendicular offsets, and (2) Oblique offsets.

Perpendicular offsets are the lateral distances taken at right angles (90°) to the chain line. These are also known as offsets.

Lateral distances measured at any angle other than 90° to the chain line are called oblique offsets.

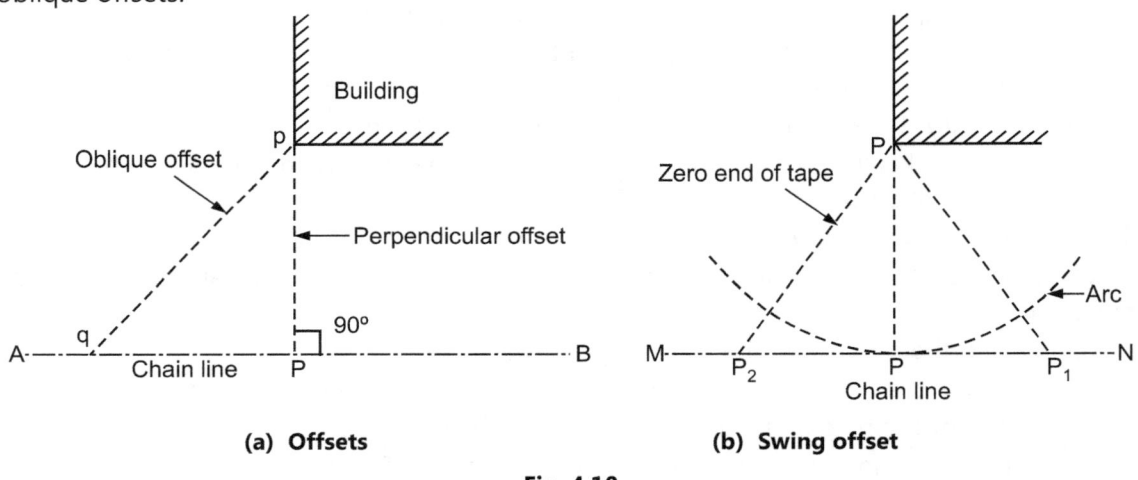

(a) Offsets   (b) Swing offset

Fig. 4.10

Generally, metallic tape is used for measuring offset distance. For greater accuracy, steel tape is also used.

Every offset is characterised by two measurements:

1. Chainage of chain/tape line at which the offset is taken (Ap), and
2. Length of the offset (Pp), as shown in Fig. 4.9 (a).

4.3.3.1 Offset Measurements-Types

(i) Short and Long Offsets: Offsets upto a distance of 15 m are called short offsets and those longer than 15 m are called long offsets.

(ii) Swing offset: A swing offset is the one which is obtained by swinging the tape from outside point along a chain line. Short offset can be set out and measured by swinging the tape along the chain line. The position of the offset on chain line MN is located by swinging the tape from P and the point where the arc is tangential to the chain line, is the required foot of offset. In the figure, Pp is the swing offset.

4.4 EQUIPMENTS

1. Pegs:

Wooden pegs are used to mark the positions of the stations. They are made of stout timber, generally 2.5 cm or 3 cm square and 15 cm long, tapered at the end. They are driven in the ground with a hammer and kept about 4 cm projecting above the ground.

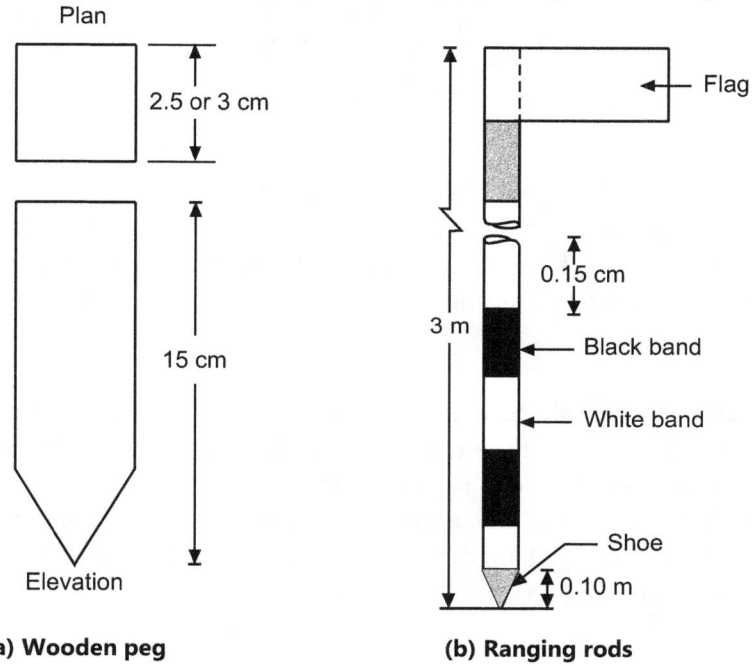

(a) Wooden peg   (b) Ranging rods

Fig. 4.11

2. Ranging Rods:

These are generally 2 to 3 m in length and are painted with alternate bands of black and white or red and white, 3 m length being more common. They are octagonal or circular in cross section with an iron shoe provided at lower end. The pointed shoe enables the rod to be planted in ground firmly. They may be used with flag on top. They may be made of timber or hollow steel pipe.

3. Line Ranger:

It is an optical instrument to obtain an intermediate point on a given line.

4. Open Cross Staff:

It is the simplest instrument used for setting out right angles. It consists of a head in the form of wooden block or metallic frame with two pairs of vertical slits and is mounted on a pole.

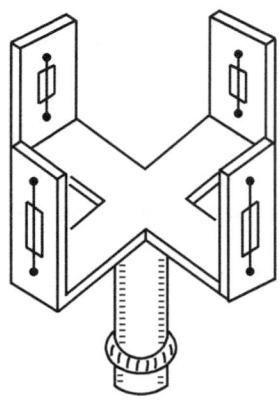

Fig. 4.12: Open cross staff

It is provided with two pairs of vertical slits. Each pair of slits forms a line of sight. Thus two lines of sight at right angles to each other are formed. The frame or head is mounted on a pole. [Fig. 4.12]. The height of the open cross staff can be adjusted to suit the observer's eye level.

Procedure:

(i) **To set out a right angle to a chain/tape line:** For this, the open cross staff is held at the required chainage say M' on the chain line PQ. The instrument is turned till one of the lines of sight passes through the ranging rod at the other end of the line i.e. Q. The line of sight through the other pair of slits will be a line at right angles to the survey line PQ. A ranging rod is erected at say M in the direction of other line of sight. Thus MM' is a perpendicular to the chain line at M'. See. Fig. 4.13 (a).

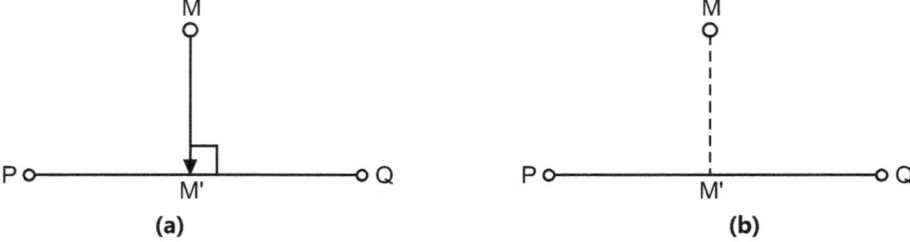

Fig. 4.13

(ii) **To find the foot of perpendicular on the chain/tape line:** In case a perpendicular offset is to be laid from a given object say M to the chain line PQ, then open cross staff is held vertically on the chain line at a point where the foot of perpendicular offset is likely to occur. It is then turned so that one line of sight passes through the ranging rod, fixed at the end of survey line i.e. Q. Looking through the other pair of slits, it is seen if the point from which the offset is to be laid is bisected. If not, the cross staff is moved forward or backward on the chain line, till the line of sight also passes through the point M'. M' is the foot of perpendicular offset. See Fig. 4.13 (b). Thus for laying perpendicular offset by open cross staff, two persons are required simultaneously at the instrument; which is rather a disadvantage.

5. Optical Square

Optical square is an instrument based on the principles of optics. The perpendicular offsets can be set to the chain line with this instrument. It consists of a circular box about 50 mm in diameter and 12.5 mm in depth, with a sight or eye hole (E), a horizon sight [window H] and an index sight [window I]. The box is provided with a small rod at the bottom. Inside the circular box as shown in Fig. 4.14, aa' is horizon mirror, which is half silvered and half unsilvered, bb' is the index mirror fixed opposite to index sight and makes an angle of 45° with mirror aa'.

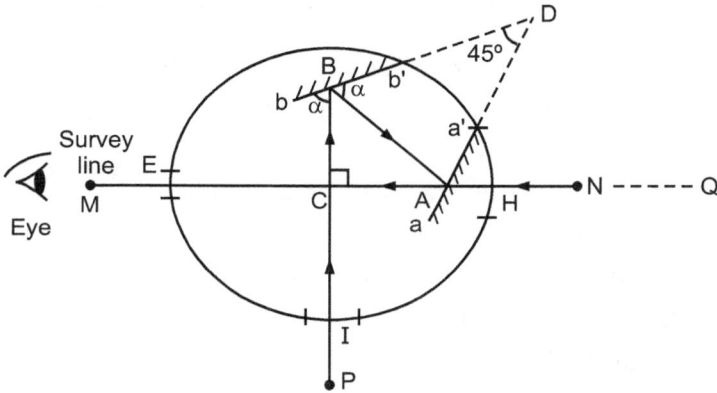

Fig. 4.14: Optical square

4.5 INTRODUCTION TO COMPASS

Surveying is concerned with the relative positions of points on, above or below the surface of the earth. It is therefore becomes necessary to start from known points on a line. If the location of two points is known, a third point may be located by measuring the distances from the already located points or direction. **The direction of survey line is measured with the help of an instrument known as 'compass'.**

Angular measurements means measurements of angles made either directly or indirectly by using some instruments. If the area to be surveyed is large, measuring the length of survey lines becomes tedious and inconvenient. Hence, it becomes necessary to fix directions of survey lines. Similarly, if chaining cannot be done due to certain obstructions, then fixing directions of survey lines by some angle measuring instruments becomes essential. These instruments are prismatic compass, theodolite etc. The survey work carried out using compass is called compass survey.

4.6 DEFINITIONS

Meridian: The reference line with respect to which horizontal angle of survey line is measured is known as 'meridian'.

The meridians are classified as follows:
(1) True meridian
(2) Magnetic meridian
(3) Grid meridian
(4) Arbitary meridian

Bearing: It is the horizontal angle between the reference meridian and the survey line measured in clockwise or anticlockwise direction. The bearing of a line is obtained with the aid of whole circle bearing (azimuth), reduced bearing and grid bearing (in geodetic survey).

True Meridian: The line or plane passing through the geographical north pole, geographical south pole and any point on the surface of the earth is known as the 'true meridian' or 'geographical meridian'. The true meridian at a station is constant. The true meridians passing through different points on the earth's surface are not parallel, but converge towards the poles (Fig. 4.15). For surveys in small areas, the true meridians passing through different polls are assumed parallel.

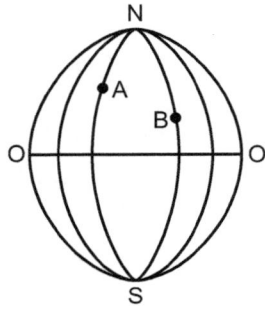

Fig. 4.15: True meridian

True Bearing: The horizontal angle measured between the true meridian and the survey line is called 'true bearing' of the line. It is also known as 'azimuth' (Fig. 4.16).

Magnetic Meridian: It is the direction indicated by a freely suspended and balanced magnetic needle unaffected by local attractive forces. The location of the magnetic poles is constantly changing, hence the direction of magnetic meridian also changes. Magnetic meridian is employed as a line of reference for rough surveys.

Magnetic Bearing: The angle between the magnetic meridian and a line is known as the 'magnetic bearing' (Fig. 4.16).

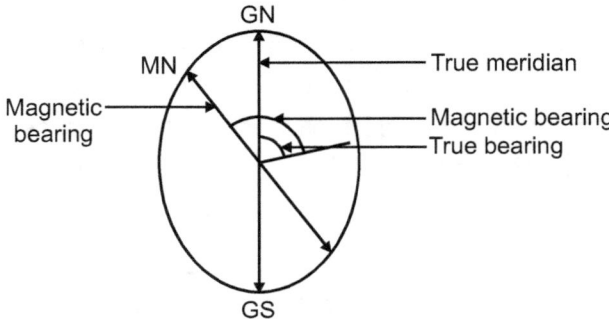

Fig. 4.16: True bearing and magnetic bearing

Grid Meridian: Sometimes, for preparing a map, state agencies assume several lines parallel to the true meridian for a particular zone. These lines are termed as 'grid lines' and the central line the 'grid meridian'.

Grid Bearing: The horizontal angle which a line makes with the grid meridian is called 'grid bearing'.

Arbitrary meridian: It is any convenient direction, usually from a survey station to some well-defined permanent object. This is used for small area survey or to determine the relative directions of small traverse.

Arbitrary bearing: The horizontal angle measured with respect to the arbitrary meridian is called 'arbitrary bearing'.

4.7 PRISMATIC COMPASS

Parts of Prismatic Compass: Fig. 4.17 (a) shows the parts of prismatic compass and Fig. 4.17 (b) shows the pictorial view of prismatic compass.

(i) It consists of a circular metal brass box about 100 mm in diameter with a hard steel pivot at the centre.

(ii) A magnetic needle is freely suspended on the pivot and carries a graduated aluminium ring. The graduations are marked from 0° to 360° in clockwise direction. Each degree is subdivided into two parts so that the minimum reading of the scale is 30'. The zero is placed at the south end and 180° at the North end and the graduations are marked in the inverted fashion. The reason for inverted graduations is that when the reading is taken through the reflecting prism, the graduations will be seen erect.

(iii) A reflecting prism carries a sighting slit and the object vane has a vertical horse hair for bisection of the object. The object vane and the reflecting prism are placed diametrically opposite to each other. The prism and the object vane can be folded so as to lie on the glass cover of compass.

(iv) The glass cover at the top prevents the entry of dust inside the compass.

(v) The object vane carries an adjustable mirror which can be slided on the object vane. The objects too high or too low can be sighted by reflection by giving suitable inclination to this mirror.

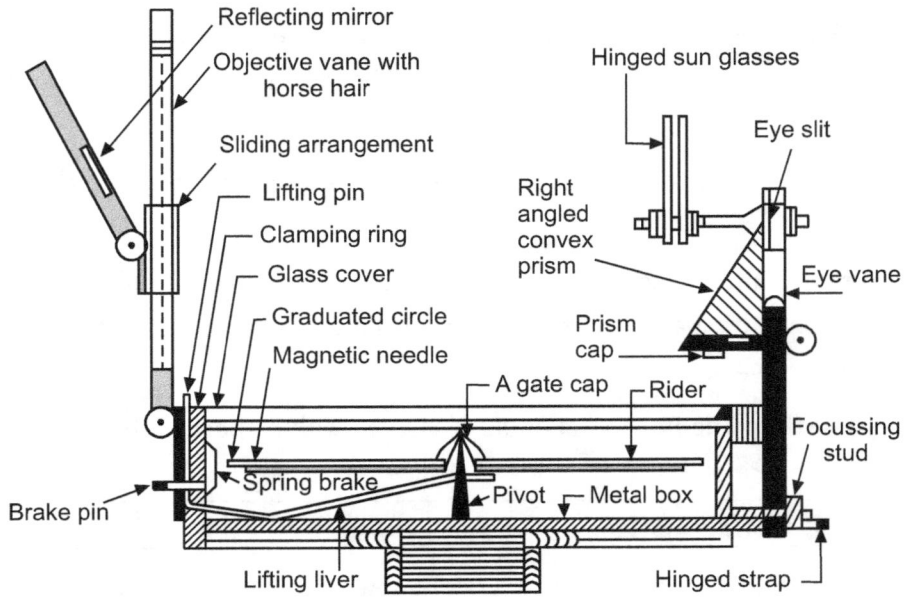

(a) Sectional view of prismatic compass

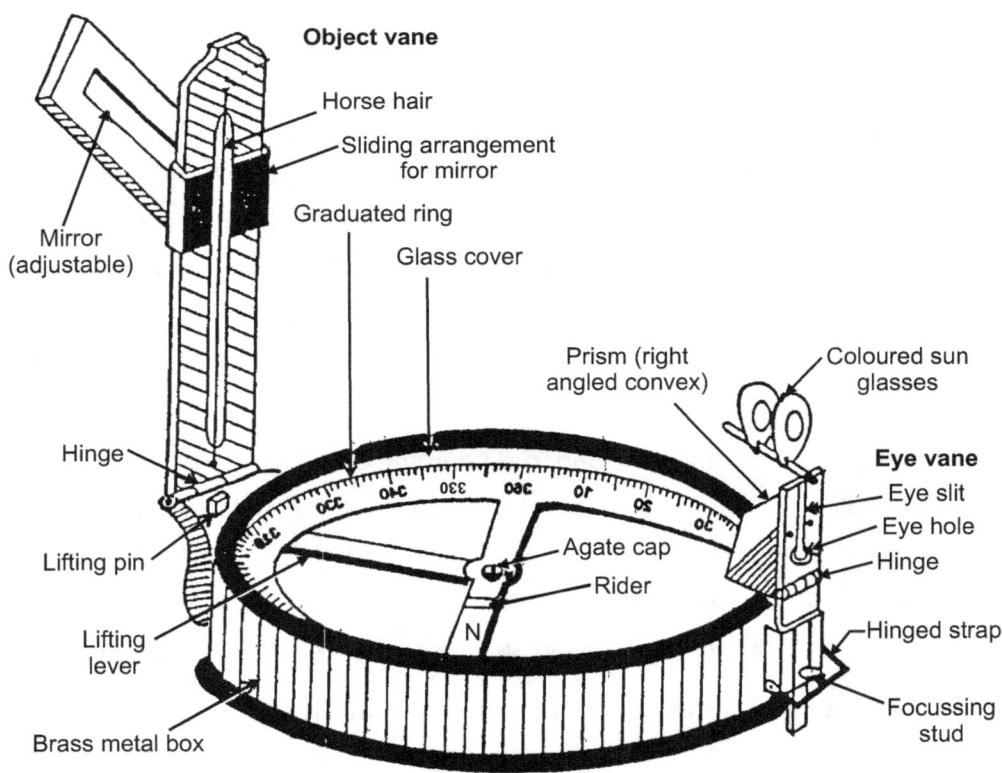

(b) Pictorial view of prismatic compass

Fig. 4.17

(vi) Hinged sun glasses usually red and blue are attached to the frame of prism. These coloured glasses can be interposed into the line of sight when brighter objects are to be sighted.

(vii) A brake pin is provided on the side of compass box to damp the oscillations of the graduated circle with needle.

(viii) When the compass is not in use, the object vane when folded presses against the lifting pin which lifts the needle from the pivot and holds it against the lid. Thus undue wear of the pivot point is prevented.

4.8 TAKING OBSERVATIONS OR MEASURING BEARINGS WITH PRISMATIC COMPASS

The prismatic compass is fixed to the top of a tripod by a ball and socket arrangement. The compass is required to be centred over a station point before bearings are observed. Hence, certain temporary adjustments are carried out at each station where the compass is set up over a station point.

1. Temporary Adjustments:

(i) Centering: It is the operation in which the compass is to be set exactly over the station peg. This is checked by dropping a small piece of stone or pebble from the underside of the compass. If the stone falls on the top of peg, then centering is correct. Otherwise the legs of the tripod are adjusted in two positions at right angles to each other.

(ii) Levelling: The levelling is checked by keeping a circular pencil on the glass cover of compass. If the pencil does not roll, the compass is in level. Otherwise, it can be done by ball and socket arrangement till the graduated ring moves freely inside the compass box.

2. Observing the bearing of a line:

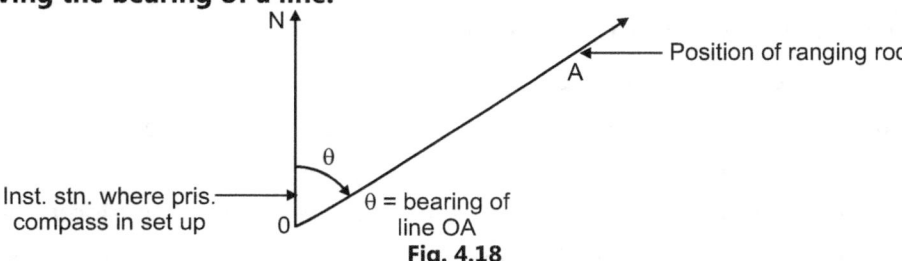

Fig. 4.18

Suppose the bearing of line OA is to be observed. The compass is centred over station O as explained in 1 (i) above and levelling is checked as explained in 1 (ii) above. Let the ranging rod be fixed at 'A'. Turn the compass in the direction of line OA. See through the eye vane and bisect the ranging rod at 'A' by the middle hair of object vane. Let the needle i.e. graduated ring come to rest. The reflecting prism is adjusted to the eyesight of observer by raising or lowering the stud. The reading under the vertical hair through prism is taken which gives the bearing of line OA. The bearings obtained in the prismatic compass are whole circle bearings.

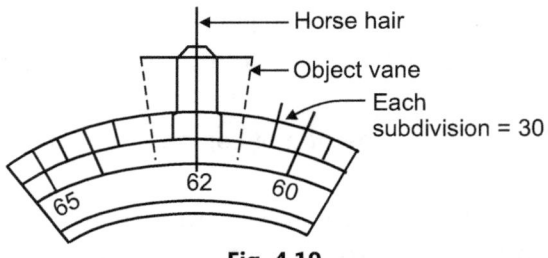

Fig. 4.19

4.9 SURVEYOR'S COMPASS

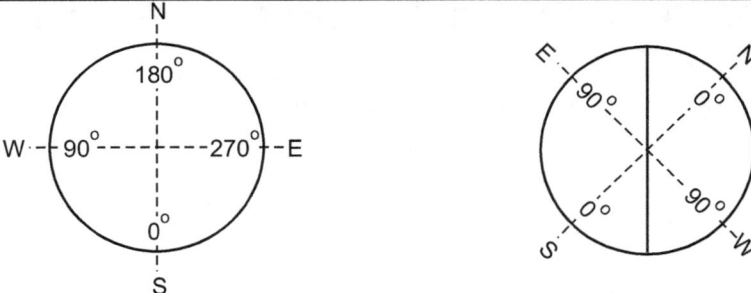

(a) Figure for graduations on prismatic compass

(b) Figure for graduations on surveyor's compass

Fig. 4.20

This is another type of compass in which graduations vary from 0 to 90°. The other peculiarities are as follows:

(i) The graduated card is attached inside the box to the bottom and the card moves with the movement of compass.

(ii) The graduations are marked in erect position.

(iii) The magnetic needle is of edge bar type.

(iv) After the object is bisected, the observer has to go round the box to take readings through the top of compass.

(v) Surveyor's compass cannot be held in hand but is mounted on tripod. The bearings obtained are the reduced bearings.

However, this compass has become obsolete now-a-days.

Reference Meridians:

Earlier, the bearing of a line is defined as the horizontal angle made by a survey line with some reference direction in a clockwise direction. This reference direction is called a Meridian and the meridians are classified as follows.

(i) True Meridian: This is a line obtained by the intersection of a plane passing through a given point and North and South poles of the earth with the surface of the earth. When the reference direction is True Meridian, the horizontal angle made by a survey line with True meridian is called True bearing of a line or azimuth. For a given point on the surface of earth, the direction of True Meridian is always same.

(ii) Magnetic Meridian: A freely suspended and properly balanced magnetic needle will always point to the Magnetic North or Magnetic Meridian. The angle made by a survey line with the magnetic North, in the clockwise direction is called Magnetic bearing of a line.

(iii) Arbitrary Meridian: When it is not possible to measure bearings of lines either with respect to True North or Magnetic North, some convenient line is chosen as Arbitrary Reference direction and angle made by lines with this Arbitrary Meridian is termed as an arbitrary bearing of the line. This Arbitrary Meridian can be chosen as a line and flag pole etc. joining the survey station with some well defined object on the ground such as an electric pole.

4.10 DESIGNATION OF BEARINGS

The bearings of survey lines are expressed in the following systems:

(i) Whole Circle Bearing System: When the bearing of a line measured in clockwise direction from North varies from 0° to 360°, it is termed as whole circle bearing. The bearings obtained using prismatic compass are the whole circle bearings.

(ii) The Reduced Bearing or Quadrantal Bearing System: The space is divided into four quadrants and the bearings of survey lines are always measured with respect to North and South line either in clockwise or anticlockwise direction towards East or West. In the Fig. 4.21, α_1 is the reduced bearing of line OA and it is written as N α_1^0 E. It is essential to write the directions before and after the value of angle. This helps to identify the quadrant in which the line lies. The maximum value of bearing in the quadrantal system is 90°. It is also called as Reduced bearing of a line. The bearings obtained using Surveyor's compass are Reduced Bearings.

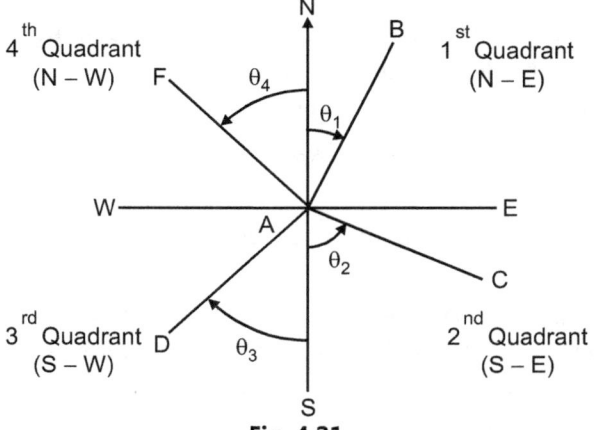

Fig. 4.21

4.11 CONVERSION OF BEARINGS FROM ONE SYSTEM TO OTHER

The whole circle bearings can be converted to Quadrantal bearings and quadrantal bearings can be converted to whole circle bearings by referring to the following Table 4.1.

Table 4.1: Conversion from W.C.B. to R.B.

W.C.B. lying between	Quadrant in which line lies	Rule for conversion to Reduced Bearing	Quadrant
(1) 0° to 90°	I	R.B. = W.C.B.	N – E
(2) 90° to 180°	II	R.B. = 180° – W.C.B.	S – E
(3) 180° to 270°	III	R.B. = W.C.B. – 180°	S – W
(4) 270° to 360°	IV	R.B. = 360° – W.C.B.	N – W

4.11.1 Fore Bearings and Back Bearings

The bearing of a survey line observed in the direction of progress of survey is called fore bearing of the line while the bearing of the same line observed from the other end or observed in the reverse direction is called back bearing of the same line.

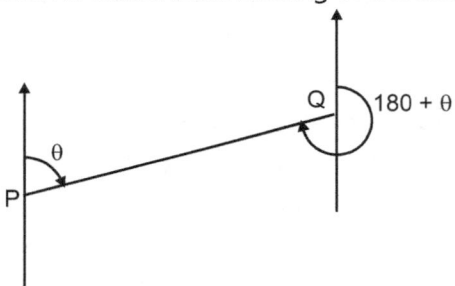

Fig. 4.22

In the Fig. 4.22, $\theta°$ is the forebearing of line PQ observed from P to Q and if the prismatic compass is shifted from P to Q and the bearing of the same line is observed from Q to P i.e. in the reverse direction then $(180° + \theta°)$ will be the back bearing of the line PQ. Thus, it can be seen that for the same line, the difference between fore bearing and back bearing of the same line is always 180° or it can be stated as under.

Back Bearing of a line = Fore Bearing ± 180°

The negative sign is to be used when the fore bearing exceeds 180°. The above rule is true for whole circle system.

In the quadrantal system, the fore and back bearings of a line are numerically same but with opposite directional signs.

In the Fig. 4.23, S $\theta°$ E is the fore bearing of line OM and the back bearing of OM is N $\theta°$ W. Similarly, the fore bearings of lines lying in the other quadrants can be converted to back bearings with change of directional signs knowing that reference meridian in case of quadrantal bearings is North-South line.

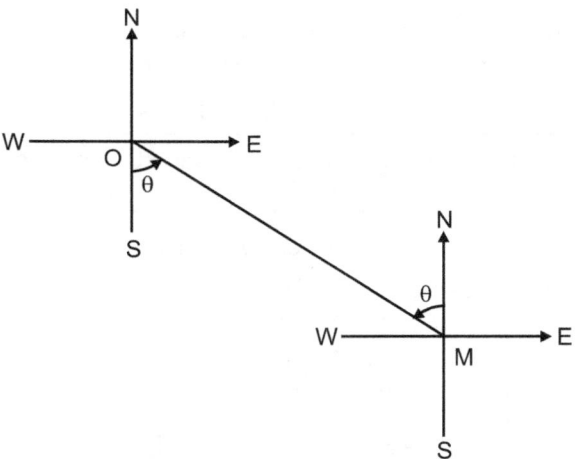

Fig. 4.23: F.B. of OM and B.B. of OM in quadrantal system

SOLVED EXAMPLES

Example 4.1: Convert the following whole circle bearings to reduced bearings.

(i) 72° 30' (ii) 128° (iii) 248° 30' (iv) 325° 15'

Solution: It is better to draw figures for such problems and knowing the quadrant in which the line lies, the conversion to quadrantal system will be easier.

(i) In the first quadrant, Whole circle Bearing = Reduced Bearing

∴ Reduced Bearing = N 72° 30' E as shown in Fig. 4.24.

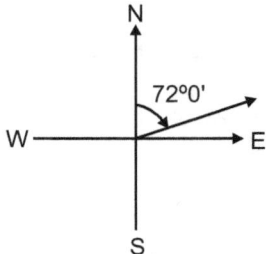

Fig. 4.24

(ii) In the second quadrant (making use of Table 4.1)

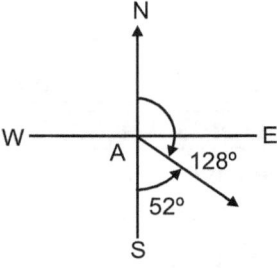

Fig. 4.25

Reduced Bearing = 180° – 128° = S 52° E as shown in Fig. 4.25.
(iii)   Reduced Bearing = (248° 30') – (180°) = S 68 30' W
(iv)   Reduced Bearing = (360°) – (325° 15') = N 34° 45' W

Example 4.2: Convert the following reduced bearings to whole circle bearings.
(i) N 23° W (ii) S 37° 30' E (iii) S 52° W (iv) N 44° 30' E

Solution: (i)   N 23° W = W.C. Bearing 360° – 23°
                    W.C. Bearing = 337°

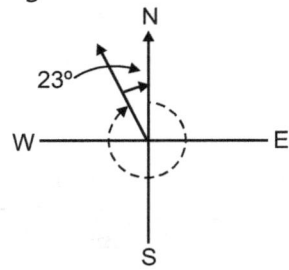

Fig. 4.26

(ii) S 37° 30' E,   W.C. Bearing = 180° – 37° 30' = 142° 30'
(iii) S 52° W

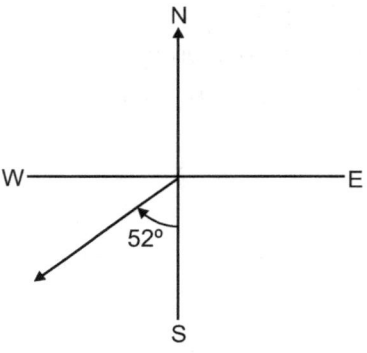

Fig. 4.27

Whole Circle Bearing = 180° + 52° = 232°

This will be clear from Fig. 4.41.

(iv) N 44° 30' E

Whole Circle Bearing = 44° 30' (being the first quadrant)

4.12 CALCULATION OF INCLUDED ANGLES FROM BEARINGS

I. The included angle between two consecutive lines can be calculated from their observed bearings. It can be interior or exterior angle.

(a) When the whole circle bearings of two lines measured from their point of intersection are known:

The included angle = Difference between the W.C. bearing of two lines provided the difference is less than 180°.

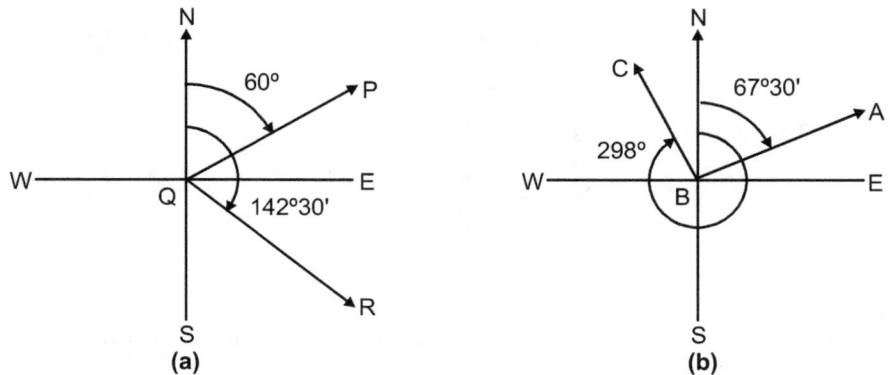

Fig. 4.28

To illustrate the above rule, let the lines PQ and QR meet at Q as shown in Fig. 4.28 (a).

The included ∠ PQR = (142° 30') − (60°) = 82° 30'

i.e.   F.B. of QR − F.B. of QP = ∠ PQR

(ii) If the difference exceeds 180°, it is the exterior angle between the two lines.

The included angle = 360° − (Difference of the W.C. bearings between the two lines).

In the Fig. 4.28 (b), F.B. of BC is 298° and F.B. of BA = 67° 30'.

∠ ABC = (298°) − (67° 30') = 230° 30'

Since the difference between the bearings is greater than 180°, it is the exterior angle.

∴   Included ∠ CBA = 360° − (230° 30') = 129° 30'

(b) When the W.C. bearings of two lines are given:

The rule given in (a) can be applied only when the bearings are expressed as if measured from the point where the lines meet.

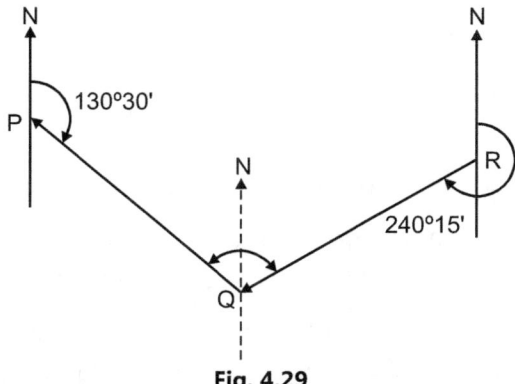

Fig. 4.29

The following example illustrates the calculation of included angle when the fore bearings of two lines are given.

Given: F.B. of PQ is 130° 30' and F.B. of RQ is 240° 15' as shown in Fig. 4.29. Looking at the Fig. 4.29.

To calculate ∠ PQR = F.B. of QR − F.B. of QP

Now F.B. of QP = B.B. of PQ = 130° 30' + 180° = 310° 30'

F.B. of QR = B.B. of RQ = (240° 15') − (180°) = 60° 15'

∴ ∠ PQR = (60° 15') − (310° 30') = − 250° 15'

Since the difference between the fore bearings of QP and QR exceeds 180° and is negative, it is the exterior angle PQR.

Included ∠ PQR = (360°) − (250° 15')

= 109° 45'

(ii) When the reduced bearings of the lines are given, the included angles between the lines can be calculated as described below. The calculation work is simplified by showing the two lines in proper quadrant and calling the upper half of quadrant as North Meridian and the lower half of the quadrant of South Meridian.

(a) If the lines are lying on the same side of the same meridian:

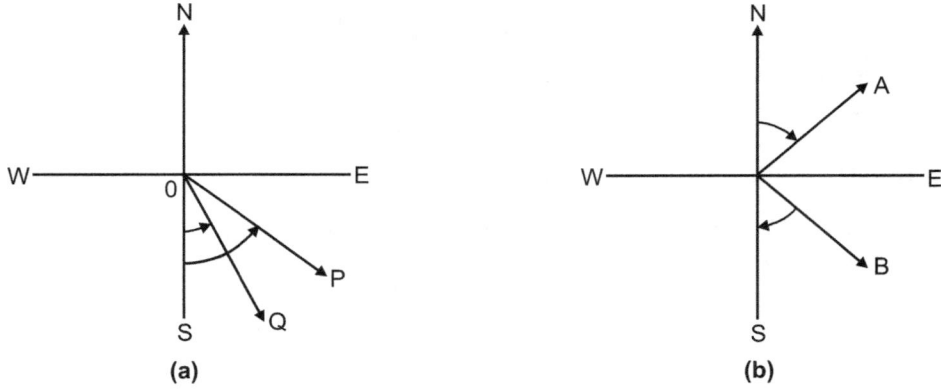

Fig. 4.30

In the Fig. 4.30 (a), ∠ POQ = Difference of Reduced bearings between OP and OQ.

(b) If the lines lie on the same side of different meridian as shown in the Fig. 4.30 (b), the included ∠ POQ = 180° − (Sum of the reduced bearings of OP and OQ).

(c) If the lines lie on the different sides of the different meridians as shown in Fig. 4.31 (a), included ∠ POQ = 180° − (Difference of the reduced bearings of OQ and OP).

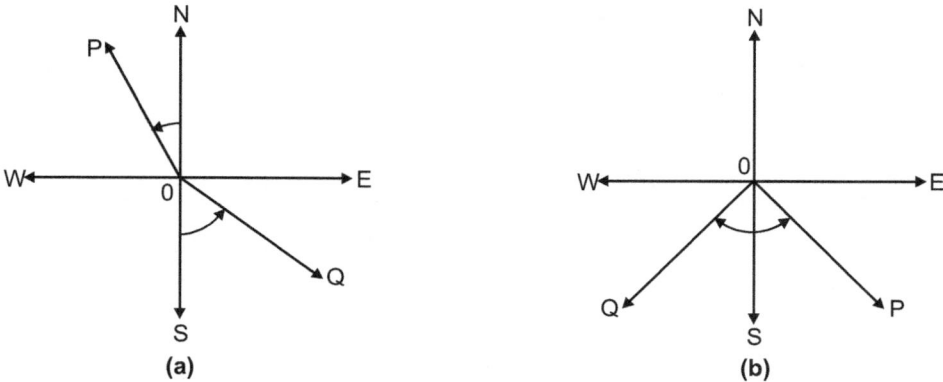

Fig. 4.31

(d) If the lines are on the opposite sides of the same meridian as shown in Fig. 4.31 (b), included ∠ POQ = Sum of the reduced bearings of OP and OQ.

4.13 CALCULATION OF BEARINGS FROM ANGLES

The bearings of lines can be calculated from the observed bearing of any one line and the included angle measured clockwise between the different lines.

Thus bearing of a line = Given bearing + Included angle

In the Fig. 4.32 (a), let F.B. of OP be 65° 30'

and let ∠ POQ be 77° 45'

Fore bearing of OQ = 65° 30' + 77° 45' = 143° 15'

(i.e. in the whole circle bearing system)

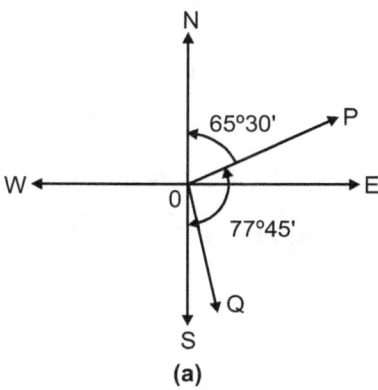

Fig. 4.32

In the Fig. 4.33 (b), let F.B. of OP be 330° 30' and let ∠ POQ = 135° 0'

∴ Fore bearings of OQ = (330° 30') + (135°) = (465° 30') − 360°

F.B. of OQ = 105° 30' (i.e. W.C.B. of OQ)

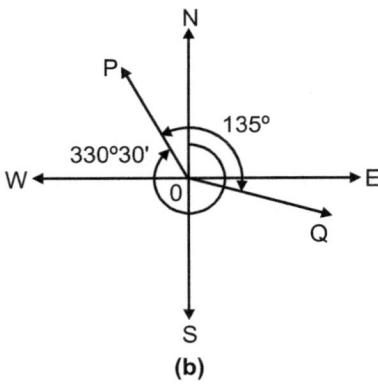

(b)

Fig. 4.33

In the Fig. 4.34.

If   F.B. of OP = N 35° E and ∠ POQ = 89° 30'

From the figure,

Fore bearing of OQ = 35° + 89° 30' = 124° 30' in the WCB system

F.B. of OQ = 180° – 124° 30' = S 55° 30' E   (i.e. in the Quadrantal system)

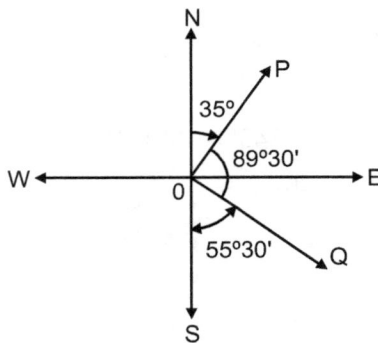

Fig. 4.34

SOLVED EXAMPLES

Example 4.3: The F.B. of AB = 106° and F.B. of BC = 296° 30'. Calculate the ∠ ABC.

Solution: From the Fig. 4.35,

$$\angle ABC = \text{F.B. of B.C.} - \text{B.B. of AB}$$
$$= 296° 30' - (106° + 180°)$$
$$= 296° 30' - 286° 0'$$
$$\angle ABC = 10° 30'$$

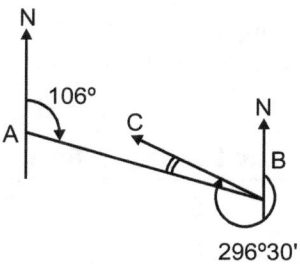

Fig. 4.35

Example 4.4: Find the included angles between the lines OP and OQ whose reduced bearings are as given below:

(i)   N 21° 30' E and S 65° W

(ii) N 32° W and S 51° 45' W

Solution: (i) Referring to Fig. 4.36,

$$\angle QOP = 180° - (65° - 21° 30') = 180° - (43° 30') = 136° 30'$$

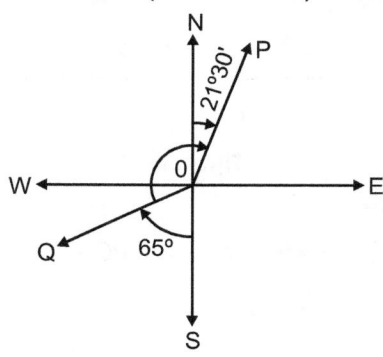

Fig. 4.36

(ii) From the Fig. 4.37

$$\angle QOP = 180° - (32° + 51° 45') = 180° - (83° 45')$$
$$\angle QOP = 96° 15'$$

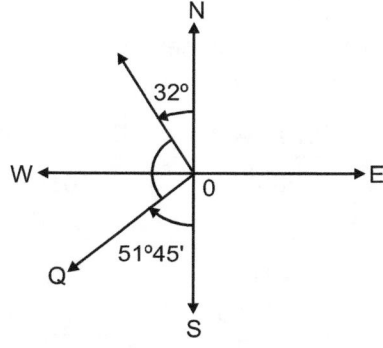

Fig. 4.37

Example 4.5: The following bearings were observed in running a closed traverse PQR in clockwise direction. Calculate the included angles to traverse.

Line	Observed	
	Fore bearing	Back bearing
PQ	115°	295°
QR	260°	80°
RP	35°	215°

Solution: Draw the sketch of closed traverse as shown in Fig. 4.51. It shows the closed traverse PQR with the marking of fore bearings as observed in the field.

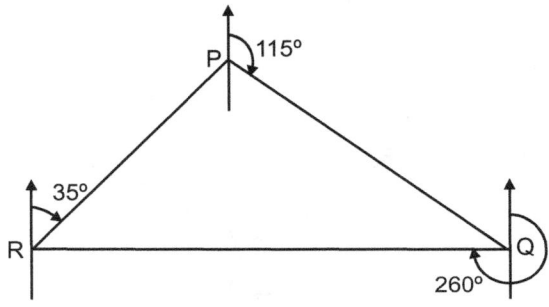

Fig. 4.38

Calculation of included angles:

$\angle Q$ = Back bearing of PQ − Fore bearing of QR
= 295° − 260° = 35°

$\angle R$ = B.B. of QR − F.B. of RP
= 80° − 35° = 45°

$\angle P$ = B.B. of RP − F.B. of PQ
= 215° − 115° = 100°

Summation of Internal Angles = $\angle Q + \angle R + \angle P$ = 35° + 45° + 100° = 180°

Example 4.6: Following bearings were observed while running a closed traverse in the clockwise direction.

Line	Fore bearing	Back bearing
AB	285° 30'	105° 30'
BC	32° 0'	212° 0'
CD	151° 0'	331° 0'
DA	198° 0'	18° 0'

Calculate the included angles at different stations and check their sum.

Solution: Draw the sketch of the traverse ABCD from the given data. Also check whether the back bearings and fore bearings differ by 180° (see Fig. 4.39).

$$\angle A = \text{B.B. of DA} - \text{F.B. of AB}$$
$$= 18° - 285° \ 30' = -267° \ 30'$$

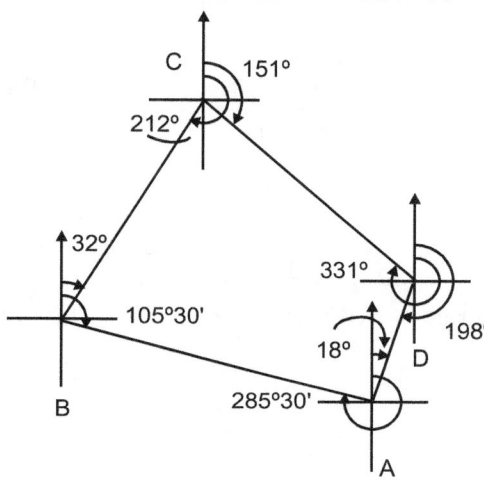

Fig. 4.39

The negative sign shows that it is an exterior angle.

∴ $\angle A = 360° - 267° \ 30' = 92° \ 30'$
$\angle B = \text{B.B. of AB} - \text{F.B. of BC} = 105° \ 30' - 32° \ 0' = 73° \ 30'$
$\angle C = \text{B.B. of BC} - \text{F.B. of CD} = 212° \ 0' - 151° \ 0' = 61° \ 0'$
$\angle D = \text{B.B. of CD} - \text{F.B. of DA} = 331° - 198° = 133°$

Sum of Internal Angles = $92° \ 30' + 73° \ 30' + 61° \ 0' + 133° \ 0' = 360° \ 0'$

Example 4.7: F.B. of line AB was measured to be 30° 15' in a closed traverse ABC which is an anticlockwise equilateral triangle. Assuming no L.A., calculate F.B. and B.B. of all lines. Tabulate your result in usual format.

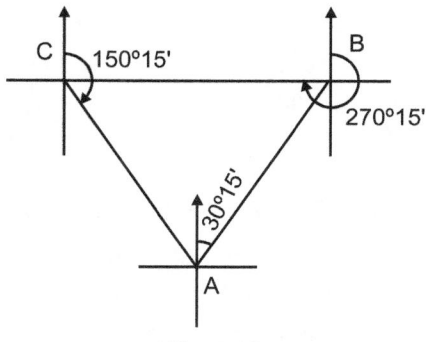

Fig. 4.40

Solution: For an anticlockwise traverse,

         Included angle = F.B. of next angle − B.B. of previous line

From the Fig. 4.53, B.B. of AB = 30° 15' + 180° 0' = 210° 15'.

∴ F.B. of BC = 270° 15'

B.B. of BC = 270° 15' – 180° = 90° 15;

F.B. of CA – 90° 15' = 60° ∴ F.B. of CA = 150° 15'

Results are tabulated as under:

Line	Fore Bearing	Back Bearing
AB	30° 15'	210° 15'
BC	270° 15'	90° 15'
CA	150° 15'	330° 15'

Example 4.8: A square ABCD was surveyed from starting station A, in a counter clockwise direction. The fore bearing of AB was observed as 130° 30'. Find out the bearings of the other sides of traverse.

Solution:

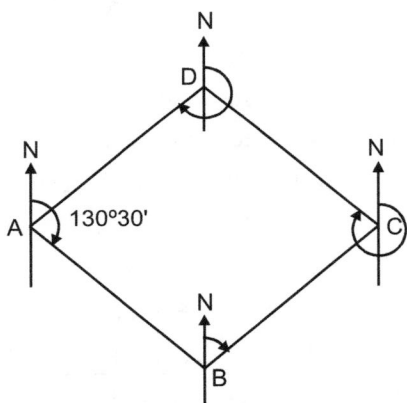

Fig. 4.41

The direction of North will be as shown in the figure since the traverse is run in counter – clockwise direction.

F.B. of AB = 130° 30'
             + 180° 0'
B.B. of A.B. = 310° 30'

From the figure, F.B. of BC = B.B. of AB – Ext. angle at B

F.B. of BC = 310° 30' – 270° = 40° 30'

B.B. of BC = 40° 30' + 180° = 220° 30'

F.B. of CD = B.B. of BC + ∠C = 220° 30' + 90° = 310° 30'

B.B. of CD = 310° 30' – 180° = 130° 30'

F.B. of DA = B.B. of CD + ∠D = 130° 30' + 90° = 220° 30'

As a check,   F.B. of AB = B.B. of DA + ∠A
= (220° 30' − 180°) + 90° = 40° 30' + 90° = 130° 30'

Results are tabulated as under.

Line	Fore bearing	Back bearing
AB	130° 30'	310° 30'
BC	40° 30'	220° 30'
CD	310° 30'	130° 30'
DA	220° 30'	40° 30'

4.14 LEVELLING

Vertical measurements are measurements which are made in the vertical plane and grouped under the term levelling.
- The operation of determining the difference of elevation of points with respect to each other on the surface of the earth is called *levelling*.
- Determination of elevations of points is necessary in selecting alignments of highways, railways, water supply and drainage pipelines and in the construction of engineering structures such as dams, bridges, industrial sheds etc.
- Levelling helps in locating industries or different shops of an automobile on a large piece of land.
- The profile of ground can be plotted in the form of longitudinal and cross-sections from spot level. This data can be used to calculate the magnitude of the cutting, filling of earth work involved in the project.

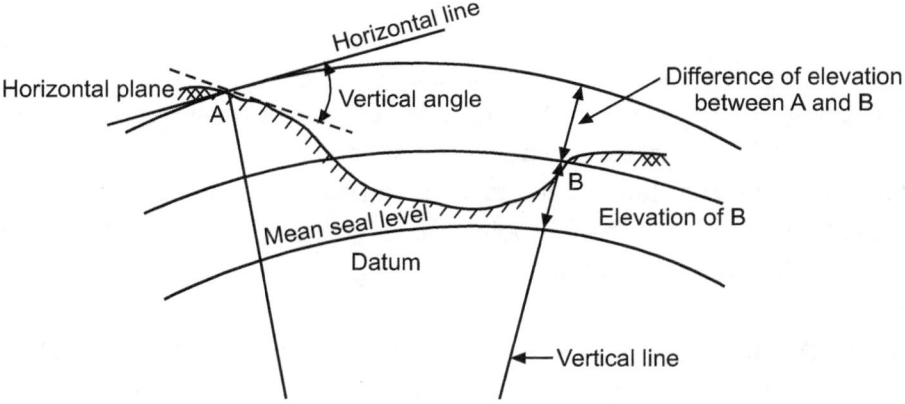

Fig. 4.42 : Levelling terms

Level Surface: A surface parallel to the mean spheroidal surface of the earth is called level surface, e.g. a still lake. It is normal to the plumb line at all points.

Level Line: It is a line lying on a level surface. It is normal to the plumb line at all the points.

Horizontal Plane: It is a plane tangential to the level surface at the point under consideration. It is perpendicular to the plumb line.

Horizontal Line: It is line lying in the horizontal plane. It is a straight line tangential to the level line.

Vertical Line: It is a line from any point on the earth's surface to the centre of the earth. It is commonly considered to be the line defined by a plumb line.

Datum Surface: It is an arbitrarily assumed level surface from which vertical distances are measured. The mean sea level at Karachi is taken as the datum surface for India or datum level from which G.T.S. bench marks are established.

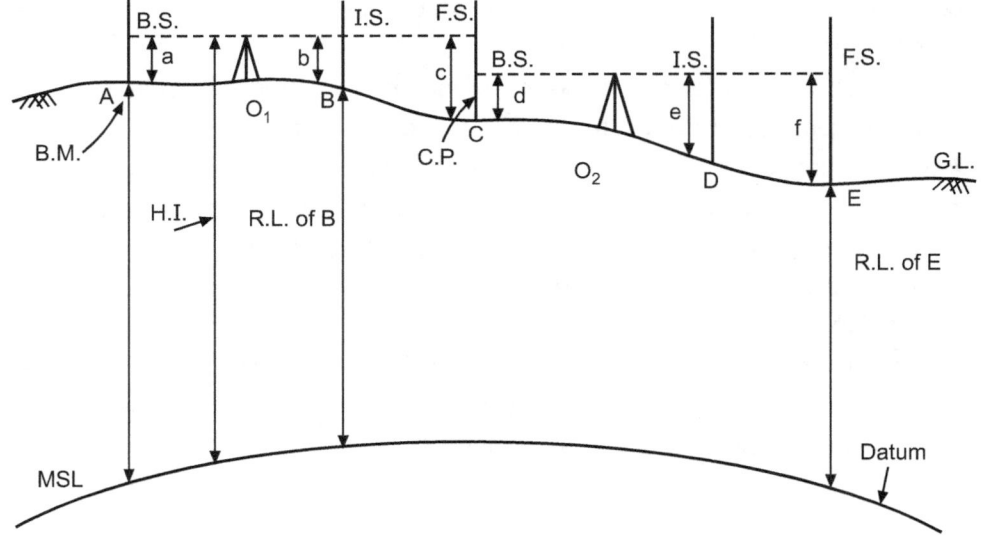

Fig. 4.43

Reduced Level (R.L.): It is the vertical distance of a point measured above or below the datum. It is also called as elevation of a point. It is abbreviated as R.L.

Back Sight (B.S.): It is a staff reading taken on a point of known elevation e.g. sight on a benchmark (station A) or on a change point, i.e. station C. In Fig. 4.43, 'a' and 'd' are back sights. It is also called a **plus** sight since the reading is added to the reduced level of the bench mark.

Fore Sight (F.S.): It is a staff reading taken on a point whose elevation is to be determined e.g. a sight on a change point i.e. station C and E. In Fig. 4.43, 'c' and 'f' are fore sights. It is also called as **minus** sight since this reading is subtracted from the reduced level of collimation plane to get the R.L. of point.

Intermediate Sight (I.S.): It is a staff reading taken on a point of unknown elevation between back sight and fore sight e.g. a sight on station B and D. In Fig. 4.43, 'b' and 'e' are the intermediate sights. It is also called as minus sight since this reading is subtracted from the reduced level of collimation plane to get the R.L. of the point.

Change Point (C.P.) or Turning Point (T.P.): It is a point on which fore sight and back sight readings are taken. Change point indicates the shifting of the level. Any well defined object whose top surface is level such as boundary stone, man hole cover, kilometre stone can be selected as change point. It is also called as Turning point. In Fig. 4.43, station C is the change point.

Height of Instrument (H.I.): It is the elevation of the plane of collimation when the instrument is levelled. It should be noted that the height of an instrument does not mean the height of the centre of the telescope above the ground, where the level is set up.

Bench Mark (B.M.): It is a fixed reference point of known elevation. Levelling work is started with bench mark.

4.14.1 Classification of Levelling

Levelling has been classified into different types, depending on the purpose for which it is carried out. The different types are as follows:

1. Profile Levelling: It is the method of levelling in which the elevations of points are determined along some fixed line at some common interval. Thus, the accurate profile of the ground is obtained along the centre line of proposed railway, highway and sewer. This is also called as *longitudinal sectioning*.

2. Cross-sectioning: This is the process of levelling which is carried out to determine the outline of the ground surface traverse to the alignment of proposed road or railway. Cross-sectioning is usually carried out alongwith the longitudinal sectioning.

3. Check Levelling: This levelling is carried out to check the reduced levels of points which have been already fixed. To check the levelling work on particular day, a line of levels is run returning back to the bench mark with a view to check the work on that day.

4. Reciprocal Levelling: When it is not possible to set up the levelling instrument midway between the two points, the difference in reduced levels between the two points is accurately found out by two sets of observations (reciprocal observations) from the two station points. This method of levelling is called *Reciprocal levelling*.

5. Trigonometric Levelling: In the Trigonometric levelling, the elevations of survey stations are obtained by measuring vertical angles and horizontal distances in the field.

6. Barometric Levelling: This is the method of levelling wherein the elevations of points are obtained with the help of a barometer.

4.14.1.1 Simple Levelling

When it is desired to find the difference in elevation between two points which are visible from the same position of the instrument station, this method is adopted. It is called as simple levelling, as shown in Fig. 4.44.

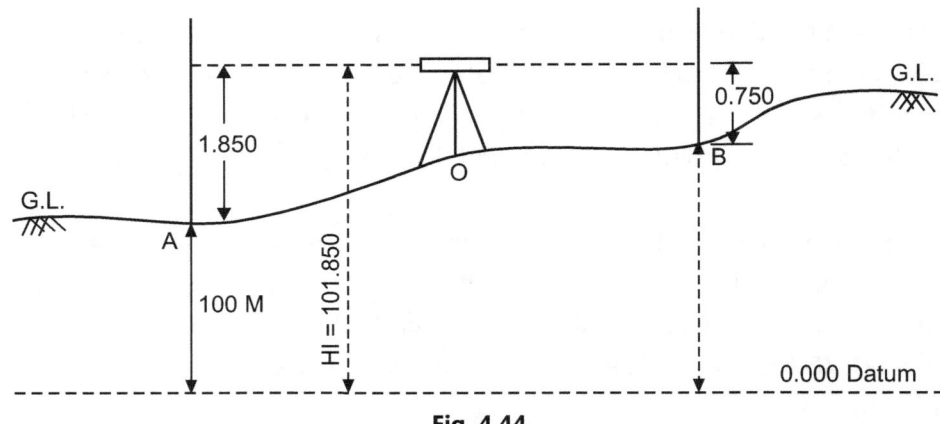

Fig. 4.44

Procedure:
(i) Setup the level approximately mid-way between A and B and carry out all the temporary adjustments.
(ii) Take the readings on the staff held at A and B. The reading on the staff is taken at which the central horizontal hair appears to cut the staff. Let the reading at A be 1.850 and that at B be 0.750.
(iii) Let the reduced level of point A be 100.00 m. Then the reading on 'A' will be back sight reading and the reading on B will be fore sight reading.
∴ Height of Instrument at 'O' will be R.L. of A + B.S. reading
= 100 + 1.850 = 101.850 m
(iv) R.L. of B = Height of Instrument – F.S. reading on B
= 101.850 – 0.750
= 101.100 m

Looking to Fig. 4.44, it will be observed that when point A is lower than point B, the reading on the staff of A is more than the reading at 'B' due to steepness of ground.

4.14.1.2 Differential Levelling

Applied to determine the elevation of point which is some distance apart from B.M. i.e. the unknown elevation of a point cannot be determined in a single setup of instrument. Thus, in this method, instrument gets setup number of times, to observe reading along a route in between observed points. For each setup, staff readings are taken back to a point of known elevation and final sight to the terminal station.

Procedure:
(i) Let us consider a station B whose elevation is to be determined with reference to a B.M. station A, quite a distance apart. In establishing the station B as B.M. differential levelling is carried out starting from A and terminating at B.

(ii) In order to carry out the levelling, first the instrument is setup at some location say O_1, in such a way that back sight reading taken on A can be read clearly as shown in Fig. 4.45.

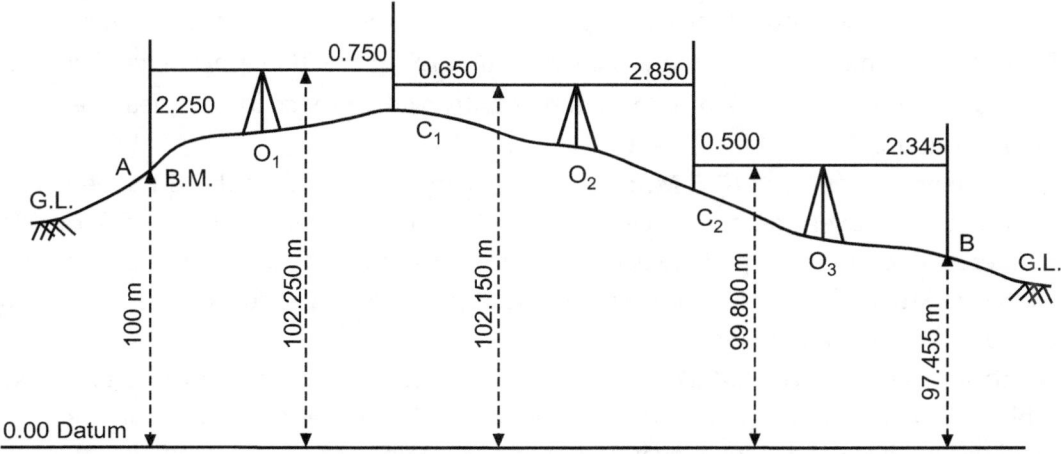

Fig. 4.45: Differential levelling

(iii) The staffman is then directed to move forward towards B and choose a point, say C_1 which is firm and stable. It is preferable that the distance of C_1 from O_1 be the same as that of station A from O_1. After proper selection of the point C_1, staff is held to take the fore sight reading for this instrument setup.

(iv) The instrument is then shifted to some other position in forward direction, say O_2 towards B, and then take the back sight reading C_1. Thus, point C_1 is used as turning point. From O_2 fore sight reading is taken to another well choosen turning point C_2.

(v) Finally, from O_3 back sight is taken on C_2 and last sight is at the terminal point B.

$$\begin{aligned}
\text{H.I. at St. } O_1 &= \text{R.L. of A + B.S. on A} \\
&= 100 + 2.250 = 102.250 \text{ m} \\
\text{R.L. at St. } C_1 &= \text{H.I. at St. } O_1 - \text{F.S. on St. } C_1 \\
&= 102.250 - 0.750 \\
&= 101.500 \text{ m} \\
\text{H.I. at St. } O_2 &= \text{R.L. at St. } C_1 + \text{B.S. on St } C_1 \\
&= 101.500 + 0.650 \\
&= 102.150 \text{ m} \\
\text{R.L. at St. } C_2 &= \text{H.I. at St. } O_2 - \text{F.S. on St. } C_2 \\
&= 102.150 - 2.850 = 99.30 \text{ m} \\
\text{H.I. at St. } O_3 &= \text{R.L. at St. } C_2 + \text{B.S. on St. } C_2 \\
&= 99.300 + 0.500 \\
&= 99.800 \text{ m} \\
\text{R.L. at St. B} &= \text{H.I. at St. } O_3 - \text{F.S. on St. B} \\
&= 99.800 - 2.345 = 97.455 \text{ m}
\end{aligned}$$

4.14.2 Bench Marks

There are four types of bench marks in a levelling work.

1. **Great Trigonometric Survey Bench Mark (G.T.S.B.M.):** These bench marks are established throughout the country with high precision by the Survey of India Department. Their elevations are shown in a G.T.S. map. These are established at an interval of about 100 km all over the country with respect to the mean sea level at Karachi datum.

2. **Permanent Bench Mark (P.B.M.):** These are established between the G.T.S. bench marks by the state government agencies like Public Work Department (P.W.D.) on clearly defined and permanent points such as the top of a parapet wall of a bridge or culvert, kilometre stone, railway platform etc. Its exact location and reduced level is marked on the top of permanent object.

3. **Arbitrary Bench Mark (A.B.M.):** These are reference points whose elevations are arbitrarily assumed for small levelling operations. Their elevations do not refer to any fixed datum. It is used when elevation difference is important rather than elevation.

4. **Temporary Bench Mark (T.B.M.):** These are the reference points on which a day's work is closed and from where levelling is continued the next day. Such a B.M. is carefully established on permanent objects like kilometre stones, parapets etc.

4.14.3 Study and Use of Dumpy Level

Instruments required for levelling are:

1. **A Level:** Level is an instrument used to obtain horizontal line of sight while observing the readings on levelling staff.
2. **A Levelling Staff:** It is used to measure the vertical distances of points below or above the horizontal line of sight.

Types of Levels:

1. Dumpy level
2. Modern tilting level
3. Automatic level.

1. Dumpy Level:

The dumpy level is commonly used for levelling work because it is compact and stable type of instrument. It consists of a telescope mounted upon a level bar which is rigidly fastened to the spindle. Inside the tube of the telescope there are objective and eye piece lens at the either end of the tube. A diaphragm fitted with cross-hairs is present near the eye piece end. A focusing screw is attached with the telescope. A level tube housing a sensitive plate bubble is attached to the telescope and parallel to it. The levelling head consists of tribrach and trivet with three foot screws known as levelling screws in between. The trivet is attached to a tripod stand.

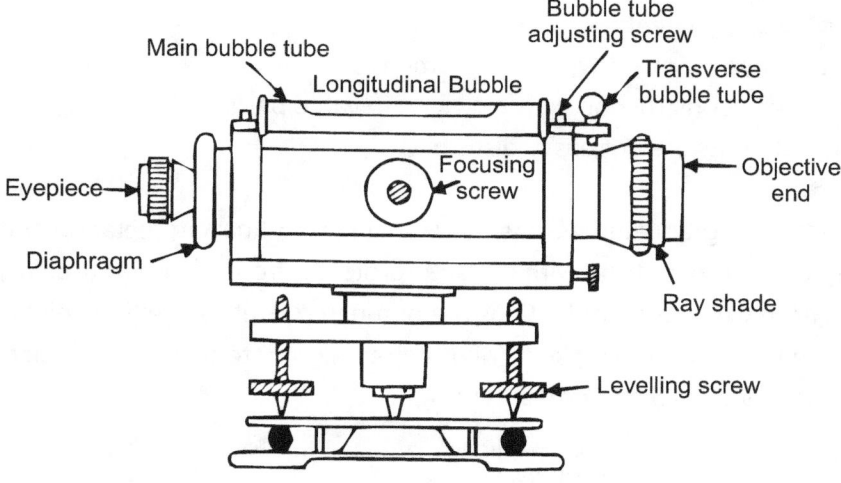

(a) Dumpy Level and its Parts

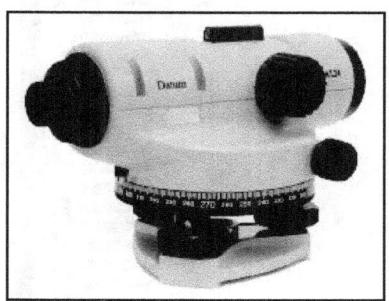

(b) Dumpy Level

Fig. 4.46

Functions of Salient Parts:

1. **A Levelling Head:** To bring the bubble in the centre of its run.
2. **Telescope:** Used to sight a staff placed at desired station and to read staff distinctly.
3. **Diaphragm:** Holds the cross hairs (fitted with it).
4. **Eye Piece:** Magnifies the image formed in the plane of the diaphragm and thus to read staff during levelling.
5. **Level Tube:** Used to make the axis of the telescope horizontal and thus the line of sight.
6. **Levelling Screws:** To adjust instrument (level) so that the line of sight is horizontal for any orientation of the telescope.
7. **Tripod Stand:** To fix the instrument (level) at a convenient height of an observer.

Advantages of Dumpy Level:
1. It is stable and compact type of instrument.
2. It is simple in construction with very few movable parts.
3. The adjustments are not easily disturbed.

Levelling Staff:

It is a self-reading graduated wooden or aluminium rod having rectangular cross-section. The lower end of the rod is stood with metal to protect it from wear and usually point of zero measurement from which the graduations are numbered. Staff are either solid (having single piece of 3 metre height or folding staff (of 4 metre height into two or three pieces). The least count of a levelling staff is 5 mm or 0.005 m.

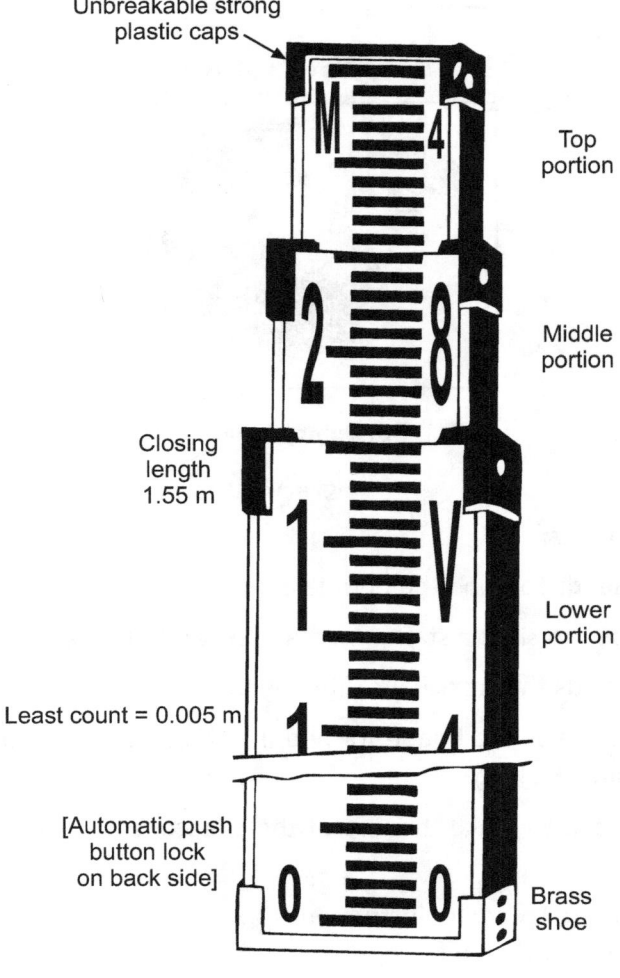

Fig. 4.47: Telescopic staff

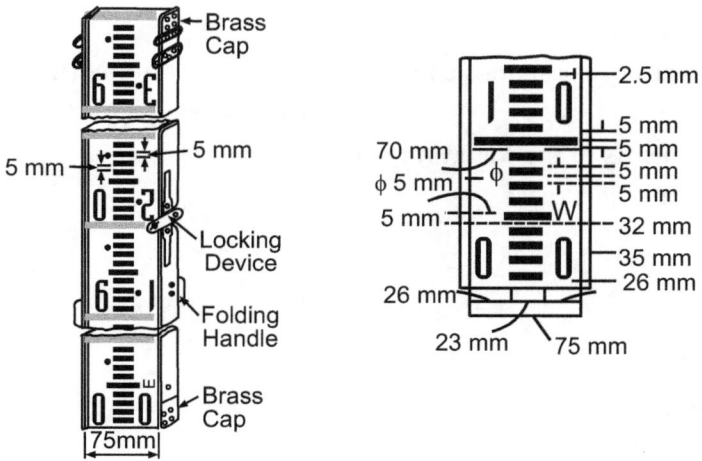

Fig. 4.48: Folding staff

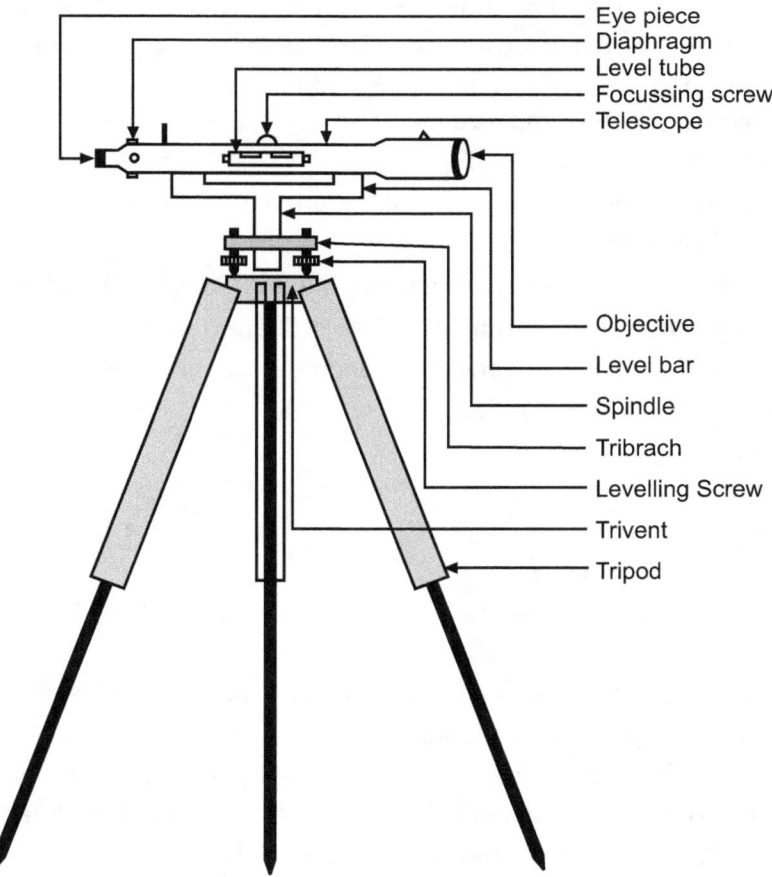

Fig. 4.49: Schematic diagram of an engineer's level

Telescope of Dumpy Level:

There are two types of telescopes used in the levelling instruments:
1. External focusing type.
2. Internal focusing type.

The telescope consists of the following parts:
(i) Objective or object glass
(ii) Body
(iii) Eye piece
(iv) Diaphragm
(v) Diaphragm screws
(vi) Ray shade
(vii) Focusing screw.

The object glass forms a real inverted image infront of the eye piece which magnifies the image to produce an inverted virtual image. The cross-hairs are placed infront of the eye piece where the real inverted image is produced by the objective. However, in modern telescopes, the erect image of the levelling staff is obtained.

4.14.3.1 Adjustments of the Dumpy Level

There are two types of adjustments:
1. Temporary adjustment.
2. Permanent adjustment.

1. Temporary Adjustment:

These adjustments are done at each setup of the level before taking the readings on the staff. These are necessary at each setting of the level. There is no need of centring the level at any station and should be placed on any commanding position.

These are done in the following steps:
(a) Setting up
(b) Levelling up
(c) Focusing:
(i) Focusing the eye piece
(ii) Focusing the objective glass.

(a) Setting Up:

(i) During setting, the tripod stand is setup at a convenient height having its head horizontal (through eye estimation).
(ii) The instrument is then fixed on the head by rotating the lower part of the instrument with right hand and holding firmly the upper part with left hand.
(iii) Before fixing, the levelling screws are required to be brought in between the tribrach and trivet.
(iv) Circular bubble, if present, is then brought to the centre by adjusting the tripod legs.

(b) Levelling:

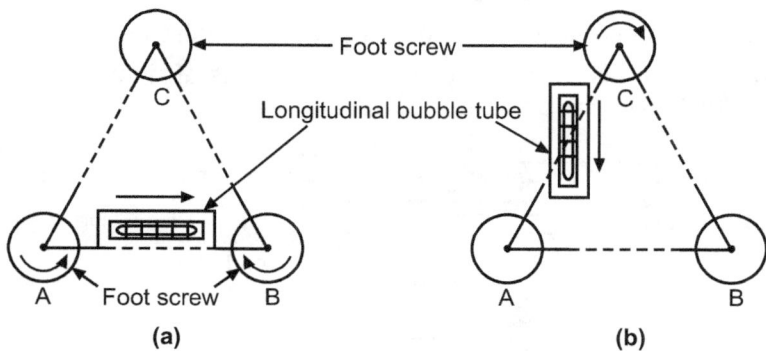

Fig. 4.50

Levelling of the instrument is done to make the vertical axis of the instrument truly vertical. It is achieved by carrying out the following steps:

Step 1: The level tube is brought parallel to any two of the foot screws, by rotating the upper part of the instrument. (Fig. 4.50 (a))

Step 2: The bubble is brought to the centre of the level tube by rotating both the foot screws either inward or outward.

Step 3: Rotate the telescope clockwise through 90° so that it lies over the third foot screw. (Fig. 4.50 (b))

Step 4: The bubble is then again brought to the centre of the level tube by rotating the third foot screw either inward or outward.

Step 5: Repeat step 1 by rotating the upper part of the instrument and then step 2.

Step 6: Repeat step 3 by rotating the upper part of the instrument and then step 4.

Step 7: Repeat step 5 and 6, till the bubble remains central in both the positions.

Step 8: Now, turn the telescope through 180° and observe the bubble. If it does not remain in the centre, the instrument needs to be corrected for its permanent adjustment.

(c) Focusing:

Focusing is required to be done in order to form image through objective lens at all the plane of the diaphragm and to view the clear image of the object through eye-piece. This is being carried out by removing parallex by proper focusing of objective and eye piece.

(i) Focusing the Eye piece: The telescope is first pointed towards the sky or hold a piece of white paper infront of the eye piece and observe the cross hairs. If the cross-hairs are not clearly seen, move the eye piece in or out till the cross-hairs are distinctly seen.

(ii) Focusing the Object Glass: Look through the eye piece towards the staff and bring the image of staff in the plane of cross-hairs by moving the focusing screw. Parallax is said to be eliminated when there is no change in the staff reading when the eye is moved up and down. Now, the instrument is ready for taking observations.

4.14.3.2 Fundamental Lines of a Level

There are three fundamental lines in a level instrument. These are:

(i) Vertical axis.   (ii) Axis of the level tube.   (iii) Line of sight.

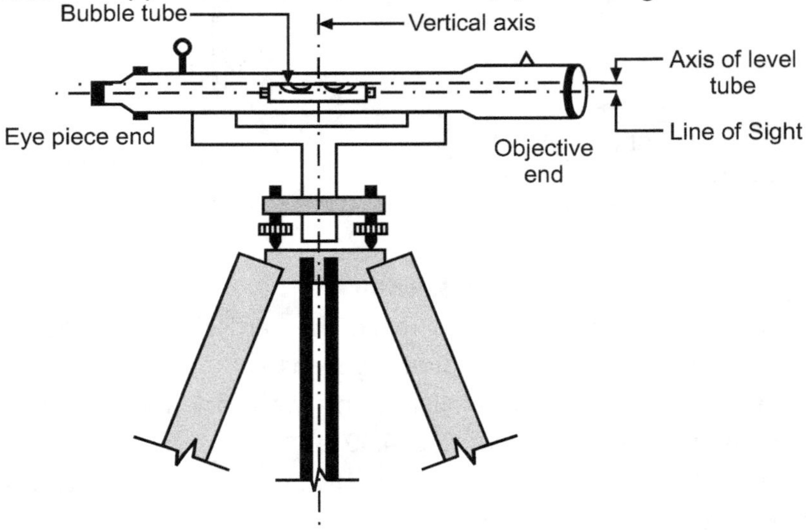

Fig. 4.51: Fundamental Lines in a Level

Relations among Fundamental Lines:

In a properly adjusted dumpy level, desired relations among fundamental lines are:
1. Axis of the level tube is perpendicular to the vertical axis.
2. Horizontal cross hair should lie in a plane perpendicular to the vertical axis, so that it will lie in a Horizontal plane when the instrument is properly levelled.
3. The line of sight is parallel to the axis of the level tube.

Permanent Alignment of Dumpy Level:

If any fundamental relation is found to be disturbed in a dumpy level, the cross-hairs and level tube are adjusted so that the fundamental relations get satisfied. The reference line for the adjustments in dumpy level is the vertical line which remain fixed in direction, as it depends upon the direction of gravity.

4.14.4 Reduction of Levels

There are two methods of calculation of reduced level or elevation of points from the staff readings observed in the field.

(a) Collimation plan or height of instrument method (H.I.)
(b) Rise and Fall.

(a) Collimation Plane Method or Height of Instrument Method (H.I. Method):

In this method, the reduced level of the collimation plane is found out for each setup of dumpy level and then the reduced levels of other points are found out with respect to the respective plane of collimation.

The procedure of finding R.L. is as given below:
1. First take a reading on bench mark and then find the R.L. of collimation plane by adding back sight reading and R.L. of bench mark.
   Height of Instrument = R.L. of collimation plane
   = R.L. of bench mark + B.S.
2. Calculate the reduced levels of intermediate points or change point by subtracting the I.S. or F.S. readings from the R.L. of collimation plane.
3. After the instrument is shifted and setup and levelled at new position, take a back sight reading on change point. Determine the R.L. of new collimation plane.
   R.L. of new collimation plane = R.L. of change point + B.S. reading
4. Obtain the reduced levels of the remaining points from the R.L. of new collimation plane.
5. Repeat the procedure till all the levelling work is finished.

On completing the observations, the arithmetical check is applied as given below:

$$\Sigma \text{ B.S.} - \Sigma \text{ F.S.} = \text{Last R.L.} - \text{First R.L.}$$

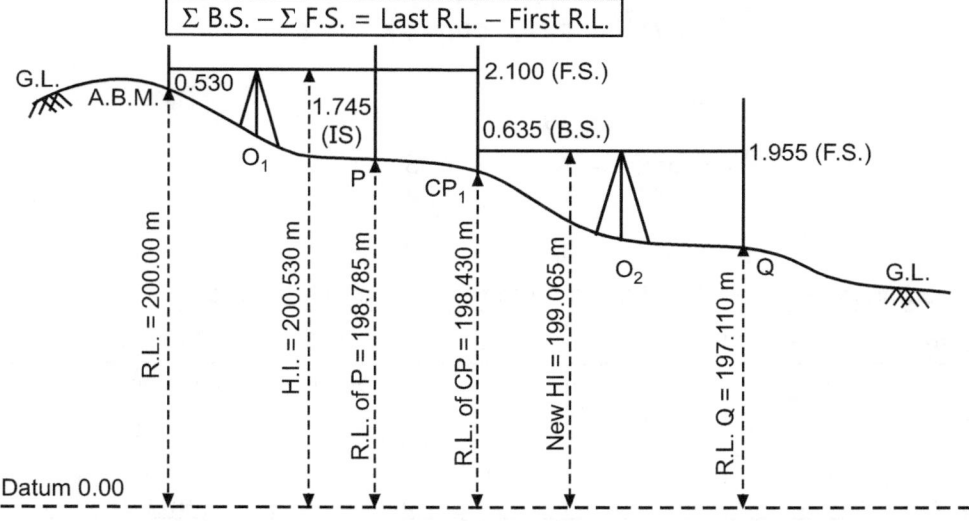

Fig. 4.52: Sketch illustrating collimation plane or H.I. method

Sketch illustrates collimation plane or H.I. method.
- Let the dumpy level height setup at O_1 and all the temporary adjustments are done.
- The telescope will revolve in a horizontal plane and reading is taken on Arbitrary Bench Mark (A.B.M.) which is 0.530 m.
- It is required to find the reduced levels of P and Q.
- R.L. of A.B.M. is 200.000 m.
- Then readings are taken at station P and change point (CP_1) respectively i.e. 1.745 and 2.100 m.

- Dumpy level is shifted to new position O_2 and all the temporary adjustments are done.
- Back sight reading is taken on CP_1 i.e. 0.635 m and fore sight reading taken on station Q i.e. 1.955 m.

∴ Height of Instrument or R.L. of collimation plane at O_1
= R.L. of ABM + B.S.
= 200.000 + 0.530
= 200.530 m

R.L. of St. P = H.I. − I.S.
= 200.530 − 1.745
= 198.785 m

R.L. of CP_1 = H.I. − F.S.
= 200.530 − 2.100
= 198.430 m

New H.I. at O_2 = R.L. of CP_1 + B.S.
= 198.430 + 0.635
= 199.065 m

R.L. of Q = New H.I. − F.S.
= 199.065 − 1.955
= 197.110 m

The readings will be tabulated as under in the page of a level book.

Station	B.S.	I.S.	F.S.	H.I.	R.L. (m)	Remark
–	0.530	–		200.530	200.000	ABM
P	–	1.745	–	–	198.785	–
	0.635	–	2.100	199.065	198.430	CP_1
Q	–		1.955	–	197.110	–
Σ	1.165	–	4.055	–	–	–

Arithmetical Check:

Σ B.S. − Σ F.S. = Last R.L. − First R.L.
1.165 − 4.055 = 197.110 − 200.000
− 2.890 = − 2.890

(b) Rise and Fall Method:

In this method, the difference of elevation between two consecutive points is determined by comparing each point after the first with that immediately preceding it, i.e. two consecutive staff readings.

Rise or Fall = Previous Reading − Current Reading

If difference is + ve → Rise

If difference is − ve → Fall

Reduced level of any point = Reduced level of preceding point ± Rise or fall

+ → when Rise

− → when Fall

The R.L. of collimation plane is not required to find out. The difference of readings will indicate a rise or a fall depending on whether the staff reading at that point is smaller or greater than that at the preceding point.

The arithmetical check in the reduction of level is applied as follows:

$$\Sigma \text{ B.S.} - \Sigma \text{ R.S.} = \Sigma \text{ Rise} - \Sigma \text{ Fall} = \text{Last R.L.} - \text{First R.L.}$$

Thus, there is a check on the intermediate reduction of levels.

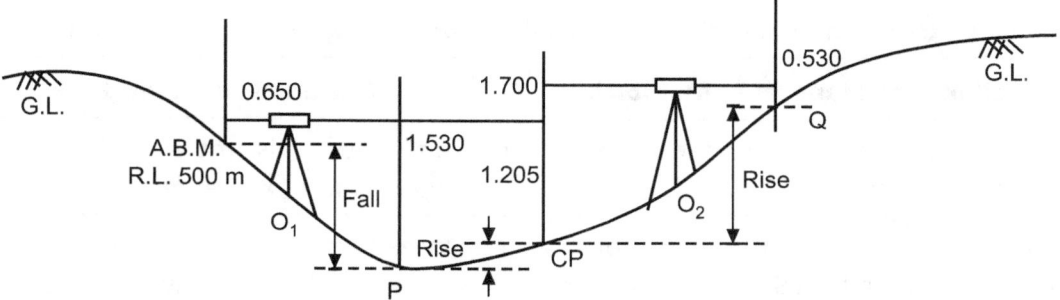

Fig. 4.53: Illustrative sketch of rise and fall method

Rise or Fall between ABM and P = Previous reading − Current reading

= 0.650 − 1.530

= − 0.880 m

R.L. of P = R.L. of AMB ± Rise or Fall

= 500 − 0.880

= 499.120 m

Rise or Fall between P and CP = 1.530 − 1.205 = 0.325 m

R.L. of CP = R.L. of P ± Rise or Fall

= 499.120 + 0.325

= 499.445 m

Rise or Fall between CP and Q = 1.700 − 0.530

= 1.170 m

R.L of Q = R.L. of CP ± Rise or Fall

= 499.445 + 1.170

= 500.615 m

Station	B.S.	I.S.	F.S.	Rise	Fall	R.L. (m)	Remark
–	0.650	–			–	500.000	ABM
P	–	1.530	–	–	0.880	499.120	–
–	1.700	–	1.205	0.325	–	499.445	CP
Q	–	–	0.530	1.170	–	500.615	–
Σ	2.350	–	1.735	1.495	0.880	–	–

Arithmetic Check:

$$\Sigma \text{ B.S.} - \Sigma \text{ F.S.} = \Sigma \text{ Rise} - \Sigma \text{ Fall} = \text{Last R.L.} - \text{First R.L.}$$
$$2.350 - 1.735 = 1.495 - 0.880 = 500.615 - 500.000$$
$$\therefore \qquad 0.615 = 0.615 = 0.615$$

Comparison between Collimation Plane (H.I) Method and Rise and Fall Method

Collimation Plane (H.I.) Method	Rise and Fall Method
1. It is more rapid and involve less number of calculations.	1. This method is more tedious as it involves more calculations.
2. Since there is no check on R.L. of I.S., errors if any, in the I.S. are not detected.	2. Since there is complete check on the R.L. of I.S., errors if any, in the I.S. are also detected.
3. Most suited for longitudinal or cross-sectional levelling and controlling.	3. It is well suited for determining the difference of levels of two points where precision is required. e.g. establishing new bench marks.
4. There are two arithmetical checks. Σ B.S. − Σ F.S. = Last R.L. − First R.L.	4. There are three arithmetical checks. Σ B.S. − Σ F.S. = Σ Rise − Σ Fall = Last R.L. − First R.L.

4.14.5 Recording the Staff Readings in the Level Book

The tabular form of the page of a level book is as shown in the illustrative example:

The following points should be considered while making entries in the level book.

1. On each page of a level book, the first entry is always a back sight and last entry is always a fore sight.

2. When change point is taken, the fore sight and back sight readings should be written in the same line.

3. When transferring the readings from one page to another, if the last entry on previous page happens to be an intermediate sight, it is entered in both intermediate sight and fore sight readings on previous page and is written under back sight and intermediate sight column as first entry.

4. Specific mention of benchmarks, change points, prominent features along the alignment of engineering structures such as roads, canals, railway lines etc. should be made in 'Remarks column'.

Note: In the continuously sloping ground, it is to be noted that change point occurs at the point where the reading abruptly changes from smaller value to bigger value as in the case of rising ground or from bigger value to smaller value abruptly as in the case of a falling ground.

SOLVED EXAMPLES

Example 4.9: Determine the Reduced Levels of all the stations by H.I. method from the following. The readings during a road profiling working from a point P to another point Q, 2 km apart using a dumpy level and a 4 m levelling staff were:

0.500, 1.525, 2.150, 0.985, 0.450, 0.870, 1.850, 2.585, 1.710, 2.850, 3.415, 3.855

While obtaining the above readings, the instrument was shifted after fourth, sixth and tenth readings. Enter all the readings in a level field book page. The R.L. of 1st point P was happened to be a P.B.M. with R.L. = 150.000 m. Also apply usual Arithmetic check.

Solution:

- The readings are entered in a level book page by noting that the instrument was shifted after 4th, 6th and 10th readings. Therefore, 4th, 6th and 10th readings (0.985, 0.870 and 2.850) will be entered in fore sight column.
- Consequently 5th, 7th and 11th readings (i.e. 0.450, 1.850 and 3.415) will be entered in back sight column.
- The first reading is entered in the B.S. column, whereas, the last reading is entered in the fore sight column. The remaining readings are entered in intermediate sight column.
- It is noted that number of B.S. readings is equal to the number of F.S. readings on a level book page.
- Here No. of B.S. = No. of F.S. = 4.

Station	B.S.	I.S.	F.S.	H.I. (Collimation plane)	R.L. in m	Remark
P	0.500	-	-	150.500	150.000	P.B.M.
1	-	1.525	-	-	148.975	-
2	-	2.150	-	-	148.350	-
3	0.450	-	0.985	149.965	149.515	CP_1
4	1.850	-	0.870	150.945	149.095	CP_2
5	-	2.585	-	-	148.360	-
6	-	1.710	-	-	149.235	-
7	3.415	-	2.850	151.510	148.095	CP_3
Q	-	-	3.855	-	147.655	Last Pt.
SUM (Σ)	6.215		8.560	-	-	-

The R.L.s of staff stations are calculated as follows by using Collimation Plane Method (H.I.)

1.   First H.I. = R.L. of P.B.M + B.S. on station P
                                            = 150.00 + 0.500
                                            = 150.500 m
2.   R.L. of St. 1 = H.I. – I.S. on St. 1
                                            = 150.500 – 1.525
                                            = 148.975 m
3.   R.L. of St. 2 = H.I. – I.S. on St. 2
                                            = 150.500 – 2.150
                                            = 148.350 m
4.   R.L. of St. 3 [CP_1] = H.I. – F.S. on St. 3
                                            = 150.500 – 0.985
                                            = 149.515 m

Now the instrument is shifted, hence new H.I. will be calculated.

5.   Second H.I. = R.L. of CP_1 (St. 3) + B.S. on St. 3
                                            = 149.515 + 0.450
                                            = 149.965 m
6.   R.L. of St. 4 [CP_2] = Second H.I. – F.S. on St. 4
                                            = 149.965 – 0.870
                                            = 149.095 m

As the instrument is shifted; third H.I. is to be found out.

7.   Third H.I. = R.L. of St. 4 [CP_2] + B.S. on St. 4
                                       = 149.095 + 1.850
                                       = 150.945 m

8.   R.L. of St. 5 = Third H.I. – I.S. on St. 5
                                       = 150.945 – 2.585
                                       = 148.360 m

9.   R.L. of St. 6 = Third H.I. – I.S. on St. 6
                                       = 150.945 – 1.710
                                       = 149.235 m

10.   R.L. of St. 7 = Third H.I. – F.S. on St. 7
                                       = 150.945 – 2.850
                                       = 148.095 m

As the instrument is shifted, fourth H.I. is to be found out.

11.   Fourth H.I. = R.L. of St 7 [CP_3] + B.S. on St. 7
                                       = 148.095 + 3.415
                                       = 151.510 m

12.   R.L. of St. Q = Fourth H.I. – F.S. on St. Q
                                         = 151.510 – 3.855
                                         = 147.655 m

Note: It can be noted from above calculations that B.S. is always 'plus' sight and is always added; whereas R.S. and I.S. are 'minus' sights and are always subtracted.

Check: The arithmetical check on calculation is

                Σ B.S. – ΣF.S. = Last R.L. – First R.L.
                6.215 – 8.560 = 147.655 – 150.000
                    – 2.345 = – 2.345

Example 4.10: Readings taken successively on staff positions in a levelling work are: 2.065, 1.470, 1.226, 3.198, 2.458.

Level was shifted after second reading. If R.L. of first staff position is 260 M, find the R.L.s of other staff positions. Use rise and fall method. Show arithmetical check and simple calculations.

Solution: From the data, first reading (i.e. 2.065) will be entered in back sight column. The level was shifted after second reading (i.e. 1470), so it will come in fore sight column and next consecutive reading 1.226 will come in back sight column in the same row as it is change point.

Last reading (i.e. 2.458) will be in fore sight column and remaining will be in intermediate sight column.

Explanation of Calculation:

In the rise and fall method, each staff reading is compared with respect to previous one, to find out whether it is a rise or fall of next point. The rise or fall is added to or subtracted from the R.L. of previous point to get R.L. of next point.

Station	B.S.	I.S.	F.S.	Rise	Fall	R.L. (m)	Remark
1	2.065	-	-	-	-	260.000	First Pt.
2	1.226	-	1.470	0.595	-	260.595	C.P.1
3	-	3.198	-	-	1.972	258.623	-
4	-	-	2.458	0.740	-	259.363	Last Pt.
Sum (Σ)	3.291	-	3.928	1.335	1.972	-	-

1. For station 2 rise will be = B.S. on St. 1 − F.S. on St. 2
   = 2.065 − 1.470
   = 0.595

   The second reading being smaller than previous one indicates that it is rise.

2. ∴ R.L. of St. 2 = R.L. of St. 1 + Rise of St. 2
   = 260.00 + 0.595
   = 260.595 m

3. As I.S. of station 3 is greater than B.S. of station 2, so it indicates that it is fall.
   For St. 3 fall = B.S. on St. 2 − I.S. on St. 3
   = 1.226 − 3.198
   = 1.972

4. R.L. of St. 3 = R.L. of St. 2 − Fall
   = 260.595 − 1.972
   = 258.623 m

5. As F.S. of station 4 is smaller than I.S. of station 3, so it is rise
   For St. 4, Rise = I.S. on St. 3 − F.S. on St. 4
   = 3.198 − 2.458
   = 0.740

6. R.L. of St. 4 = R.L. of St. 3 + Rise of St. 4
   = 258.623 + 0.740
   = 259.363 m

Arithmetical Check:

Σ B.S. − Σ F.S. = Σ Rise − Σ Fall = Last R.L. − First RL
3.291 − 3.928 = 1.335 − 1.972 = 259.363 − 260.000
− 0.637 = − 0.637 = − 0.637

Example 4.11: During a fly levelling work the staff readings were obtained at a regular interval of 25 m. The readings were as under –

B.S. → 0.565, 0.990, 2.775 and 2.350
F.S. → 1.685, 1.350, 2.055 and 3.450

The work was beginned with a point whose R.L. known to be 255.555. Enter the readings for Rise and Fall method to determine the R.L.s of all stations. Also, find the nature and magnitude of gradient. Apply usual check.

Solution: From the data of B.S. and F.S. readings, it is observes that there are continuous change points. Readings are tabulated accordingly.

Station	B.S.	I.S.	F.S.	Rise	Fall	R.L. (m)	Remark
0	0.565	-	-	-	-	255.555	ABM
25	0.990	-	1.685	-	1.120	254.435	CP_1
50	2.775	-	1.350	-	0.360	254.075	CP_2
75	2.350	-	2.055	0.720	-	254.795	CP_3
100	-	-	3.450	-	1.110	253.695	-
Σ	6.680	-	8.540	0.720	2.580	-	-

$$\text{Gradient} = \frac{\text{Last R.L.} - \text{First R.L.}}{\text{Horizontal distance}}$$

$$= \frac{-1.860}{100}$$

$$= 0.0186 \text{ or } 1 \text{ in } 53.76 \quad \text{(Falling gradient)}$$

Arithmetical Check:

Σ B.S. $-$ Σ F.S. $=$ Σ Rise $-$ Σ Fall $=$ Last R.L. $-$ First R.L.
∴ 6.680 $-$ 8.540 $=$ 0.720 $-$ 2.580 $=$ 253.695 $-$ 255.555
∴ $-$ 1.860 $=$ $-$ 1.860 $=$ $-$ 1.860

Example 4.12: A fly levelling work was carried out, starting from a P.B.M. of R.L. 239.685 (Refer Fig. 4.54) and finishing the work on C. Tabulate the readings shown in Fig. 4.54 and find R.L. of A, B and C. Use any method of your choice. Apply usual check.

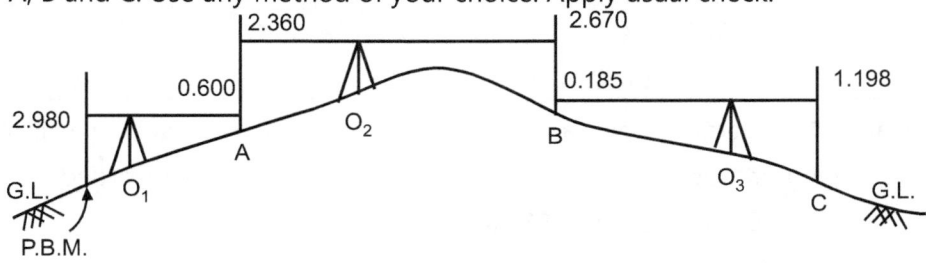

Fig. 4.54: Fly levelling (Not to Scale)

Solution: As Fly levelling work was carried out, so they will be only back sight and fore sight and no intermediate sight. The problem is solved by collimation plane (H.I.) method.

Station	B.S.	I.S.	F.S.	H.I. (Collimation plane)	R.L. in m	Remark
-	2.980	-	-	242.665	239.685	P.B.M.
A	2.360	-	0.600	242.425	242.065	CP_1
B	0.185	-	2.670	241.940	241.755	CP_2
C	-	-	1.198	-	240.742	-
Sum (Σ)	5.525	-	4.468		-	-

Arithmetical Check:

$$\Sigma \text{ B.S.} - \Sigma \text{ F.S.} = \text{Last R.L.} - \text{First R.L.}$$
$$5.525 - 4.468 = 240.742 - 239.685$$
$$1.057 = 1.057$$

The problem can also be solved by rise and fall method.

Station	B.S.	I.S.	F.S.	Rise	Fall	R.L. (M)	Remark
-	2.980	-	-	-	-	239.685	P.B.M.
A	2.360	-	0.600	0.2380	-	242.065	CP_1
B	0.185	-	2.670	-	0.310	241.755	CP_2
C	-	-	1.198	-	1.013	240.742	-
Sum (Σ)	5.525	-	4.468	2.380	1.323	-	-

Arithmetical Check:

∴ $\Sigma \text{ B.S.} - \Sigma \text{ F.S.} = \Sigma \text{ Rise} - \Sigma \text{ Fall} = \text{Last R.L.} - \text{First R.L.}$
$$5.525 - 4.468 = 2.380 - 1.323 = 240.742 - 239.685$$
∴ $1.057 = 1.057 = 1.057$

Example 4.13: Starting from an A.B.M. of R.L. = 200 m, levelling was done on a continuous sloping ground and following readings were successfully recorded.

3.090, 3.840, 1.370, 2.660, 3.410, 0.955 and 1.820

Rule out the page of a level book for Collimation Plane Method' outer the readings and calculate R.L. value of each staff station. Apply usual check show two simple calculations.

Solution: In the continuously sloping ground, change point occurs where the reading abruptly changes from bigger value to smaller value abruptly as in the case of a falling ground.

Station	B.S.	I.S.	F.S.	H.I. (Collimation plane)	R.L. in m	Remark
1	3.090	-	-	203.090	200.000	A.B.M.
2	1.370	-	3.840	200.620	199.250	CP_1
3	-	2.660	-	-	197.960	-
4	0.955	-	3.410	198.165	197.210	CP_2
5	-	-	1.820	-	196.345	-
Σ	5.415	-	9.070	-	-	-

Arithmetical Check:

$$\Sigma\ B.S. - \Sigma\ F.S. = \text{Last R.L.} - \text{First R.L.}$$
$$5.415 - 9.070 = 196.345 - 200$$
$$-3.655 = -3.655$$

1. First H.I. = R.L. of A.B.M. + B.S.
   = 200 + 3.090
   = 203.090 m
2. R.L. of St. 2 = H.I. − F.S. on St. 2
   = 203.090 − 3.840
   = 199.250 m
3. Second H.I. = R.L. of CP_1 + B.S. on St. 2. (CP_1)
   = 199.250 + 1.370
   = 200.620 m
4. R.L. of St. 3 = Second H.I. − I.S. on St. 3
   = 200.620 − 2.660
   = 197.960 m

Example 4.14: The following staff readings were observed on the continuously sloping ground along the centre line of a road, with the help of a dumpy level and 4 m staff of 20 m interval. The first staff reading was taken on B.M. and the second reading was taken on the starting point of the road. Reduced level of B.M. was 350.00 m, 0.540, 0.935, 1.245, 3.885, 0.450, 1.635, 2.220, 3.665, 0.775, 1.555, 2.785, 3.450.
  (a) Enter the readings in a level field book page.
  (b) Calculate the reduced level by rise and fall method.
  (c) Determine the gradient of road.

Solution:

Distance	B.S.	I.S.	F.S.	Rise	Fall	R.L. (m)	Remark
0	0.540	–	–	–	–	350.000	BM
20	–	0.935	–	–	0.395	349.605	First point on road
40	–	1.245	–	–	0.310	349.295	–
60	0.450	–	3.885	–	2.640	346.655	CP$_1$
80	–	1.635	–	–	1.185	345.470	–
100	–	2.220	–	–	0.585	344.885	–
120	0.775	–	3.665	–	1.445	343.440	CP$_2$
140	–	1.555	–	–	0.780	342.660	–
160	–	2.785	–	–	1.230	341.430	–
180	–	–	3.450	–	0.665	340.765	–
Σ	1.765	10.375	11.000	–	9.900	3454.205	–

Arithmetical Check:

$$\Sigma \text{B.S.} - \Sigma \text{F.S.} = \Sigma \text{Rise} - \Sigma \text{Fall} = \text{Last R.L.} - \text{First R.L.}$$

$$1.765 - 11 = 0 - 9.235 \quad = 340.765 - 350.00$$

$$-9.235 = -9.235 \quad = -9.235$$

$$\text{Gradient of Road} = \frac{\text{Last R.L.} - \text{First R.L.}}{\text{Distance between first and last point}}$$

$$= \frac{340.765 - 350.000}{180} = \frac{-9.235}{180}$$

$$= 0.0513 \quad \text{(Falling gradient)}$$

$$= 1 \text{ in } 19.491$$

Example 4.15: Find the missing values marked as X in the below levelling page of book. Also carryout the arithmetical check.

Station	B.S.	I.S.	F.S.	Rise	Fall	R.L. (m)	Remark
1	0.930	-	-	-	-	200.00	BM
2	-	2.820	-	-	1.890	X	-
3	X	-	X	X	-	198.580	CP$_1$
4	0.935	-	1.850	0.230	-	X	CP$_2$
5	-	X	-	-	X	197.495	-
6	-	-	2.785	-	0.535	X	Last Pt.

Solution: Starting from the known data of reduced levels, the missing readings are Calculated as under:

1.   R.L. of Stn. 2 = R.L. B.M. − Fall Stn. 2
                                      = 200 − 1.890
                                        = 198.110 m

2. As we know R.L. of Stn. 2 and Stn. 3, the difference between these two R.L.s will give amount of Rise of Stn. 3

                Rise of Stn. 3 = R.L. of Stn. 3 − R.L. of Stn. 2
                                 = 198.580 − 198.110
                                 = 0.470 m

3.   Rise of Stn. 3 = I.S. of Stn. 2 − F.S. on Stn. 3
                          0.470 = 2.820 − F.S. on Stn. 3
∴   F.S. on Stn. 3 = 2.350 m

4.   Rise of Stn. 4 = B.S. of Stn. 3 − F.S. on Stn. 4
                          0.230 = B.S. of Stn. 3 − 1.850
∴   B.S. of Stn. 3 = 2.080 m

5.   R.L. of Stn. 4 = R.L. of Stn. 3 + Rise of Stn. 4
                                = 198.580 + 0.230
                                = 198.810 m

6.   Fall of Stn. 5 = R.L. of Stn. 4 − R.L. of Stn. 5
                                = 198.810 − 197.495
                                = 1.315 m

7.   I.S. of Stn. 5 = B.S. of Stn. 4 + Fall of Stn. 5
                                = 0.935 + 1.315
                                = 2.250 m

8.   R.L. of Stn. 6 = R.L. of Stn. 5 − Fall of Stn. 6
                                = 197.495 − 0.535
                                = 196.960 m

Arithmetical Check:

∴ Σ B.S. − Σ F.S. = Σ Rise − Σ Fall = Last R.L. − First R.L.
                    3.945 − 6.985 = − 0.700 − 3.740 = 196.960 − 200.000
∴   − 3.040 = − 3.040   = − 3.040

The result in tabulated form:

Station	B.S.	I.S.	F.S.	Rise	Fall	R.L. (m)	Remark
1	0.930	-	-	-	-	200.00	BM
2	-	2.820	-	-	1.890	198.110	-
3	2.080	-	2.350	0.470	-	198.580	CP_1
4	0.935	-	1.850	0.230	-	198.810	CP_2
5	-	2.250	-	-	1.315	197.495	-
6	-	-	2.785	-	0.535	196.960	Last Pt.
Sum Σ	3.945	-	6.985	0.700	3.740	-	-

Example 4.16: Find the values shown as X in the following level field book page. Also show usual arithmetic check.

Station	B.S.	I.S.	F.S.	H.I.	R.L. in M	Remark
P	X	-	-	X	105.000	P.B.M.
Q	-	1.525	-	-	X	-
R	-	1.600	-	-	104.250	-
S	X	-	2.450	X	103.400	X
T	-	1.250	-	-	103.050	-
U	-	1.855	-	-	X	-
V	-	-	-	-	101.315	Last Point

1.   H.I. at Stn. P = R.L. of Stn. R + Fall on Stn. R
                           = 104.250 + 1.600
                           = 105.850 m
2.   B.S. on Stn. P = H.I. − R.L. of Stn. P
                           = 105.850 − 105.000
                           = 0.850 m
3.   R.L. of Stn Q = H.I. − I.S. on Stn. Q
                           = 105.850 − 1.525
                           = 104.325 m
4.   H.I. at Stn. S = R.L. of Stn T + I.S. on Stn. T
                           = 103.050 + 1.250
                           = 104.300 m

5.　　　　　　　　B.S. on Stn S　=　H.I. at Stn. S – R.L. of Stn. S
　　　　　　　　　　　　　　　　=　104.300 – 103.400 = 0.900 m
6.　　　　　　　　R.L. of Stn U　=　H.I. at Stn S – I.S. on Stn. U
　　　　　　　　　　　　　　　　=　104.300 – 1.855 = 102.445 m
7.　　　　　　　　F.S. on Stn Y　=　H.I. at Stn. S – R.L. of Stn V
　　　　　　　　　　　　　　　　=　104.300 – 101.315 = 2.985 m

Station	B.S.	I.S.	F.S.	H.I.	R.L. (m)	Remark
P	0.850	-	-	105.850	105.000	P.B.M.
Q	-	1.525	-	-	104.325	-
R	-	1.600	-	-	104.250	-
S	0.900	-	2.450	104.300	103.400	CP_1
T	-	1.250		-	103.050	-
U	-	1.855	-	-	102.445	-
V	-	-	2.985	-	101.315	Last Point
(Σ)Sum	1.750	-	5.435	-	-	-

Arithmetical Check:

　　　　　Σ B.S. – Σ F.S. = Last R.L. – First R.L.
　　　　　1.750 – 5.435 = 101.315 – 105.000
　　　　　　　– 3.685 = – 3.685

Example 4.17: The following readings were taken with a 4 m levelling staff. The staff was held inverted at 3rd reading. Readings were 1.585, 2.630, 2.465, 3.285. Calculate the R.Ls. of the staff stations. The first reading was taken on a B.M. of R.L. 200.000 m.

Solution: The problem is solved by collimation plane method. Since, the instrument was not shifted during the exercise, only one H.I. will be obtained.

1.　　　　　　　　　　　H.I.　=　R.L. of B.M. + B.S. on B.M.
　　　　　　　　　　　　　　　=　200.000 + 1.585
　　　　　　　　　　　　　　　=　201.585 m
2.　　　　　　R.L. of Stn. 2　=　H.I. – I.S. on Stn. 2
　　　　　　　　　　　　　　　=　201.585 + 2.630
　　　　　　　　　　　　　　　=　198.955 m
3.　　　　　　R.L. of Stn. 3　=　H.I. – (–I.S. on Stn. 3)
　　　　　　　　　　　　　　　=　201.585 + 2.465
　　　　　　　　　　　　　　　=　204.050 m

Here, the I.S. is added to H.I. as the staff is held inverted at the point-. Therefore, the point is above the line of sight i.e. H.I. and hence the staff reading will have to be added to get R.L. of the point above H.I. as shown in Fig. 4.55.

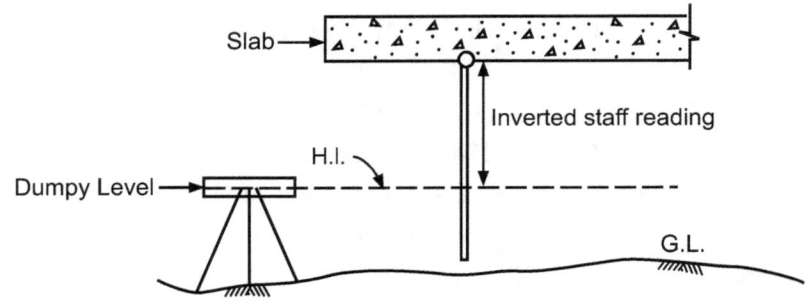

Fig. 4.55

4. R.L. of Stn. 4 = H.I. − F.S. on Stn. 4
    = 201.585 − 3.285
    = 198.300 m

The readings are entered as follows. The reading of staff held inverted is entered as negative since, it is above H.I.

Station	B.S.	I.S.	F.S.	H.I.	R.L. in M	Remark
1	1.585	-	-	201.585	200.000	B.M.
2	-	2.630	-	-	198.955	-
3	-	−2.465	-	-	204.050	Inverted staff
4	-	-	3.285	-	198.300	Last Point
Σ	1.585	-	3.285	-	-	-

Arithmetical Check:

Σ B.S. − Σ F.S. = Last R.L. − First R.L.
1.585 − 3.285 = 198.300 − 200.000
− 1.700 = − 1.700

Example 4.18: Find the height of a Tee-beam above the floor level. The R.L. of the floor is 100.855 m and the staff reading on the floor is 2.055 m. The reading on the staff held upside down against the under side of the beam is 3.565 m.

Solution: R.L. of plane of collimation,

H.I. = 100.855 + 2.055 = 102.910 m

R.L. of the under side of Tee-beam

= 102.910 + 3.565 = 106.475 m

Hence, the height of the Tee-beam above the floor level,

= 106.475 − 100.855
= 5.620 m

Example 4.19: During a levelling work started from A.B.M. of known R.L. = 100.000 m, the following staff readings were obtained:
1. 0.850   2. 1.555   3. 1.725
4. 0.455   5. 1.800   6. 1.750
7. 0.950   8. 1.555

The instrument was shifted after 3rd and 6th readings. Enter correctly all the readings in a field book page and determine the reduced levels of all stations showing calculations by Rise and Fall method. Apply usual arithmetic check.

Solution: The readings are entered in a field book page by noting that the instrument was shifted after 3rd and 6th reading will be entered in fore sight column and consequently 4th and 7th reading will be entered in back sight column.

The first reading is entered in back sight column, whereas last reading will be entered in fore sight column and remaining readings in intermediate sight column.

Station	B.S.	I.S.	F.S.	Rise	Fall	R.L. in m	Remark
1	0.850	-	-	-	-	100.000	A.B.M.
2	-	1.555	-	-	0.705	99.295	-
3	0.455	-	1.725	-	0.170	99.125	CP_1
4	-	1.800	-	-	1.345	97.780	-
5	0.950	-	1.750	0.05	-	97.830	CP_2
6	-	-	1.555	-	0.605	97.225	Last point
(Σ) Sum	2.255	-	5.030	0.050	2.825	-	-

Arithmetical Check:

Σ B.S. $-\Sigma$ F.S. $=\Sigma$ Rise $-\Sigma$ Fall = Last R.L. $-$ First R.L.

∴   2.255 $-$ 5.030 = 0.050 $-$ 2.825 = 97.225 $-$ 100

∴ $-$ 2.775 = $-$ 2.775 = $-$ 2.775

EXERCISE

1. Explain the various principles of survey.
2. Define : (a) Base line, (b) Offsets, (c) direct ranging, (d) Indirect ranging.
3. Differentiate between direct and indirect ranging.
4. Explain with neat sketch the line ranger.
5. Explain with neat sketch the open cross staff.
6. Compare Rise and Fall Method and Height of instrument method.
7. Describe temporary adjustments of level.
8. Compare the Height of collimation and Rise and Fall method.

9. Draw a neat sketch showing the optical parts inside and the internal focusing telescope of a dumpy level.
10. Explain the following bench marks.
    (i) Permanent B.M.
    (ii) Temporary B.M.
    How are bench marks established?
11. Define the following terms:
    (i) Datum
    (ii) Station
    (iii) Reduced level
12. Write a brief note on the necessity of change point in levelling work. And show C.P with the aid of a sketch.
13. Define four types of Bench marks used in levelling.

PROBLEMS

1. The following consecutive reading were taken with a levelling instrument at intervals of 20 m. The instrument was shifted after the fourth and eighth reading. The last reading was taken on a BM of RL 110.200 m. Find the RL of all the points 2.375, 1.730, 0.615, 3.450, 2.835, 2.70, 1.835, 0.985, 0.435, 1.160, 2.255 and 3.630 m.

2. The fallowing reading were taken with a dumpy level and a 4M levelling staff 1.260, 1.435, 1.670, 0.640, 1.920, 2.560, 1.845, 2.210, 0.965 and 1.325. The instrument was shifted after 3rd and 8th reading. The R.L. of the station where first reading was taken was 150. 000 m. Calculate the R.L. of the other points by collimation plane method. Apply the usual check.

3. In an operation of compound levelling, following staff reading in meters are observed 1.725, 1.950, 1.285, 0.895, 0.500, 2.300, 2.825, 1.500, 3.100 and 3.800.
First reading is taken on P.B.M. of R.L. 120.00 m. Instrument is shifted after 4th, 8th and 10th reading. Fill the page of a level book and compute R.L.s of all stations using rise and fall method. Apply usual arithmetic check. Also mention necessary points in the remark column.

4. In levelling operation following readings were recorded 1.230, 1.900, 3.535, 2.170 and 2.135. The instrument was shifted to a new position after 3rd reading. Last reading was taken on an inverted staff held at the bottom of a slab. First reading was taken on a B.M. R.L. 250.000. Enter the above data in a level book page and complete it by using Rise and Fall method with the usual check.

5. Following readings were successively taken along a continuously sloping ground with a 4 m staff and Dumpy level: 3.555, 2.225, 0.675, 3.445, 2.885, 1.115, 0.775, 3.775 and 2.935 m. R.L. of last station was known to be 506.390 m. Rule out the page of level field book for the 'collimation plane' method and enter all the readings properly. Hence, calculate R.L. of all other staff stations. Apply the usual arithmetical check.

6. The following staff readings were observed on continuously sloping ground along the centreline of a road, with the help of a dumpy level and 4 m staff at 20 m interval. The first reading was taken at the starting point of the road having R.L. 350.000 m, 0.540, 1.245, 2.375, 3.885, 1.245, 2.560, 3.780, 0.875, 1.625, 2.960.
   (i) Enter the readings in a page of the level book.
   (ii) Find R.L.s by Rise and fall method. Apply the usual checks.
   (iii) Determine longitudinal gradient of the road.

7. A levelling work was conducted between T.B.M.A. (R.L. 508.905 m) and T.B.M. (R.L. 500.690 m). The readings taken were 0.750, 1.780, 2.935, 3.410, 0.425, 3.685, 0.685 and 2.975. The instrument was shifted after the 4th and 6th reading. Book the entries in tabular form, reduce the levels and exercise the arithmetic check. (Solve by collimation plane method).

8. The following readings were taken with a 4 m levelling staff. The staff was held inverted at 4th reading, touching the Soffit it of the slab. Readings were 1.025, 1.930, 2.525, 3.125 and 2.980. Calculate the R.L.s of the staff station. The first reading was taken on a Bench Mark of R.L. 590.00 M.

9. Fly levels were taken with a dumpy level and 4 m levelling staff as follows 1.550, 2.690, 1.850, 0.850, 2.770. The value of B.M. is 150.380 M. Enter the above readings in the usual form. Calculate R.L.s and apply usual checks.

10. Following table shows some reading in a check levelling work. Calculate the missing reading shown as 'X'. Tabulate the same and apply usual arithmetic check.

Sr. No.	BS	IS	FS	Rise	Fall	RL	Remark
1.	X	–	–	–	–	463.875	BM1
2.	–	X	–	0.550	–	X	–
3.	0.965	–	3.655	–	X	X	CP1
4.	X	–	1.400	–	X	461.885	CP2
5.	–	–	1.025	X	–	463.875	BM1

11. The following consecutive readings were taken with a 4 m levelling staff on a continuously sloping ground on points at an interval of 20 m, 0.525, 1.380, 2.160, 3.805, 0.460, 2.960, 3.060, 0.345, 1.925 and 2.190. The RL of the last point was 639.280. Calculate: RL of all other points by the collimation plane method.

❏❏❏

WATER RESOURCES ENGINEERING

5.1 INTRODUCTION OF WATERSHED

Watershed is a natural unit drain, draining run-off water to a common point, by a system of streams or rivers. A watershed is a closed hydrological unit, consisting of the geographical area that feeds a river or stream. Thus, watershed development consists of the integrated treatment of this unit. These treatments include measures to reduce soil erosion, increase rain water retention and conservation, regeneration of the depleted biomass through a forestation, improving soil quality, fertility and water retention capabilities of farmlands, social participation and sustainability.

Watershed is defined as 'that geographical area which feeds water to a drainage line (like a rivulet, stream, river etc.)'. However, more than being only a geographical area, it is also the area from where the community draws sustenance. The quality and health of a watershed, therefore directly affects the quality of the life of the people. Watershed development involves the conservation, regeneration and judicious utilization of natural resources. It seems to bring about an optimum balance between the demand and use of resources. It therefore involves interactions between various components like Human Resources Development (Community Development; with particular attention gender specificities), soil and land management, water management, crop management, a forestation, posture and fodder management, live stock management and related areas.

Bringing about a balance between the often-competing demands of these various sectors requires a consensus among all those living within a particular watershed and commonality of purpose on how to meet these demands in sustainable manner.

5.1.1 Aim and Necessity

(A) Protect, conserve and improve the land resources for efficient and sustained production.

(B) Protect and enhance water resource, moderate floods and reduce silting up of tanks, increase irrigation and conserving rainwater for crops and thus mitigate draughts.

(C) To utilize the natural local resources for improving agriculture and allied occupation or industries. To improve socio-economic conditions of the local people.

5.1.2 Objective of Watershed Management

The main goal of Watershed Management – sustainable management of natural resources to improve the quality of living for the population – is to be accomplished by the following objectives:

- supply and securing of clean and sufficient drinking water for the population;
- provision and securing of access to sanitation;
- improvement and restoration of soil quality and thus, raising productivity rates;
- reducing the impact of natural hazards (especially in the context of climate change);
- improvement of the income of the population with simultaneous regeneration of natural resources;
- improvement of infrastructure for storage, transport and agricultural marketing;
- improvement of physical health (supported by clean drinking water, access to sanitation improved nourishment);
- advancement of (environmental) education and self-help;
- improvement of an effective management of the financial resources available for environmental and international co-operation.

5.1.3 Program of Watershed Development

(a) Obstructing the rainwater and increasing ground water storage.

(b) Development of ground water resources at low level.

(c) Watershed development program can be done on a scientific basis.

5.2 TYPES OF WATERSHED

(i) Mini watershed
(ii) Intermediate watershed
(iii) Macro watershed

(i) Mini Watershed: A watershed covering an area ranging 25 hectors to 150 hectors, is termed as Mini watershed.

(ii) Intermediate Watershed: A watershed covering an area ranging 150 hectors to 750 hectors, is termed as Intermediate watershed.

(iii) Macro Watershed: A watershed covering an area ranging 750 hectors to 1500 hectors, is termed as Macro watershed.

5.3 DEMARCATION OF WATERSHED

The watershed can be marked from source of the stream i.e. from the ridge to the basin. Most of the time the village boundary is considered as the watershed boundary in between two villages.

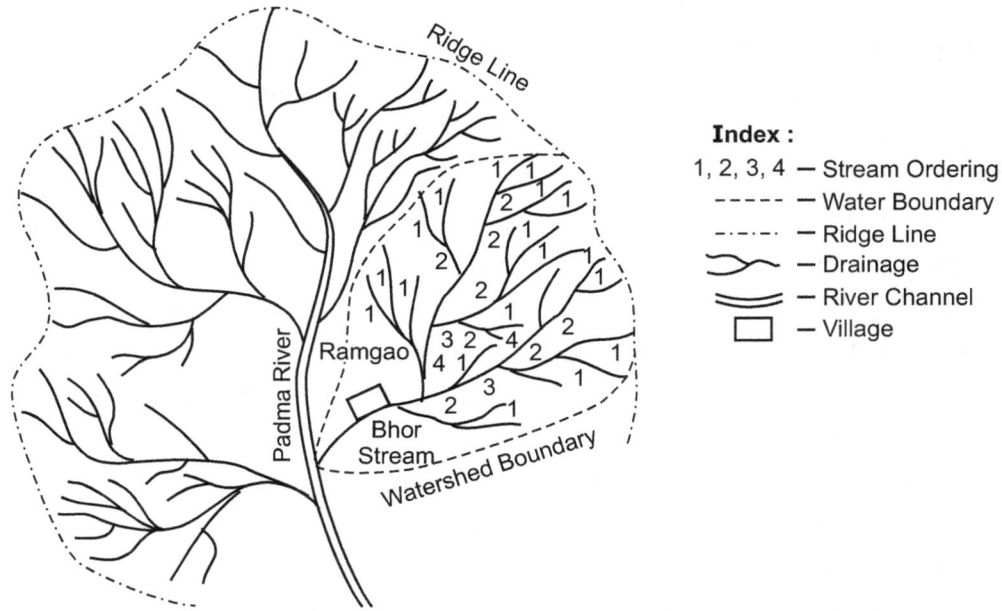

Fig. 5.1

The demarcation of a watershed is made in such a way that all the gullies and drains in the watershed from source (ridge line) to the basin (bottom) should be collected in a single drain and accordingly the boundary can be marked (Fig. 5.1). For example in Fig. 5.1, a Bhor stream is a tributary of a main river i.e. Padma river. It is 4th order stream, comes under Ramgaon village boundary. Therefore, a village boundary becomes a watershed boundary. But most of the times a watershed can have more than one village boundary.

Topography and geological conditions of the area play important role in creating groundwater potential. This aspect is described as –

(i) Hilly, (ii) Undulating, (iii) Plain.

5.4 WATER STRUCTURES

5.4.1 Present Status of the Measures on the Watershed Development
Project Study:

Different measures have been taken on the watershed project study. These measures have been taken for conservation of soil and to increase the ground water potential. The effectiveness of these measures depends upon the technical knowledge used during the construction, according to the purpose of the measures taken, and quality of the construction.

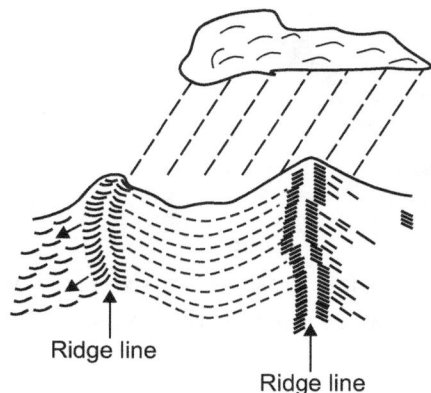

Fig. 5.2: Soil conservation structures

As mentioned above, following measures have been taken for the conservation of soil and to increase groundwater potential.

5.4.2 Measures Taken for Soil Conservation
(a) Gully Plugs
(b) Continuous/Staggered Contour trenches and
(c) Contour Bunds

5.4.3 Measures Taken for the Increase of Ground Water Potentials (Water Conservation Structures)
(a) Nala Bunds
(b) Earthen check dams
(c) Masonry check dams
(d) Gabions and Percolation Tank

These structures have been constructed very recently on five micro watersheds.

Development projects studied and it is expected that they would function effectively for a long time in future. From these points of view, the observation of these measures is carried out. These observations are given below in brief.

Gully plugs:
- Gully plugs, by using random rubble; have been constructed across the gullies on the hill slopes almost on all the watershed development projects studied.
- In the area of Siddeshwarwadi, beneficial Gully plugs constructed by the forest department have become very much beneficial.
- Towards upstream of the gully plugs, soil is deposited in the gullies which have become shallow.
- On the bank of the gullies, grass and bushes area grow vigorously due to the increase of soil moisture.

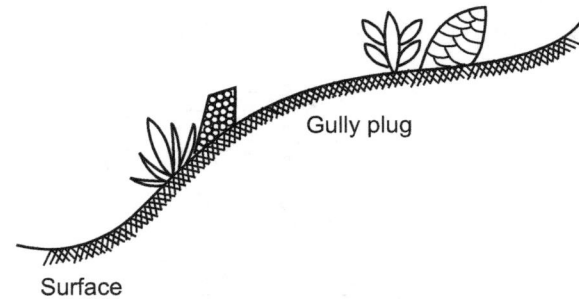

Fig. 5.3

- It is a common observation that, loose rocks used in construction of gully plugs are dislodged and are carried away along with the water and is laid down on the bed of the gully.

Continuous/Staggered Contour Trenches:

- Soil is an important material in the development of watershed, hence it is essential to control soil erosion. Therefore, Continuous Contour Trenches is one of the best solutions for the same.
- Contour trenches should be aligned along the contour so that, rain water remains accumulated for sometime in the contour trench and gradually percolates in the downstream region of the contour trench.

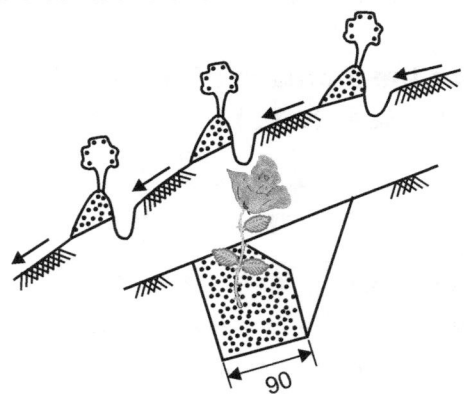

Fig. 5.4: Refilled continuous contour trenches (C.C.T.)

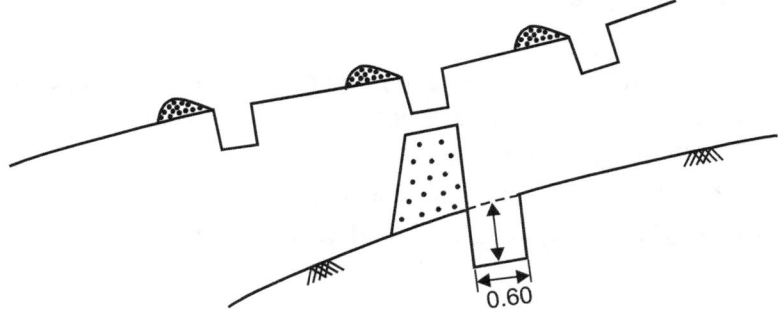

Fig. 5.5: Open continuous contour trenches

- On the southern slopes of the hill, contour trenches that are taken by the forest department can be considered as ideal ones.
- The soil is deposited in the trench and tress of Subabhul grow luxuriantly on the mountain. While on the slope of the hills in Mandwa ghat on way to Ambajogai, it is clearly seen from distance that contour trenches divert from the contour.

Loose Boulders:

In upper reaches area the loose boulder structures are constructed to reduce the velocity of water flowing on hill.

Mounds:

The soil and the murum excavated from the trench is stacked along the downstream edge of the trench forming small ridge or mound, on which forest trees are planted.

Fig. 5.6: Earthen mounds

Staggered Contour Trenches:
- In the area, where slope of hill is rather steep and intensity of rainfall is high, in that region staggered contour trenches are taken.
- The length of every contour trench is about 4 m having interval little less than 4 m between the two.
- Another row of contour trenches is taken alternatively to the previous ones at the lower level.
- The dimensions of these staggered contour trenches are similar to the continuous contour trenches.

Crescentric Contour Trenches:

They are also provided in the foot hill regions. The arms of the crescent always point towards the higher level whereas the kink of the crescent is at the lower. Therefore the maximum height of the bund is always at the kink and gradually it becomes less and less towards the arms.

Contour Bunds:

In the region of foot hills where slopes are flat and are covered by medium to coarse-grained soil, continuous contour bunds are provided. These bunds are very short and are constructed by scrapping the soil from the same area. As these bunds are aligned along the contour, the velocity of the water coming from the higher reaches gets reduced and whatever soil is removed from the higher level gets deposited towards upstream of the bunds.

Vanrai Bandhara: This structure is constructed by using cement bags. It is a temporary and low cost structure, constructed on the stream slope within 3% and 1 to 1.5 m stream bank height.

Gabbian Structure: The structure which is constructed by using stones randomly and is covered with mesh is known as gabbian.

The structure is constructed across the stream which has width of not more than 10 m. The height of the stream is not more than (1 m or) 1/3 of depth of stream.

Nala Bund: This is a masonry structure constructed across the stream. For this structure the required width of stream bed ranges from 30 m - 5 m.

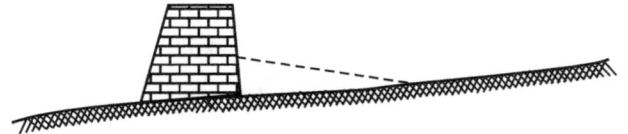

Fig. 5.7: Nala bund

Earthen Dams:

It is made up of earth material and has length equal to the width of the stream. This is known as an earthen structure. During construction of earthen check dam, engineering principle such as zone and quality should be controlled.

It is observed, in a number of watershed areas that the earthen check dams have been constructed without following engineering principles for providing zones and without observing quality control while using the material for construction.

At the earthen check dam, outlet is located at the side of the higher level, where rock occurring is to release excess quantity of water that cannot be stored in the check dam.

- If erodable rock occurs in the region of outlet and along the tail channel extensive, erosion to tail channel takes place - forming waterfalls.

- Sometimes erosion of the tail channel occurs almost touching the body of the earthen dam. If proper maintenance is not carried out, there is every possibility, that entire earthwork would be washed away.

- It is also observed that the extensive silting has occurred in majority of the earthen check dams, creating watertight blanket over the floor of the reservoir, and therefore no percolation takes through the reservoir area.

Masonry Check Dams:

- Masonry check dams constructed in the watershed area are of different dimension.
- Across the major Nalas, high masonry check dams are constructed where as, across the minor Nalas small and short check dams are constructed.

- It is observed that while constructing the check dams across the major streams some engineering principles are followed. However, while constructing small overflow structures, no engineering principles have been followed.
- It is also observed that in case of some check dams, quality control was not taken into account during the construction. In case of Check Dam, voids occur in the body of Check Dam, through which water percolates and Check Dam becomes empty. Similarly, at another Check Dam, no proper bond between the foundation rock and the base of the Check Dam was achieved. Therefore, Check Dams become empty by developing leakage from the junction between the foundation rock and back base of the check dam.
- It is also observed that in some of the Check Dams constructed on various watershed development projects, erosion at the toe has taken place. This indicates that supervision and maintenance are lacking.

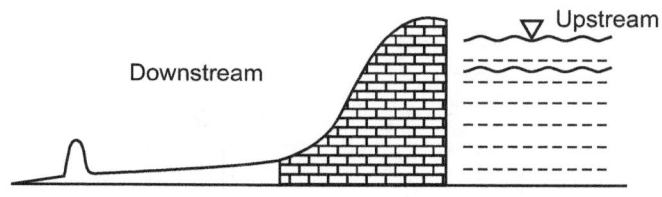

Fig. 5.8: Masonry check dam

If these structures continue to function for a long time to serve the purpose for which they have been constructed, their repairs are necessary for which suggestions have been made afterwards.

Percolation Tanks:

- The percolation tank is a major structure constructed in watershed areas for recharging the ground to increase the ground water potential. Therefore, geological conditions play important role in their functioning.
- Percolation tanks have been constructed side by side across the tributaries of the main stream.
- The percolation conditions are very much favourable at the site of percolation tank but cut-offs have been taken only upto shallow depth. Therefore, as soon as water starts accumulating in the percolation tank it becomes empty by developing profuse leakage through foundation.

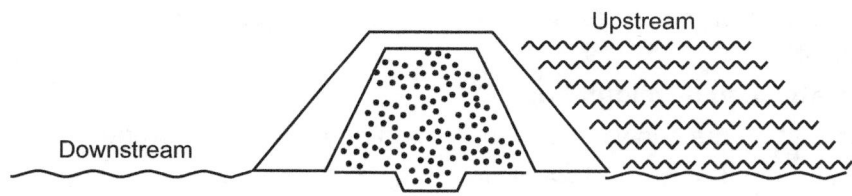

Fig. 5.9: Percolation tank

- A deep cut-off has been taken by the villagers immediately towards upstream of the wall of the percolation tank to stop profuse leakage that was taking place from the foundation rock. However, by taking new deep cut-off the percolation from the foundation rock is almost stopped and the area immediately towards downstream of percolation tank is deprived of getting any benefit.
- From the above observations of the present status of the measures taken in various watershed areas, it is clear that measures certainly require repairs and modification to make them meaningful and useful.

Farm Pond: The pond constructed at higher elevation in farmer's field to collect the extra flowing water during rain is known as farm pond. It stops surface run-off and stores large amount of water which result in ground water recharge and increase in yield of field.

It is a geographical unit draining at a common point by a system of streams, called watershed.

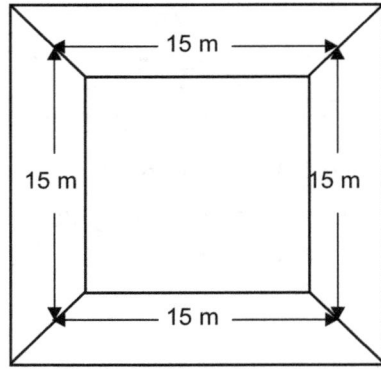

Fig. 5.10: Farm pond

Aim and Objective:
(i) Protect, conserve and improve the land resources for efficient and sustained production.
(ii) Protect and enhance water resource, moderate flood and reduce silting up of tanks, increase irrigation and conserving rainwater for crops and thus mitigate draughts.
(iii) To utilize the natural local resources for improving agriculture and allied occupation or industries, so as to improve socio-economic conditions of the local residents.

Program of watershed development:
(i) Obstructing the rainwater and increasing ground water storage.
(ii) Development of ground water resources.
(iii) Watershed development program can be done on the scientific basis.

Gulley Plug   **Continuous Contour Trenches CCT**

Check Weir   **Farm Pond**

Check Dam   **K. T. Weir**

Photos

K. T. Weir (Kolhapur Type Weir):

Kolhapur type weir is a typical water conservation structure, in which open gates are provided for easy operation to dispose the excess water during flood condition.

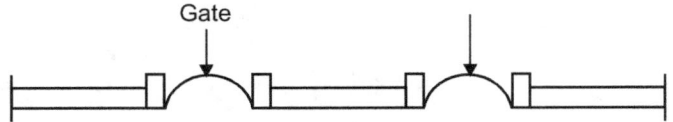

Fig. 5.11: Kolhapur type weir

5.5 ELEMENTS OF WATERSHED

Topography:

Topography of the area play important role in increasing ground water potential. The geomorphic structure present in the area should be described. The altitudinal range in the watershed projects such as highest and lowest elevation, should be reported. The type of the drainage pattern and slope of the area is also studied under this section.

It is categorized as (i) Hilly, (ii) Undulating and (iii) Plain topography.

Rainfall data:

As referred in the criteria for selection of watershed, the area for proposed watershed should be a draught prone area, and there should be a scarcity of rainfall. So last 20 years rainfall data of watershed area is collected to know the back history of the same. For the selection of watershed, this rainfall data should be below the average rate. Rainfall is very important parameter to recharge the watershed.

Climatic Conditions:

Data is collected from the nearest meteorological station. The following data is collected to check the climatic conditions of the study area:

1. Normal rainfall of the area in a year.
2. Highest intensity/hour of rainfall in the last 10 years (mm).
3. Highest rainfall in 24 hours in last 10 years (mm) and average rainfall is calculated.
4. Temperature maximum and minimum in three seasons i.e. summer, monsoon and winter.

During climatic studies following points are taken into consideration:

(i) Whether the climate is hot or cold.
(ii) Dry or moist.
(iii) Microclimatic zone boundaries within the watershed are also studied.

5.6 ROOF TOP RAIN WATER HARVESTING

Rooftop Rain Water Harvesting is the technique through which rain water is captured from the roof catchments and stored in reservoirs. Harvested rain water can be stored in sub-surface ground water reservoir by adopting artificial recharge techniques to meet the household needs through storage in tanks.

The Main Objective of rooftop rain water harvesting is to make water available for future use. Capturing and storing rain water for use is particularly important in dryland, hilly, urban and coastal areas. In alluvial areas energy saving for 1 m rise in ground water level is around 0.40 kilo watt per hour.

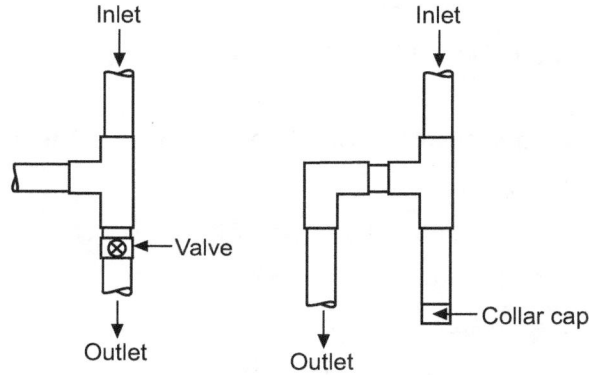

Fig. 5.12: Rainwater harvesting

5.6.1 Need for Rooftop Rain Water Harvesting

1. To meet the ever increasing demand for water.
2. To reduce the runoff which chokes storm drains.
3. To avoid flooding of roads.
4. To augment the ground water storage and control decline of water levels.
5. To reduce ground water pollution.
6. To improve the quality of ground water.
7. To reduce the soil erosion.
8. To supplement domestic water requirement during summer, drought etc.

5.6.2 Advantages of Rain Water Harvesting

1. Provides self-sufficiency to your water supply.
2. Reduces the cost for pumping of ground water.
3. Provides high quality water, soft and low in minerals.
4. Improves the quality of ground water through dilution when recharged to ground water.

5. Reduces soil erosion in urban areas.
6. The rooftop rain water harvesting is less expensive.
7. Rainwater harvesting systems are simple which can be adopted by individuals.
8. Rooftop rain water harvesting systems are easy to construct, operate and maintain.
9. In hilly terrains, rain water harvesting is preferred.
10. In saline or coastal areas, rain water provides good quality water and when recharged to ground water, it reduces salinity and also helps in maintaining balance between the fresh-saline water interface.
11. In Islands, due to limited extent of fresh water aquifers, rain water harvesting is the most preferred source of water for domestic use.
12. In desert, where rain fall is low, rain water harvesting has been providing relief to people.

5.6.3 Simple Formula to Workout the Run-off from a Catchment Area

$$Q = A \times I \times C$$

where,
- Q = Total quantity of water to be collected (cu.m.)
- A = Roof top area (sq.m.)
- I = Average monsoon rainfall (m)
- C = Co-efficient of run-off

Collection Efficiency: Efficiently the rainfall can be collected depends on several considerations. Collection efficiencies of 80% are often used depending on the specific design.

5.6.4 Components of the Roof Top Rainwater Harvesting System

The illustrative design of the basic components of roof top rainwater harvesting system is given in the following typical schematic diagram.

The system mainly constitutes of following sub components:

1. Catchment.
2. Transportation.
3. First flush.
4. Filter.

5.6.4.1 Catchment

The surface that receives rainfall directly is the catchment of rainwater harvesting system. It may be terrace, courtyard, or paved or unpaved open ground. The terrace may be flat RCC/stone roof or sloping roof. Therefore the catchment is the area, which actually contributes rainwater to the harvesting system.

5.6.4.2 Transportation

Rainwater from rooftop should be carried through downtake water pipes or drains to storage/harvesting system. Water pipes should be UV resistant (ISI HDPE/PVC pipes) of required capacity. Water from sloping roofs could be caught through gutters and down take pipe. At terraces, mouth of the each drain should have wire mesh to restrict floating material.

5.6.4.3 First Flush

First flush is a device used to flush off the water received in first shower. The first shower of rains needs to be flushed-off to avoid contaminating storable/rechargeable water by the probable contaminants of the atmosphere and the catchment roof. It will also help in cleaning of silt and other material deposited on roof during dry seasons. Provisions of first rain separator should be made at outlet of each drainpipe.

5.6.4.4 Filter

There is always some skepticism regarding Roof Top Rainwater Harvesting since doubts are raised that rainwater may contaminate groundwater. There is remote possibility of this fear coming true if proper filter mechanism is not adopted. Secondly all care must be taken to see that underground sewer drains are not punctured and no leakage is taking place in close vicinity. Filters are used for treatment of water to effectively remove turbidity, colour and microorganisms. After first flushing of rainfall, water should pass through filters. There are different types of filters in practice, but basic function is to purify water.

5.6.4.5 Sand Gravel Filter

These are commonly used filters, constructed by brick masonry and filleted by pebbels, gravel and sand as shown in the Fig. 5.13. Each layer should be separated by wire mesh.

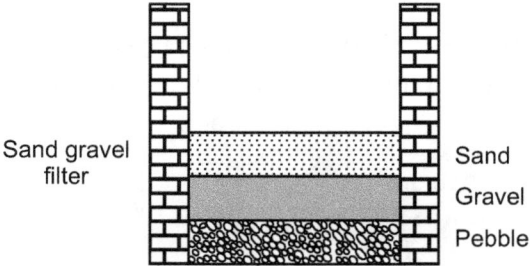

Fig. 5.13: Sand gravel filter

5.6.4.6 Charcoal

Charcoal filter can be made in-situ or in a drum. Pebbles, gravel, sand and charcoal as shown in the Fig. 5.14 should fill the drum or chamber. Each layer should be separated by wire mesh. Thin layer of charcoal is used to absorb odour if any.

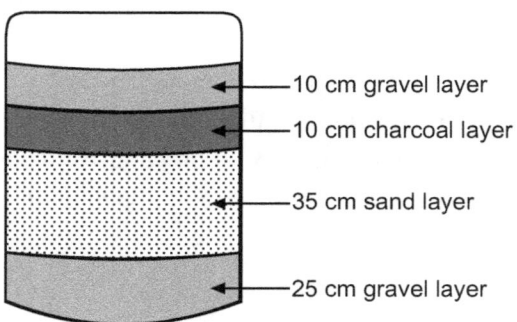

Fig. 5.14

5.6.4.7 PVC- Pipe Filter

This filter can be made by PVC pipe of 1 to 1.20 m length; Diameter of pipe depends on the area of roof. Six inches diameter pipe is enough for a 1500 Sq. feet roof and 8 inches diameter pipe should be used for roofs more then 1500 Sq. feet pipe is divided into three compartments by wire mesh. Each component should be filled with gravel and sand alternatively as shown in the Fig. 5.15. A layer of charcoal could also be inserted between two layers. Both ends of filter should have reduce of required size to connect inlet and outlet. This filter could be placed horizontally or vertically in the system.

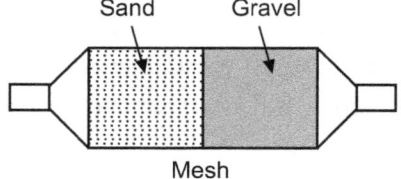

Fig. 5.15: PVC pipe filter

5.6.4.8 Sponge Filter

It is a simple filter made from PVC drum having a layer of sponge in the middle of drum. It is the easiest and cheapest form of filter, suitable for residential units.

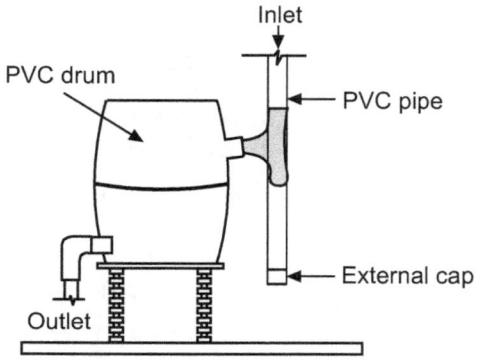

Fig. 5.16: Sponge filter

5.7 METHODS OF ROOF TOP RAINWATER HARVESTING

Storage of Direct Use

In this method, rain water collected from the roof of the building is diverted to a storage tank. The storage tank has to be designed according to the water requirements, rainfall and catchment availability. Each drainpipe should have mesh filter at mouth and first flush device followed by filtration system before connecting to the storage tank. It is advisable that each tank should have excess water overflow system.

Excess water could be diverted to recharge system. Water from storage tank can be used for secondary purposes such as washing and gardening etc. This is the most cost effective way of rainwater harvesting. The main advantage of collecting and using the rainwater during rainy season is not only to save water from conventional sources, but also to save energy incurred on transportation and distribution of water at the doorstep. These also conserve groundwater, if it is being extracted to meet the demand when rains are on.

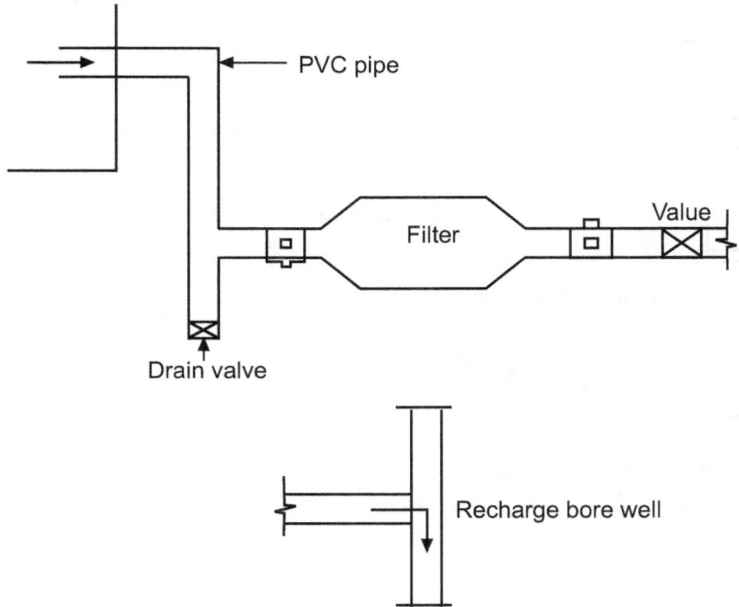

Fig. 5.17: Flow diagram of rainwater harvesting

5.7.1 Recharging Ground Water Aquifers

Ground water aquifers can be recharged by various kinds of structures to ensure percolation of rainwater in the ground instead of draining away from the surface. Commonly used recharging methods are:

(a) Recharging of bore wells,

(b) Recharging of dug wells,

(c) Recharge pits,

(d) Recharge trenches,

(e) Soak ways or Recharge shafts,

(f) Percolation tanks,

5.7.2 Recharging of Bore Wells

Rainwater collected from rooftop of the building is diverted through drainpipes to settlement or filtration tank. After settlement, filtered water is diverted to bore wells to recharge deep aquifers. Abandoned bore wells can also be used for recharge.

Optimum capacity of settlement tank/filtration tank can be designed on the basis of area of catchment, intensity of rainfall and recharge rate as discussed in design parameters. While recharging, entry of floating matter and silt should be restricted because it may clog the recharge structure. "First one or two shower should be flushed out through rain separator to avoid contamination. This is very important, and all care should be taken to ensure that this has been done."

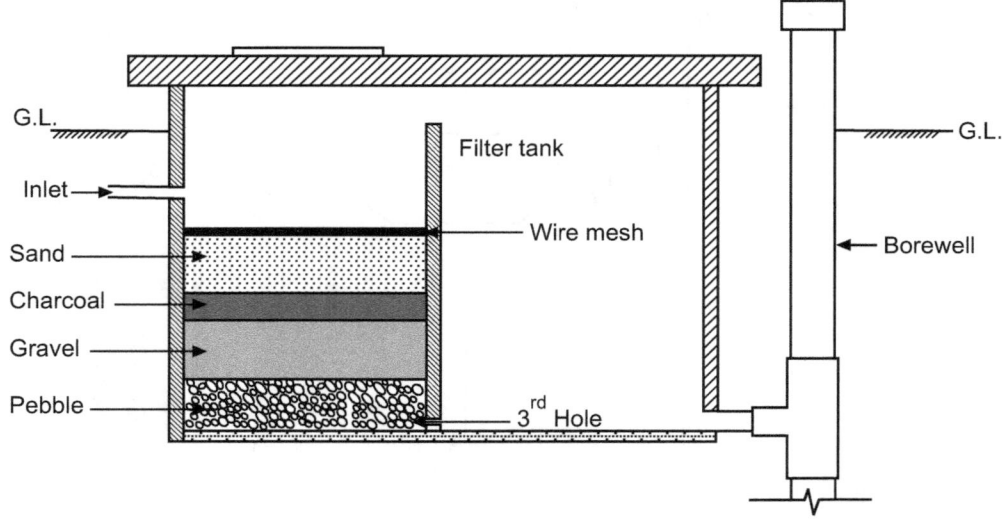

Fig. 5.18: Filtration tank

5.7.3 Recharge Pits

Recharge pits are small pits of any shape rectangular, square or circular, contacted with brick or stone masonry wall with weep hole at regular intervals. Top of pit can be covered with perforated covers. Bottom of pit should be filled with filter media.

The capacity of the pit can be designed on the basis of catchment area, rainfall intensity and recharge rate of soil. Usually the dimensions of the pit may be of 1 to 2 m width and 2 to 3 m deep depending on the depth of pervious strata. These pits are suitable for recharging of shallow aquifers and small houses.

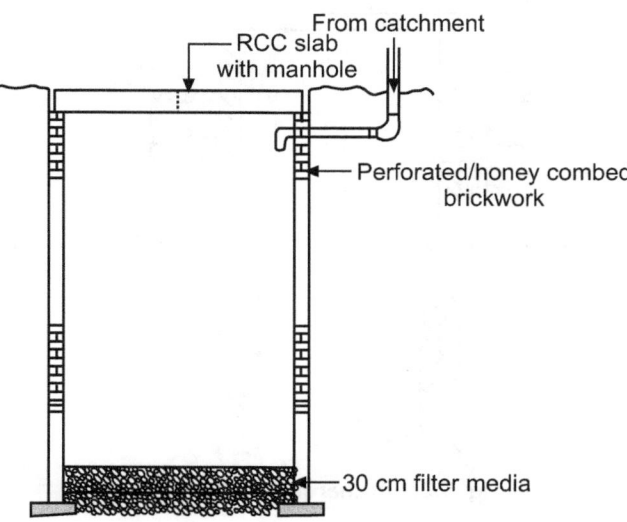

Fig. 5.19: Typical recharge pit

5.7.4 Soak Away or Recharge Shafts

Soak away or recharge shafts are provided where upper layer of soil is alluvial or less pervious. These are bored hole of 30 cm diameter upto 10 to 15 m deep, depending on depth of pervious layer. Bore should be lined with slotted/perforated PVC/MS pipe to prevent collapse of the vertical sides. At the top of soak away required size sump is constructed to retain runoff before the filters through soak away. Sump should be filled with filter media.

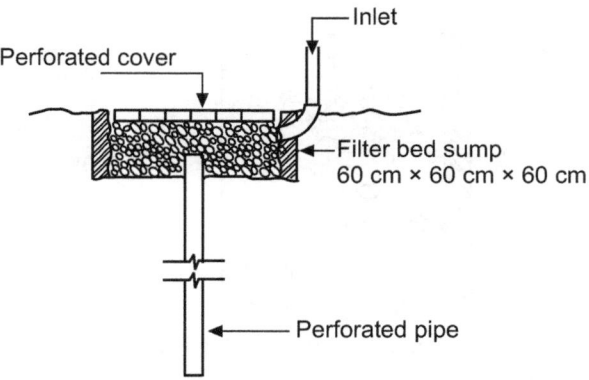

Fig. 5.20: Recharge shafts

5.7.5 Recharging of Dug Wells

Dug well can be used as recharge structure. Rainwater from the rooftop is diverted to dug wells after passing it through filtration bed. Cleaning and desalting of dug well should be done regularly to enhance the recharge rate. The filtration method suggested for bore well recharging could be used.

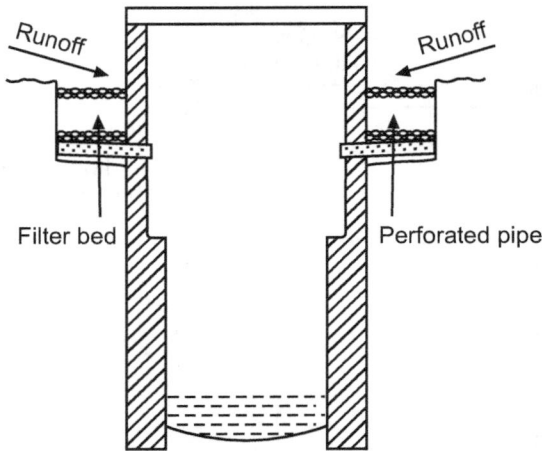

Fig. 5.21: Recharging of dug wells

5.7.6 Recharge Trenches

Recharge trench is provided where upper impervious layer of soil is shallow. It is a trench excavated on the ground and refilled with porous media like pebbles, boulder or brickbats. It is usually made for harvesting the surface runoff. Bore wells can also be provided inside the trench as recharge shafts to enhance percolation. The length of the trench is decided as per the amount of runoff expected. This method is suitable for small houses, playgrounds, parks and roadside drains. The recharge trench can be of size 0.50 to 1.0 m wide and 1.0 to 1.5 m deep.

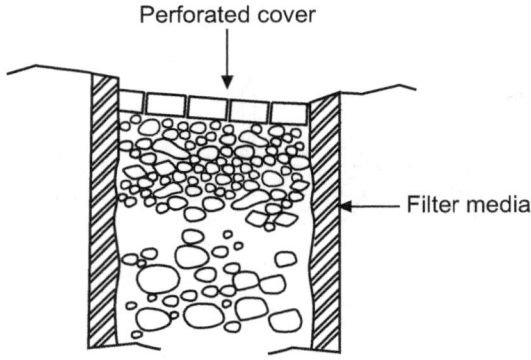

Fig. 5.22: Recharge trenches

5.7.7 Percolation Tanks

Percolation tanks are artificially created surface water bodies, submerging a land area with adequate permeability to facilitate sufficient percolation to recharge the ground water. These can be built in big campuses where land is available and topography is suitable.

Surface run-off and roof top water can be diverted to this tank. Water accumulating in the tank percolates in the solid to augment the ground water. The stored water can be used directly for gardening and raw use. Percolation tanks should be built in gardens, open spaces and roadside green belts of urban area.

5.8 INTRODUCTION OF DAM

A dam is a structure constructed across a river to store water (in the reservoir) on its upstream side. The stored water may then be utilized for water supply, irrigation, hydropower generation, navigation etc. The main purpose of a dam is to make provision for the safe retention and storage of water on its upstream side.

Dams which are unique structures, are constructed of various shapes and sizes by using various types of materials such as earth, rock, stone (masonry) or concrete. They demonstrate great complexity in their load response, depending upon the hydrology and geologic condition of the site.

As failure of a dam may result in a heavy loss of human life and property, it must be designed, constructed and maintained with utmost care. Thus safety of the dam is the first and foremost consideration. The choice of the type of a dam is often governed by site conditions and availability of funds.

5.8.1 Classification of Dams

Dams which are of numerous types may be classified into a number of different categories based upon the purpose of classification such as its use, hydraulic design or materials of construction of the structure.

(1) Classification Based on its Use:

According to the use, the dams may be classified as 'storage dams', 'diversion dams' or 'detention dams'.

- (i) **Storage dams (or weirs)** are constructed across rivers to store water in the reservoir when there is excess flow in rivers. This stored water may then be utilized during the periods of deficient supply in summer.
- (ii) **Diversion dams** are constructed to divert the whole or part of water from the river into the adjoining canal or conveyance system for carrying it to the place of use i.e. irrigation.
- (iii) **Detention dams** are primarily constructed to retard the flood flows by detaining the flood waters of river and then gradually allowing it to pass safely on the downstream side.

(2) Classification Based on the Hydraulic Design:

Based on the hydraulic design, the dams are classified as 'overflow' or 'non-overflow' dams.

- (i) **Overflow dams:** As the name suggests, overflow dams are designed to pass the (flood) discharge over their crests and are therefore to be constructed of materials that will not be eroded or washed away by such discharge e.g. masonry or concrete structures (i.e. spillways).
- (ii) **Non-overflow dams:** Non-overflow dams are those which do not allow the flood discharge to pass over it i.e. overlapping is not possible in case of non-overflow dams. Usually, some portion of the length of the dam is designed as an overflow (i.e. spillway) section and the remaining portion is designed as a non-overflow section. A 'composite dam' consists of an overflow masonry or concrete gravity dam joining the dikes of earth fill section.

(3) Classification on the Basis of Construction Material (Used):

Depending upon the type of materials of construction, dams are often classified as 'Rigid dams' and 'Non-rigid dams'.

(i) **Rigid dams:** Rigid dams are those which are constructed by making use of solid rigid materials such as (stone) masonry, concrete, steel, timber etc. and are termed as 'masonry' or 'concrete gravity dams', 'concrete arch dams', 'concrete buttress dams', 'steel or timber dams'. The Khadakwasla dam (Pune District) in Maharashtra is a stone masonry dam, whereas the Bhakra dam in Punjab is a concrete dam. Figs. 5.23, 5.24 and 5.25 indicate masonry or concrete gravity dam, concrete arch dam and concrete buttress dams respectively.

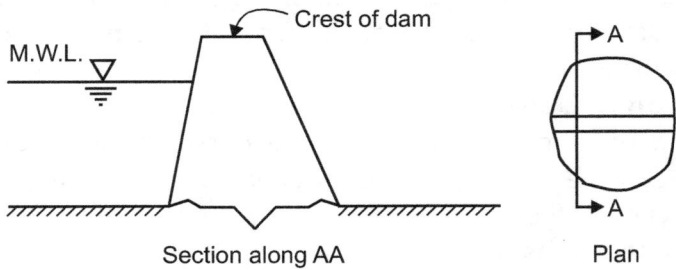

Fig. 5.23: Masonry or concrete gravity dam

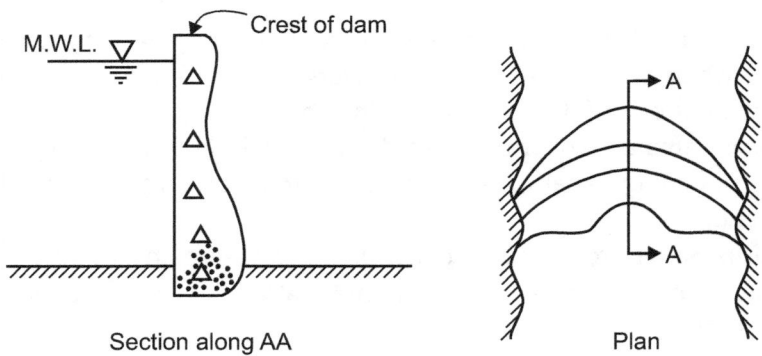

Fig. 5.24: Concrete arch dam

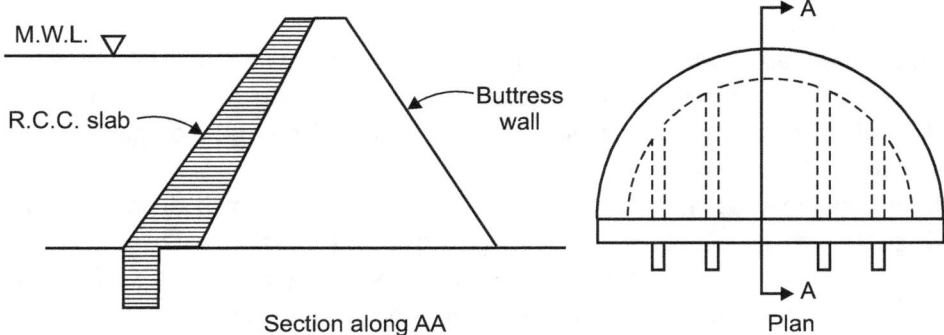

Fig. 5.25: Concrete buttress dam

(ii) Non-rigid dams: 'Non-rigid dams' are those which are constructed of materials such as earth or rock fill without any cementing material and are called as 'embankment dams' i.e. 'earth dams', 'rock fill dams' etc. Fig. 5.26 indicates an embankment type (either earth or rock fill) of dam. It may be noted that the embankment dams being economical account for about 84% of the dams constructed so far. Remaining 10% are gravity dams (either of masonry or concrete), 4.5% are arch type dams, 1% are buttress type dams and 0.5% are of multiple arch type dams.

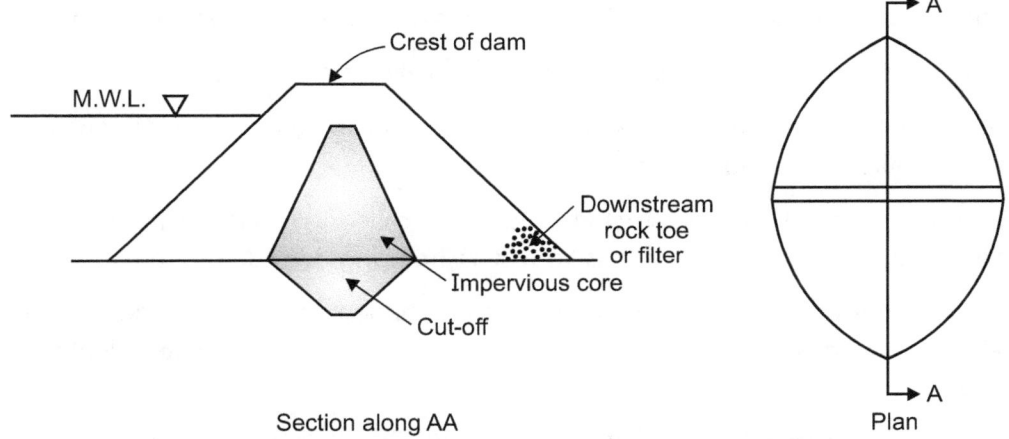

Fig. 5.26: Embankment type dam (i.e. Earth or Rock fill)

5.9 GRAVITY DAM

- A 'gravity dam' is a permanent hydraulic structure, so proportional (in its size) that it resists all the external force acting upon it by virtue of its own weight. It is therefore vertically triangular in shape and is to be constructed on solid, sound rock foundations.

- Even though its initial cost of construction is high (as compared to embankment dam), it requires very little maintenance, after its construction.

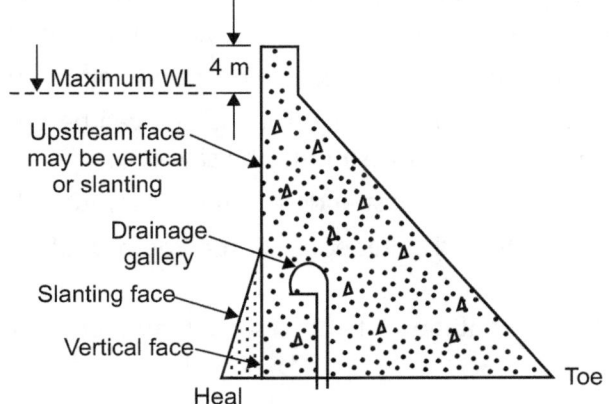

Fig. 5.27: A typical cross-section of a concrete gravity dam

- The most ancient type of gravity dam constructed in Egypt of uncemented masonry dates back to 4,000 year BC the archeological expert is of the view that this dam was maintained in perfect good condition for more than 45 centuries.
- A gravity dam may be built either in rubble masonry or concrete.
- Examples: The Khadakwasala Dam across Mutha River (Pune District) in Maharashtra and Nagarjun Sagar Dam in Andhra Pradesh has been constructed in stone masonry. However, with the advances made in the methods of construction, quality controls, curing of concrete etc. presently almost all dams are being constructed in concrete.
- Gravity dams are mostly straight in plan and are called straight gravity dams.
- Sometimes if limited degree of arch action is incorporated in the design to allow a thinner profile, it is called as 'arch gravity dam'.
- The gravity dam may be constructed solid and is called as 'solid gravity dam'. However, if it is made intentionally hollow, it is known as 'hollow gravity dam'.
- The (concrete) gravity dams are suitable for U-shaped valleys or gorges having steep side slope where solid rock foundations are encountered at reasonable depth of about 10 metres.
- The highest concrete gravity dam in the world 285 m high is - Grand Dixence Dam (1962) in the Switzerland (After Mermel 1988). The Bhakra Dam (226 m) in India (Arch gravity type) stands second in the world.
- The ratio of the base width to height of dam in these dams is far less than 1: 1.

Advantages of Gravity Dams:

The gravity dams possess the following advantages:
1. These are more suitable in steep valleys where earth's dams may tend to slip.
2. In these dams, surplus water may be discharged through the sluices provided in the body of the dam or over spillway built in a suitable location of the dam.
3. Such dams on strong foundations may be built up to a maximum practical height.
4. A gravity dam does not fail suddenly. Their failure can be predicted well in advance so that loss of property downstream may be saved.
5. Their cost of maintenance is least and benefit of cost ratio is highest.
6. These are found more advantageous in the regions of high rainfall and heavy snowfalls.
7. In these dams, sedimentation of the reservoir may be cleared through deep set sluices.

Disadvantages of Gravity Dams:
1. Their initial cost of construction is high.

2. Their construction period is comparatively more.
3. These require a strong and sound foundation.
4. Dams once constructed, cannot be raised further.
5. For the supervision of concrete dams, skilled labour is required.

5.10 EARTHEN DAM

- Earthen dams and earthen levees are the most ancient type of embankments, as they can be built with the natural materials with a minimum processing and primitive equipment.

- But in ancient days, the cost of carriage and dumping of the dam materials was quite high. However, the modern developments in earth moving equipments have considerably reduced the cost of carriage and laying of the dam materials.

- The cost of gravity dams on the other hand, has gone up because of an increase in the cost of concrete, masonry etc. while earthen dams are still cheaper as they can utilize the locally available materials and less skilled labour is required for them.

- Gravity dams require sound rocks foundations, but earthen dams can be easily constructed on earthen foundations. However, earthen dams are most susceptible to failure as compared to rigid gravity dams or arch dams.

- Before the development of the subject of soil-mechanics, these dams were being designed and constructed on the basis of experience, as on rational basis for their design was available. This led to the failure of various such earthen embankments.

- However, in these days, these dams can be designed with a fair degree of theoretical accuracy, provided the properties of the soil placed in the dam, are properly controlled. This condition makes the design and construction of such dams, thoroughly interdependent.

- Continuous field observations of deformations and pore water pressures have to be made during the construction of such dams. Suitable modifications in the design are then made during construction, depending upon these field observations.

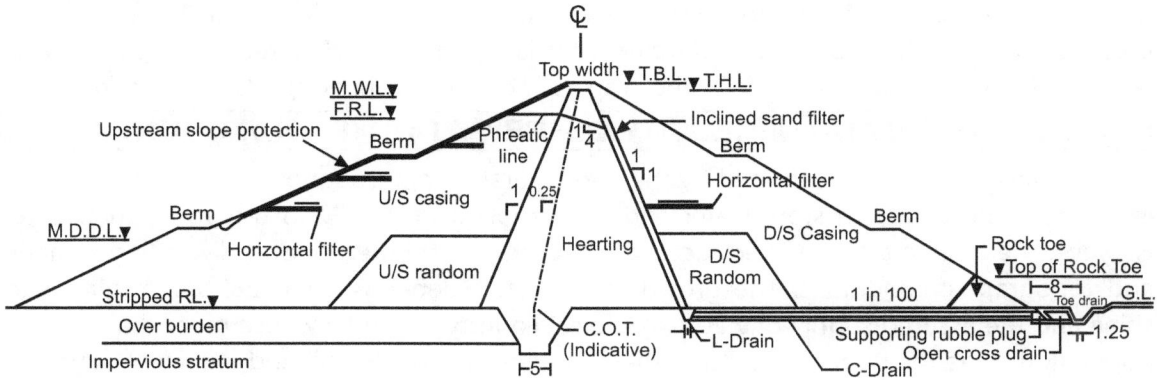

Fig. 5.28: Typical section of earth dam at (gorge)

Advantages of Earthen Dams:

Some of the outstanding advantages possessed by earthen dam over other types are as follows:

1. They can be constructed on any type of foundation such as soil, gravel, rock etc.
2. Use of locally available natural material and thus saving in the cost of transport.
3. Equally suitable for sites having very wide to steep valleys or gorges.
4. Highly mechanized and continuous process of construction.
5. The design is flexible that permits the use of different materials.
6. It is less costly as compared to other types of dams.

Disadvantages of Earthen Dams:

However, the following are some disadvantages of the earthen dams:

1. Earthen dams need supplement structures to serve as a spillway.
2. If the capacity of spillway is insufficient, dam is likely to be overlapped, which may ultimately result in its failure.
3. Subject to damage due to borrowing of animals.
4. Susceptible to concealed leakage and erosion of the foundation and dam.
5. Time required for construction of dams is more than R.C.C. dam.
6. Maintenance and operation cost is more than other type of dam.

5.11 INTRODUCTION TO IRRIGATION

A crop requires certain amount of water at different intervals throughout its growth period. If it rains as and when required by the crop, it is not necessary to supply water to it, artificially. However, as it happens in our country, it may not rain when required by the crops and sometimes it may rain in excess of its requirements thus damaging the crops. Thus, instead of depending entirely on the mercy of nature, man thought of storing the water during the excessive rainfall and utilizing it during the scanty or less rainfall period. Thus, irrigation may be defined as 'the scientific artificial application of water to the agricultural land to supply necessary moisture to the crop as and when required for its healthy growth'.

5.12 FUNCTIONS AND NECESSITY OF IRRIGATION (IN OUR COUNTRY)

If it rains as and when required by the agricultural crop, throughout its growth period, it is not at all necessary to store water and then apply it artificially to the agricultural crop. However, tie India monsoon is erratic and not evenly distributed due to diversified climatic and topographic conditions. The growth of the crop depends upon the soil fertility, sun shine and the assured supply of water. In topical country like India whose more than 70% of population depends upon agriculture, there is plenty of fertile soil and sufficient sunshine for the growth of crop. However, the rainfall is uncertain, untimely and unevenly distributed resulting in the necessity of artificial application of water by efficient irrigation system.

Irrigation is necessary for the following reasons:

(i) **Scanty Rainfall:** In India, many areas like Rajasthan receive very less rainfall. These areas need irrigation water, in such cases, irrigation work may be constructed at the places where quantity of water is available and we can convey the water to such areas where there is deficiency of water.

(ii) **Non-Uniform Rainfall:** In India, there is large spatial and temporal variation in precipitation. Thus, the rainfall is not uniform at all the zones. The rainfall during the winter is very scanty and therefore Rabi crops need the artificial supply of water by the irrigation works.

(iii) **Increasing Yield in Dry Farming:** Dry farming depends upon natural rainfall. Agriculture which deals with rainfall only, is called dry farming.

(iv) **Practicing Crop Rotation:** To bring in rotation of crops, i.e. if we want that the more number of crops should be rotated then there will be need of irrigation water.

(v) **Controlled Water supply:** As irrigation serves the following important purposes:

(a) It can save the crops from drying during short duration droughts.

(b) It washes out or dilutes salts in soil.

(c) It cools the soil and also the atmosphere and makes more favourable environment for healthy plant growth.

The construction of proper distribution system may ensure proper irrigation water supply. Thus, the yield of the crop can be increased even there is limited water supply. Proper irrigation system checks water losses during irrigation.

5.13 ADVANTAGES OF IRRIGATION

It hardly needs to emphasize the importance and benefits of irrigation when our country has to increase the overall food production to meet the food requirements of growing population Even then, some of the direct and indirect benefits of irrigation are as follows:

(A) Direct Benefits:

(i) **Increased food production:** As there is assured supply of water to the agricultural crop, there is bound to be increase in food production. This is the most important benefit for our country in view of tremendous growth in population and sizeable quantities of food grains that are to be imported every year.

(ii) **Protection from famine:** With the artificial application of water, there will be assured growth of crop resulting in protection from famine thus reducing the amount to be spent by the Government on famine relief works.

- (iii) **No necessity of mixed cropping:** In areas where irrigation facilities are not available, farmers generally adopt 'mixed cropping' system i.e. sowing together of two or more crops in the same agricultural land. If the weather conditions are not favourable to one of the crops, they may be beneficial for the other and thus the cultivator gets at least some yield from the land. When irrigation facilities are made available, farmers need not adopt the mixed cropping system.

- (iv) **Cultivation of cash crops:** With the assured supply of irrigation water, the farmers may cultivate more remunerative crops such as tobacco, sugarcane etc. in place of conventional crops such as Bajara, Jowar etc.

- (v) **Plantation:** Plantation of trees along the canal banks leads to the increase in the timber wealth of the country and also prevent the erosion of soil in such areas.

- (vi) **Navigation:** The large irrigation canals may serve as the cheapest means of transport and thus serve the useful purpose of inland navigation.

- (vii) **Appreciation of value of agricultural land:** Due to assured supply of irrigation water, the value of agricultural land in the command area gets appreciated.

- (viii) **Generation of hydro-electric power:** Water stored in the reservoirs and also from the canal falls can be used for the generation of hydro-electric power.

- (ix) **Drinking water supply:** Irrigation water stored in the reservoirs can also be used as supply of drinking water to the towns and cities.

(B) Indirect Benefits:

- (i) **Increase in revenue:** Large irrigation projects serve as a permanent sources of additional income to the government.

- (ii) **Overall development of the area:** Due to the availability of irrigation facilities, there will be overall development and prosperity and the general standard of living in the area increases.

- (iii) **Employment opportunities:** The constructions of large irrigation projects, creates employment to the people in that area.

- (iv) **Increase in the ground water table:** Irrigation facility in an area increases the general level of ground water table due to seepage of water through the reservoir and canal and thus the cost of lifting water from the adjoining open wells and tube wells gets reduced.

5.14 DISADVANTAGES OF IRRIGATION

Some of the ill-effects of irrigation are as follows:

- (i) **Water logging:** Due to over irrigation and seepage from canals the ground water table rises and in the absence of proper drainage of the soil, leads to water logging. Water logging renders the soil infertile and useless for cultivation.

(ii) Bad climate: Due to intense irrigation of an area, the climate becomes cold and damp resulting in unhealthy climate causing outbreak of malaria disease.

(iii) Increase in humidity: Excess and intense irrigation may result in increasing the humidity of the area.

(iv) Marshy land: Excess irrigation of the land with poor drainage may convert it into a marshy land.

EXERCISE

1. Explain necessity of watershed management work.
2. Explain the types of structures involved in watershed management.
3. Define watershed.
4. Explain roof top rain water havesting and ground water recharge.
5. Explain necessity of irrigation and benefits of irrigation.
6. Write short notes on the following:
    (i) Classification of dams.
    (ii) Zoned earthen embankment.
    (iii) Watershed management.
    (iv) Construction of septic tank.

UNIT 6

ENVIRONMENTAL ENGINEERING

6.0 WATER DEMAND

While designing the water supply scheme for a town or city, it is necessary to determine the total quantity of water required for various purposes by the city. As a matter of fact the first duty of the engineer is to determine the water demand of the town and then to find suitable water sources from where the demand can be met. But as there are so many factors involved in demand of water, it is not possible to accurately determine the actual demand. Certain empirical formulae and thumb rules are employed in determining the water demand, which is very near to the actual demand.

Following are the various types of water demands of a city or town:

6.1 CATEGORIES OF WATER DEMAND

Water demand may be divided into the following categories:
(a) Domestic,
(b) Institutional,
(c) Industrial,
(d) Public,
(e) Agricultural,
(f) Fire, and
(g) Compensation of losses

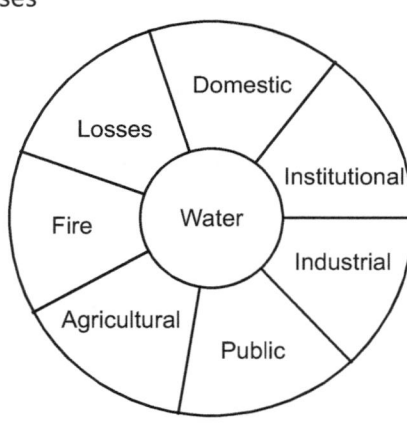

Fig. 6.1

(a) Domestic Water Demand:

Domestic water requirement may be divided as:

(i) In-house requirement

(ii) Sprinkling requirement

In-house requirement includes drinking, cooking, sanitation, house cleaning, clothes washing etc.

Sprinkling requirement includes water requirement for garden watering, lawn sprinkling, car washing etc.

Domestic water demand mainly depends upon the habits, social status, climatic conditions and customs of the people. As per IS: 1172-1963, under normal conditions, the domestic consumption of water in India is about 135 litres/day/capita. But in developed countries this figure may be 350 litres/day/capita because of use of air coolers, air conditioners, maintenance of lawns, automatic household appliances.

The details of the domestic consumption are:

(a) Drinking   5 litres
(b) Cooking   5 litres
(c) Bathing   55 litres
(d) Clothes washing   20 litres
(e) Utensils washing   10 litres
(f) House washing   <u>10 litres</u>
                        135 litres/day/capita

(b) Institution and Commercial Demand:

Universities, Institution, commercial buildings and commercial centers including office buildings, warehouses, stores, hotels, shopping centers, health centers, schools, temple, cinema houses, railway and bus stations etc. comes under this category. As per IS: 1172-1963, water supply requirements for the public buildings other than residences are as follows.

Sr. No.	Type of Building	Construction per capita per day (litres)
1.	(a) Factories where bathrooms are required to be provided.	45
	(b) Factories where no bathrooms are required to be provided	30
2.	Hospitals per bed	
	(a) Number of beds not exceeding 100	340
	(b) Number of beds exceeding 100	450

... Contd.

3.	Nurse homes and medical quarters.	135
4.	Hostels	135
5.	Offices	45
6.	Restaurants (per seat)	70
7.	Hotel (per bed)	180
8.	Cinema concert halls and theatres (per seat)	15
9.	Schools	
	(a) Day schools	45
	(b) Boarding schools	135
10.	Garden, sport grounds	35 per sq. m.
11.	Animal/vehicles	45

(c) Industrial:

Factors governing industrial water requirements depend on several factors. Such as type of industry, size of industry and number of industries for a particular water supply scheme. A water supply scheme may be planned for a residential town and amount of water requirement, may be taken care of for existing industry in the town or city likely to come up. Sometimes, a water supply scheme is planned for an industrial area where different type of industry of different sizes is located or likely to come. A case may be there, in which size of the industry is of such a giant one, that water supply scheme has to be planned for that particular industry in addition to housing and other amenities associated with the industry. Water requirement for a few industries located in a town may be taken around 60 litre/head/day but the demand may go as high as 500 litre/head/day depending on type of industry.

(d) Demand for Public Use:

Quantity of water required for public utility purposes such as for washing and sprinkling on roads, cleaning of sewers, watering of public parks, gardens, public fountains etc. comes under public demand. To meet the water demand for public use, provision of 5% of the total consumption is made designing the water works for a city.

The requirements of water for public utility shall be taken as given in Table:

Sr. No.	Purpose water	Requirements
1.	Public parks	1.4 litres/m^2/day
2.	Street washing	1.0 – 1.5 litres/m^2/day
3.	Sewer cleaning	4.5 litres/head/day
4.	Road site trees	28150 lit/km/day

(e) Agricultural Demand:

Public water supply is not used in our country for agricultural purpose. Only some farm houses, water may be used for kitchen gardens or minor agricultural purpose. In foreign countries also, private water resources are frequently used for farming, especially for irrigation of crops. Public supply is commonly used for dairies, cattle troughs, farm house purposes, horticulture and green house cultivation. An average consumption of these purposes is given in Table:

Usage	Estimated consumption
• Intensive daily farming	• 80 litres/day/hectare of grazing fully utilized or 1350 litres/day per cow.
• Average agriculture demands for mixed farming.	• 47000 litres/day per hector of farm land.
• Green house.	• 12400 litres/day per hectare in winter and three times of this value in summer.

In India, there is a great shortfall in agricultural demand and it is not in an organized sector. In foreign countries, crop irrigation demand (by sprinkling) is estimated by considering the rainfall deficiency, which can be made up by water during the growing season. Let the shortfall in rainfall in an area in four years out of five, is around 130 mm per annum. For full development of crops on one hectare 135 mm precipitation would represent 1350 m. If this much water is required for three months growing season, the average daily demand during this period will be 15 m^3 per day per hectare cultivated.

(f) Fire Demand:

Fire may take place due to faulty electric wires by short circuiting, fire catching materials, explosions, bad intension of criminal people or any other unforeseen mis-happenings. If fires are not properly controlled and extinguished in minimum possible time, they lead to serious damage and may burn cities.

All the big cities have full fire-fighting squads. As during the fire reakdown large quantity of water is required for throwing it over the fire to extinguish it, therefore provision is made in the water work to supply sufficient quantity of water or keep as reserve in the water mains for this purpose. In the cities, fire hydrants are provided on the water mains at 100 to 150 m apart for fire demand.

The quantity of water required for fire fighting is generally calculated by using different empirical formulae. For Indian conditions Kuiching's formula gives satisfactory results.

- Kuiching's formula: $Q = 3182 \sqrt{p}$
  where 'Q' is quantity of water required in litres/min
  'P' is population of town or city in thousands
- Freeman's formula: $Q = 1136 (P/5 + 10)$
  where 'Q' is quantity of water required in litres/min
  'P' is population of town or city in thousands
- Government of India recommendation: (for cities having population more than 50,000)
  $Q = 100 \sqrt{p}$
  Where 'Q' is quantity of water required in kilo litre /day and 'P' is population in thousands

(g) Compensation of losses and Wastes:

All the water, which goes in the distribution, pipes does not reach the consumers. The following are the reasons :

1. Losses due to defective pipe joints, cracked and broken pipes, faulty valves and fittings.
2. Losses due to consumers keep open their taps of public taps even when they are not using the water and allow the continuous wastage of water.
3. Losses due to unauthorized and illegal connections.

While estimating the total quantity of water of a town; allowance of 15% of total quantity of water is made to compensate for losses, thefts and wastage of water.

6.2 FACTORS AFFECTING PER CAPITA DEMAND

Factors affecting per capita demand may be summarized as

(a) Habit of inhabitants
(b) Public services
(c) Climate
(d) System of supply
(e) Metering of water supply
(f) System of drainage
(g) Availability of alternative sources
(h) Distribution pressure
(i) Industrialization
(j) Cost of water

The following are the main factors affecting for capita demand of the city or town.

(a) Climatic conditions: The quantity of water required in hotter and dry places is more than cold countries because of the use of air coolers, air conditioners, sprinkling of water in lawns, gardens, courtyards, washing of rooms, more washing of clothes and bathing etc. But in very cold countries sometimes the quantity of water required may be more due to wastage, because at such places the people often keep their taps open and water continuously flows for fear of freezing of water in the taps and use of hot water for keeping the rooms warm.

(b) Size of community: Water demand is more with increase of size of town because more water is required in street washing, running of sewers, maintenance of parks and gardens.

(c) Living standard of the people: The per capita demand of the town increases with the standard of living of the people because of the use of air conditioners, room coolers, maintenance of lawns, use of flush, latrines and automatic home appliances etc.

(d) Industrial and commercial activities: As the quantity of water required in certain industries is much more than domestic demand, their presence in the town will enormously increase per capita demand of the town. As a matter of the fact the water required by the industries has no direct link with the population of the town.

(e) Pressure in the distribution system: The rate of water consumption increase in the pressure of the building and even with the required pressure at the farthest point, the consumption of water will automatically increase. This increase in the quantity is firstly due to use of water freely by the people as compared when they get it scarcely and more water loss due to leakage, wastage and thefts etc.

(f) System of sanitation: Per capita demand of the towns having water carriage system will be more than the town where this system is not being used.

(g) Cost of water: The cost of water directly affects its demand. If the cost of water is more, less quantity of water will be used by the people as compared to when the cost is low.

6.3 PER CAPITA DEMAND

If 'Q' is the total quantity of water required by various purposes by a town per year and 'P' is population of town, then per capita demand will be

Per capita demand = $\dfrac{Q}{P \times 365}$ litres/day

Per capita demand of the town depends on various factors like standard of living, number and type of commercial places in a town etc. For an average Indian town, the requirement of water in various uses is as under:

(i) Domestic purpose   135 litres/capita/day
(ii) Industrial use   40 litres/ capita/day
(iii) Public use   25 litres/ capita/day
(iv) Fire demand   15 litres/ capita/day
(v) Losses, wastage and thefts   <u>55 litres/</u> capita/day
           Total =   270 litres/capita/day

The total quantity of water required by the town per day shall be 270 multiplied with the total population in litres/day.

6.4 DESIGN PERIOD

The complete water supply project includes huge and costly constructions such as dams, reservoir, treatment works and network of distribution pipelines which cannot be replaced on increased in their capacities, easily and conveniently. For example, the water mains including the distrusting pipes are laid underground, and cannot be replaced or added easily, without digging the roads do disrupting the traffic. In order to avoid these future complications of expansions, the various components of a water supply scheme are purposely made larger, so as to satisfied the community needs for a reasonable number of years to come. This future period or the number of years for which a provision is made in designing the capacities of the various components of the water supply scheme is known as design period. Such a scheme which is designed for a design period of say y years is supposed to satisfactorily serve the community needs up to the end of y years. Mostly water works are designed for design period of 22-30 years, which is fairly good period.

The design period should neither be too long nor should it be too short. The design period cannot exceed the useful of the component structure, and is guided by the following consideration.

6.4.1 Factors Governing the Design Period

1. Useful life of component structures and the chances of their becoming old obsolete.
2. Amount and availability of additional investment likely to be incurred for additional provisions. For example, if the funds are not available, one has to keep a smaller design period.
3. The rate on investment and funds available or any subsides from other sources.
4. Anticipated rate of population growth, including possible shifts in communities, industries and commercial establishments, for examples, if the rate of increase of population is less, a higher figure for the design period may be chosen.

6.5 NEED FOR FORECASTING POPULATION

The population of every town or city goes on increasing every year. If water supply scheme is designed for the present population, it will be inadequate within few coming years, as the population increases continuously. All components of water supply scheme when once constructed cannot be made larger or replaced easily in future. Hence, various components of the water supply scheme are designed to supply water to the population which will be existing at the end of design period. Therefore, it is necessary to find the population of the town or city at the end of the design period (generally 30 years). It is done from the past census data generally available with the local bodies like punchayat, municipality or corporation.

In short *"Finding probable population of a city at a future date, from census data of previous decades is known as forecasting of population"*.

6.5.1 Methods of Population Forecast

Following methods are generally used to estimate the future population:
1. Arithmetical Increase Method
2. Geometrical Increase Method
3. Incremental Increase Method
4. Declining growth or Decrease Rate of Growth Method
5. Simple graphical or Graphical Extension Method
6. Graphical Comparison Method
7. Zoning Method or Master Plan Method
8. The Logistic Curve Method
9. The Ratio Method or Apportionment Method.

6.5.2 Arithmetical Increase Method

It is based on the assumption that the average rate of increase in population from decade to decade is constant. Mathematically, it can be expressed as $\frac{dP}{dT}$ = constant, where, $\frac{dP}{dT}$ is the rate of change of population. From the previous census data, the increase in population between consecutive decades is found and from this average increase per decade is worked out. Future population, as shown below, is then worked from the present population.

Let 'P' be the present population, 'd' is the average increase per decade and P_n is the future population after the period of 'n' decades (1 decade = 10 years). It is given by the following relation.

$$P_n = P + nd$$

This method is suitable when (a) The design period for the town is small and (b) When the town is old and large and also reached its saturation population due to maximum development.

This method is unsuitable for towns which are developing at a faster rate as compared to its past development. It gives lower results of future population. The following example will illustrate this method.

6.5.3 Geometrical Increase Method

This method is also called as uniform percentage method. It is based on the assumption that the average percentage increase in population from decade to decade is constant. From the census date of previous four, five decades the percentage increase between consecutive decade is found out and then its average is worked out.

If 'P' is the present population, 'r' is the average percentage increase per decade, then 'P_n' the population after n decades is given by the relation

$$P_n = P\left[1 + \frac{r}{100}\right]^n$$

Derivation of the formula:

$$\text{Population after one decade} = P_1 = P + \frac{r}{100} \times P = P\left[1 + \frac{r}{100}\right]$$

$$\text{Population after two decades} = P_2 = P_1 + \frac{r}{100} \times P_1$$

$$= P_1\left[1 + \frac{r}{100}\right]$$

$$= P\left[1 + \frac{r}{100}\right]\left[1 + \frac{r}{100}\right]$$

$$= P\left[1 + \frac{r}{100}\right]^2$$

Similarly, population after three decades $= P_3 = P\left[1 + \frac{r}{100}\right]^3$

Hence, population after 'n' decades $= P_n = P\left[1 + \frac{r}{100}\right]^n$

This method is suitable for towns having large scope of expansion and a fairly constant rate of growth is expected.

This method gives higher results, as compared to arithmetical method.

6.5.4 Incremental Increase Method

The benefits of arithmetical as well as of geometric method is included in this method. Similar to arithmatic method average increase per decade (d) is found out. Then increase or decrease in the population change for each decade is found out and from these average incremental increase is worked. Let us call it as 't'. Then, population at the end of nth decade is given by the following relation.

$$P_n = P + nd + (1 + 2 + 3 \ldots n)t$$

or

$$P_n = P + nd + \frac{n(n + 1)}{2} \times t$$

where,

P = Present population
d = Average increase per decade
t = Average incremental increase
n = Number of decades

The method is recommended to be used for towns whose population is varying at a progressive rate and not at constant rate.

SOLVED EXAMPLES

Example 6.1 : Following is the population data for a town. Water supply scheme is to be designed for this town with a design period of 30 years. Find the population at the end of the year 2020 by arithmetical method.

Year	1950	1960	1970	1980	1990
Population	35,000	37,500	43,500	52,000	57,500

Solution:

Year	Population	Increase in population
1950	35000	
1960	37500	2500
1970	43500	6000
1980	52000	8500
1990	57500	5500
	Total	22,500

$n = \frac{1}{10}(2020 - 1990)$
= 3 decades
P = 57,500

Average increase in decade = $\frac{22500}{4}$
= 5625

Therefore, Population at the end of 2020 = P_n = P + nd
= 57,500 + 3 × 5625 = 74,375

Hence, population at the end of year 2020 will be 74,375.

Example 6.2: Solve the previous example by geometric increase method.

Solution:

Year	Population	Increase in population	Percentage increase in population
1950	35,000	2500	$\dfrac{2500 \times 100}{35,000} = 7.14\%$
1960	37,500	6000	$\dfrac{6000 \times 100}{37,500} = 16.00\%$
1970	43,500	8500	$\dfrac{8500 \times 100}{43,500} = 19.54\%$
1980	52,000	5500	$\dfrac{5500 \times 100}{52,000} = 10.58\%$
1990	57500		

Total percentage increase = 53.26

$\therefore$ Average percentage increase, $r = \dfrac{1}{4} \times 53.26 = 13.315\%$

$\therefore$ Population in the year 2020 $= P_{2020} = P\left[1 + \dfrac{r}{100}\right]^3$

$= 57,500 \left[1 + \dfrac{13.315}{100}\right]^3 = 83,662$

By arithmetical method population in the year 2020 = 74,375.

Hence, it will be seen that this method gives higher results.

Example 6.3: Solve the previous example by Incremental Increase method.

Solution:

Year	Population	Increase in population	Incremental increase
1950	35,000		
1960	37,500	2500	–
1970	43,500	6000	+ 3500
1980	52,000	8500	+ 2500
1990	57,500	5500	– 3000
		Total 22500	+ 3000

$$\text{Average per decade, d} = \frac{22500}{4} \qquad\qquad t = \frac{3000}{3}$$

$$= 5625 \qquad\qquad = 1000$$

$$\therefore \text{Population in the year 2020} = P_{2020} = P + nd + \frac{n(n+1)}{2} \times t$$

$$= 57500 + 3 \times 5625 + \frac{3(3+1)}{2} \times 1000$$

$$= 57500 + 16875 + 6000$$

$$= 80{,}375$$

Note: By comparing the results of the population for the same town by above three methods, it is seen that arithmetic method gives low population, whereas the geometrical method gives higher population. The incremental increase method gives medium population (future).

Example 6.4: With the help of following data, estimate the future population of a town in the year 2001, using incremental increase method.

Year	1911	1921	1931	1941	1951	1961
Population (in thousands)	350	466	994	1560	1623	1839

Solution:

Year	Population	Increase in population	Incremental increase
1911	350		
1921	466	116	
1931	994	528	+ 412
1941	1560	566	+038
1951	1623	063	− 503
1961	1839	216	+ 153
Total		1489	+ 100

$$n = \frac{1}{10}(2001 - 1961)$$
$$= 4 \text{ decades}$$

$$\text{Average per decade, d} = \frac{1489}{5}, \qquad t = \frac{100}{4} = 25$$

$$= 297.8$$

∴ Population in the year 2001 = P_n

$$= P + nd + \frac{n(n+1)}{2} \times t$$

$$= P_{2001}$$

$$= 1839 + 4 \times 297.8 + \frac{4(4+1)}{2} \times 25$$

$$= 1839 + 1191.2 + 250$$

$$= 3280.2 \text{ Thousand}$$

∴ Population in the year 2001 = 3280.2 Thousand

6.6 WATER TREATMENT PLANT

The complete process of removal of undesirable matter such as various impurities in order to make the water acceptable for domestic or industrial use is commonly termed as treatment of water.

6.6.1 Objective of Treatment of Water

The following are the Objective of treatment of water :

- To make water colourless, odour free and tasty.
- To make water safe and sparkling for drinking and domestic purposes.
- To remove dissolved gases and turbidity of water.
- To make it free from all objectionable impurities present in suspension, colloidal or dissolved form.
- To remove harmful bacteria.
- To remove hardness of water.
- To make water suitable for various uses such as industrial purposes.

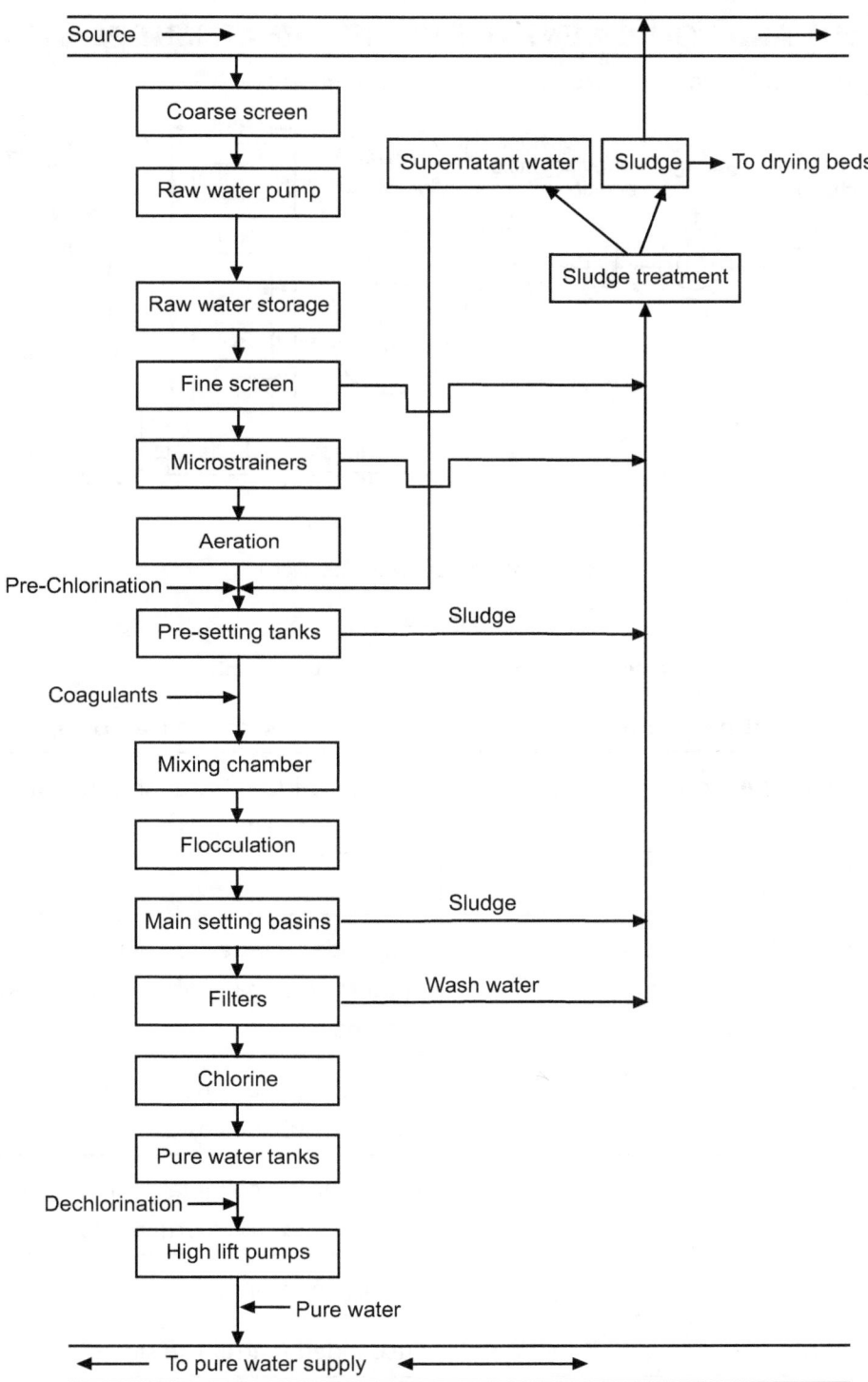

Fig. 6.2 : Flow diagram showing different treatment stages

6.7 LAYOUT AND COMPONENTS OF WATER TREATMENT PLANT

The layout of a typical water treatment plant is shown in Fig. 6.3.

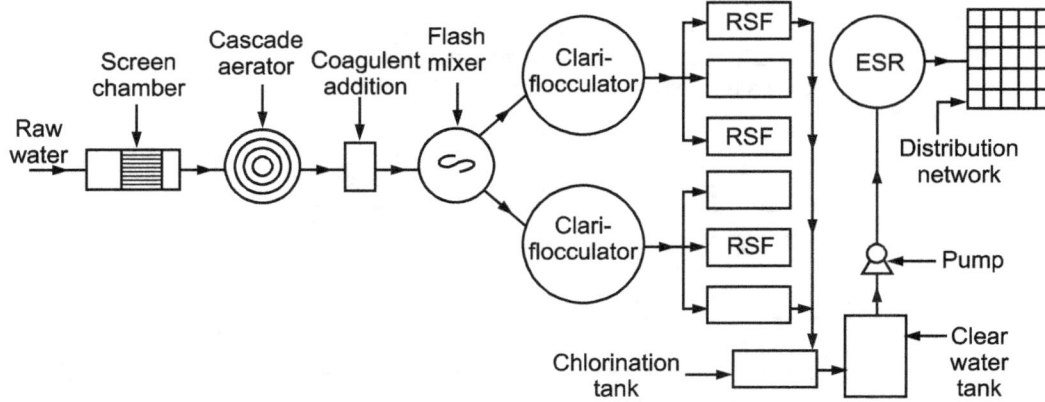

RSF = Rapid Sand Filter

ESR = Elevated Service Reservoir

Fig. 6.3

Table 6.1: Functions of water treatment units

Treatment unit	Function (removal)
Aeration, use of chemicals	Colour, odour, taste and dissolved gases like CO_2 and Fe.
Chemical methods	Iron, manganese etc.
Coagulation	Suspended matter and very fine suspended impurities a part of colloidal matter and bacterial.
Disinfection	Pathogenic bacteria, organic matter and reducing substances.
Filtration	Finer and colloidal dissolved matter, bacteria and micro organisms.
Screening	Floating matter
Sedimentation	Suspended matter like silt and sand.
Softening	Hardness.

6.7.1 Components of Water Treatment Plant

A typical water treatment plant consists of the following components:

1. **Intake well, jack well and a pump house:** The raw water is admitted from the source in these wells through inlet openings fitted with coarse screen to exclude floating matter.

2. **Screen chambers:** Raw water brought through rising main is admitted in screen chamber provided with bar screens and/or fine screen to exclude remaining floating matter.

3. **Aerators:** Through aerators the water is exposed to atmospheric air to eliminate gases like H_2S, CO_2 and mineral matters like Fe, Mn.

4. **Coagulant tank:** Here the desired coagulant is added in the water.

5. **Flash mixer:** Water containing coagulant is intimately mixed in this unit.

6. **Clariflocculator:** This is a combined unit doing the operations of flocculation and also sedimentation (often called as clarification). Water from flash mixer is admitted in the flocculation zone where with the help of moving paddles, suspended particles come together (agglomerate) and form compact settleable mass called *floc*. The water containing this floc moves to a portion of unit where sedimentation of the floc occurs.

7. **Filter beds:** These are in the form of tanks rectangular in shape. Number of such beds often called as battery of filters are provided in the big building. This building is called as filter house.

   Very fine particles and colloidal matter which have refused to settle earlier are removed through filtration.

8. **Chlorination or Disinfection unit:** Here generally chlorine is applied to filtered water to completely destroy the micro-organism escaped through filtration. This confirms the purity of water. This is the last unit of water treatment.

9. **Pumping, Elevated Service Reservoir (ESR):** Pure water is admitted in a protected clear water tank. This water is then pumped and fed to ESR through a rising main.

10. **Distribution system:** The treated water from this overhead reservoir is fed into distribution system for consumption.

Note:

1. In case of ground water source, sedimentation and filtration may not be required because the ground water is already filtered during its percolation through various layers of the soil. In such case, the disinfection through chlorination may be sufficient.

2. The nature and degree of treatment depends upon the source and some units mentioned above may not be required.

Various processes adopted in water treatment are explained in details in the next articles.

6.8 DRAINAGE OF WATER FROM BUILDING

The sewage produced in houses and buildings has to be conveyed and connecteed to the muncipal sewers by the owners of the buildings. The provision and construction of an effcient plumbing system, for collection and movement of the sewage produced in the building, till it is carried and discharged into the nearest muncipal sewer, is an important aspect of building construction.

Many of us, who are living in areas provided with sewers, might have experienced the bad or improperly designed plumbing works, which everyday possess problems, in either the kitchen drain or the wash basin or the water closed getting choked, or the foul smells escaping from somewhere or the other. A properly designed and carefully constructed plumbing system in buildings, is therefore, absolutely necessary to avoid such frequent trouble.

The arrangement provided in a house of building, for collecting and conveying waste water through drain pipes, by gravity, to join either a public sewer or a domestic septic tank, is termed as house drainage or building drainage

6.8.1 Aims of House Drainage

House darainge is privided

- To maintain healthy conditions in the building.
- To dispose off waste water as early and quickly as possible.
- To avoid the entry of foul gases from the sewer or the septic tank.
- To facilitate quick removal of foul matter.
- To collect and remove waste matters systematically.

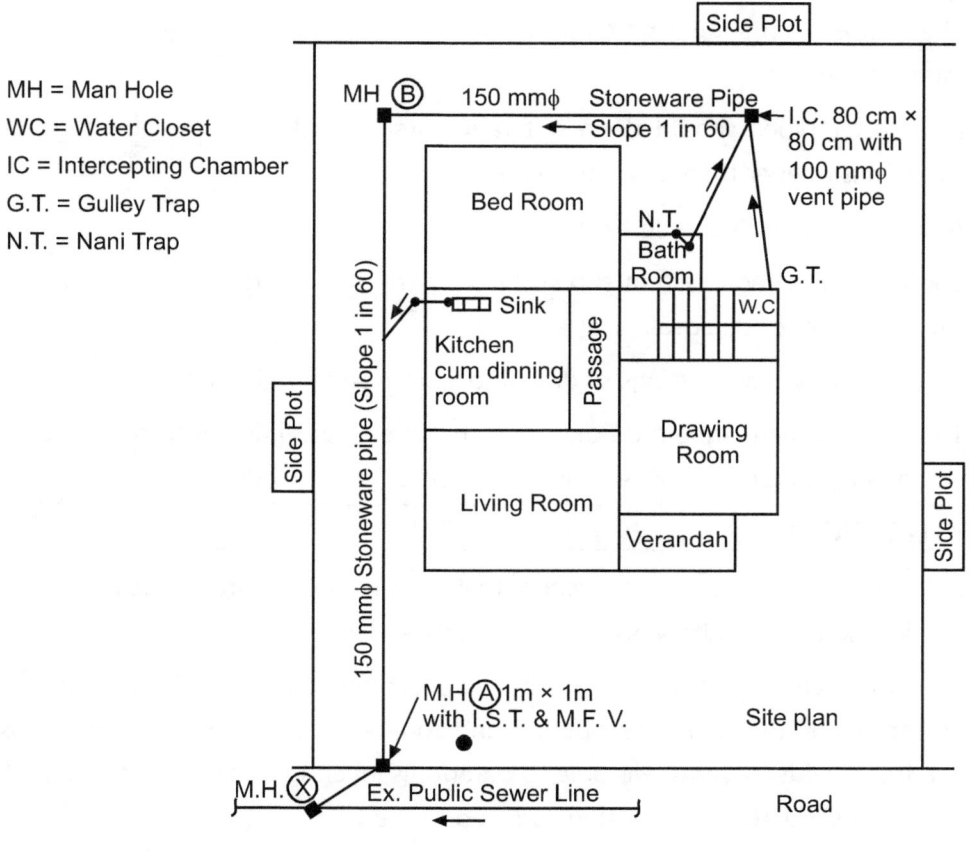

Fig. 6.4

6.8.2 Principle of Drainage of Water from Building

The following principles are adopted for the effcient drainage system:

1. The lavatory blocks should be located that the length of drainage line is minimum.
2. The drainage pipes should be laid by the side of the building rather than below the building.
3. All the drains should be laid by the side of the building rather than below the building.
4. The slope of the drain should be sufficient to develop self cleansing velocity.
5. The size of drain should be sufficient, so that flooding of the drain does not take place while handling the maximum discharge.
6. The drainage system should contain enough number of traps at suitable location.

7. The house drain should be disconnected to the pubic sewer by the provision of an intercepting trap.
8. Rain water pipes should drain out rain water directly into the street gutters from where it is deeper than the housedrain.
9. All the connections should be water tight.
10. The entire drainage system should be properly ventilated from the starting point to the final point of disposal.
11. All the materials and fittings of drainage system should IS marks.
12. The entire system should be designed that the possibilities of formation of air locks, siphonage, under deposits etc. are minimised.

6.9 SEPTIC TANK

A septic tank treats domestic sewage that is; the outlets from basins, baths, W.C.s, showers, sinks and other sanitary and domestic appliances.

In 1860, a French man called Mouras built a masonry septic tank for a house in France. After a dozen years, the tank was opened and found, contrary to all expectations, to be almost free from solids. Mouras was able to patent his invention on 2nd September, 1881. It is believed that the septic tank was first introduced to the USA in 1883, to England in 1895 and to South Africa (by the British military) in 1898.

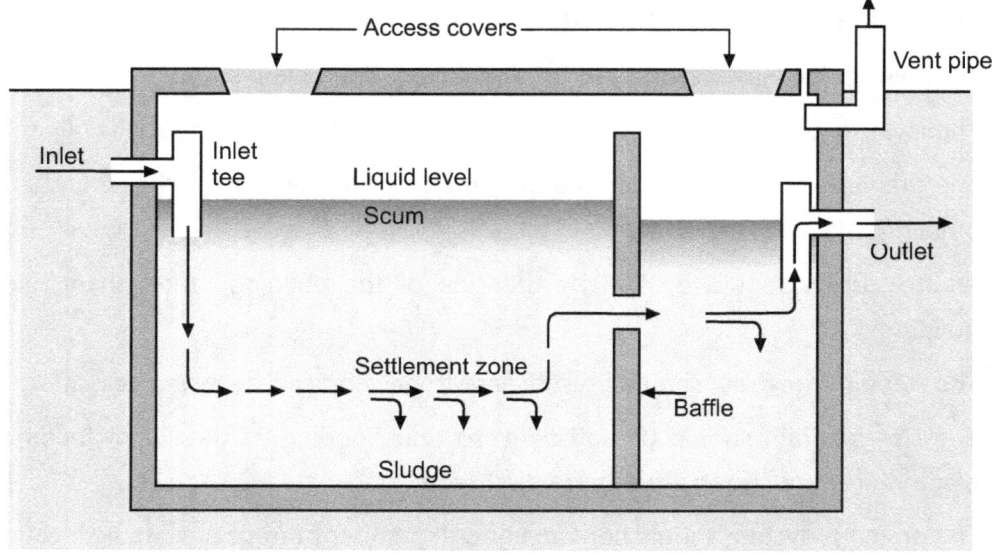

Fig. 6.5

In septic tanks the solids in the sewage settle to the bottom to form sludge. Relatively clear liquid is left which forms a layer of scum on its surface. Bacteria feed on this liquid and digest some of the matter in it. The liquid then either passes into another settlement tank before passing to a water course or is discharged underground through a network of pipes to filter through the soil in a soak away system. The solids that build up at the bottom of the tank need to be removed about once a year.

6.9.1 Digestion Process in Septic Tank

Sewage is allowed to rest in the septic tank for about 16 to 48 hours. The process of digestion in the septic tank is done by bacteria. These bacteria can be killed by certain chemicals. The process of breaking down the organic matter in sewage is called anaerobic digestion since it is largely outside the presence of air.

The digestion reduces the amount of sludge and makes the contents of the septic tank less smelly. Normally, it would take about two months to break down all the sludge in the tank so a normally used septic tank will only partially break down the contents.

Too much bleach, detergents and other household chemicals may destroy the useful bacteria. As a result the sewage will not be treated fully and may cause pollution problems. Emptying the septic tank regularly will ensure the septic tank keeps working properly. If possible use biodegradable 'septic safe' detergents.

6.9.2 Construction of Septic Tank

Septic tanks can be block/brick built or made of cement reinforced pipe. Access covers should be of durable quality to resist corrosion and must be secured to prevent easy removal. Septic tanks should prevent leakage of the contents and ingress of subsoil water and should be ventilated. Ventilation should be kept away from buildings.

6.10 SOAK PITS

Soak pit a circular covered pit, through which the effluent is allowed to be soaked or absorbed into the sorrunding soil. The soak pit may either be filled with stone aggregate or may be kept empty.

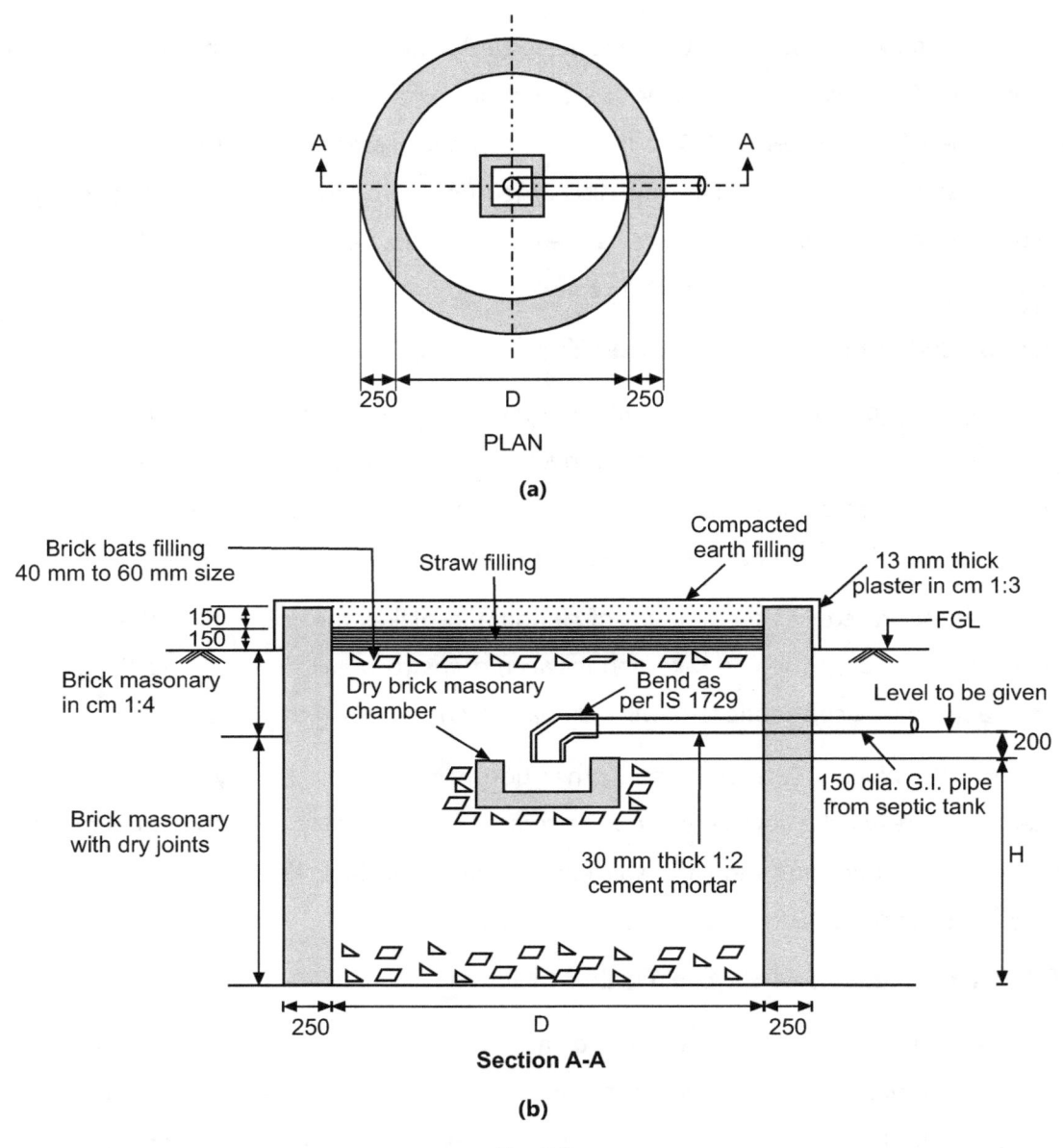

Fig. 6.6

When the soak pit is empty, the pit is lined by brick, stone or concrete block with dry open joint. In addition to this, this lining is supported the inlet level by at least 7.5 cm thick backing of course aggregate. However, when the soak pit is filled with stone or brick aggregate, no lining is required except for a top masonry ring constructed to prevent damage by flooding of the pit by surface run off.

Typical plan and cross section of septic tank are show in Fig. 6.6.

EXERCISE

1. Explain categories of water demand.
2. Draw treatment flow sheet for a typical water treatment plant.
3. Explain construction of septic tanks and soak pits.
4. Write short note on drainage of water from building.
5. Explain the factors governing the design period.
6. Write short notes on the following :
   (i) Per capita demand.
   (ii) Design period.
   (iii) Arithmetic increase.
   (iv) Geometric increase.

www.ingramcontent.com/pod-product-compliance
Lightning Source LLC
Chambersburg PA
CBHW080428230426
43662CB00015B/2221